SHAKESPEARE AND
THE HOMILIES

Shakespeare and the Homilies

And Other Pieces of Research into the Elizabethan Drama

By
ALFRED HART

But this good Sir did follow the plaine word,
Ne medled with their controuersies vaine.
All his care was, his seruice well to saine,
And to read Homelies vpon holidayes:
When that was done, he might attend his playes;
An easie life, and fit high God to please.

SPENSER, *Mother Hubberd's Tale*, ll. 390-395.

1970
OCTAGON BOOKS
New York

First published 1934

Reprinted 1970

*by permission of Melbourne University Press by
arrangement with Cambridge University Press*

OCTAGON BOOKS

A DIVISION OF FARRAR, STRAUS & GIROUX, INC.

19 Union Square West

New York, N. Y. 10003

LIBRARY OF CONGRESS CATALOG CARD NUMBER: 72-120626

PREFACE

A POLOGY is perhaps the right note for the author of any new book on the Elizabethan drama to strike in a preface; I shall content myself, if not others, with an explanation. Most of these essays originally took the form of lectures delivered before the members of the Melbourne Shakespeare Society at different periods during the past fifteen years and have been rewritten since. Running through them and giving some slight unity to rather diverse topics are dissent from much recent criticism of Shakespeare's plays and insistence upon relevant facts as the only sound basis of fruitful speculation in literature. In my essay on ' Shakespeare and the Homilies ' I have attempted to show that the dramatist took his views on divine right and the mutual relation of monarch and subjects from the official book of sermons; in that on ' The Censorship of 2 *Henry IV* ' I have given reasons for rejecting the traditional opinion that all the omissions in the quarto version were made in order to shorten the play for representation, and have fully discussed those which seem to have been struck out by order of the censor. The three essays on ' Play Abridgment ' constitute, I think, the first attempt made to reconcile the time allotted for representation and the length of plays. So many still-vexed questions have been rather sketchily discussed in these necessarily brief discussions that I do not hope for general acceptance of my opinions. The essays on the vocabularies of *Edward III* and *The Two Noble Kinsmen* suggest new methods of using the diction of Shakespeare's plays for purposes of comparative criticism. Had these or similar methods been used with honesty and judgment by the self-styled ' scientific ' literary critics and disintegrators of Shakespeare's plays, most of their books would never have been written.

Preface

My best thanks are due to the Council of the Melbourne University for a generous grant from the Publication Fund, which made the printing of this book possible, and to the Managers of the Melbourne University Press for accepting the remainder of the financial responsibility. I must also thank the proprietors of *The Review of English Studies* for permission to reprint the articles on ' Play Abridgment ' and ' The Vocabulary of *The Two Noble Kinsmen.*' I am indebted to Professor E. H. C. Oliphant for some helpful suggestions, and to Professor G. H. Cowling for advice and encouragement. I must acknowledge, too, the never-failing courtesy and help of the officers of the Melbourne Public Library, and, in particular, the bibliographical assistance of Mr. A. B. Foxcroft.

A. HART.

27th July, 1934.

CONTENTS

A NEW SHAKESPEAREAN SOURCE-BOOK

'O most gentle Iupiter, what tedious homilie of Loue haue you wearied your parishioners withall, and neuer cri'de, haue patience, good people.'   *As You Like It*, III, ii, 145-7.

MODERN research has not added much to our knowledge of the books that Shakespeare read, if he was, indeed, a reader in our sense of the word. The industry of generations of commentators has failed to discover many borrowings from authors other than those whose novels or chronicles he used as raw materials for his plays. Such loans he repaid with the usurious interest of genius; thus Cinthio Giraldi's dull story of a sordid crime grew into the miracle that is *Othello*. He was 'no pickpurse of another's wit,' and did not indulge in petty pilferings as did the tribe of sonneteers. In the Elizabethan phrase, his poetry could live of its own. Occasionally he made glorious booty of Plutarch's purple patches; his description of the meeting of Cleopatra and Antony, Volumnia's appeal to her son, the speech of Coriolanus to Aufidius transmute North's admirable prose into even more admirable poetry. But neither in *Antony and Cleopatra* nor in *Coriolanus* nor in any other play, do we find phrases, lines or passages 'lifted' or 'conveyed' from the works of any other writer than the author used for the play. The poet altered, retained, added or omitted whatever he thought fit, but such alterations or additions were his own, and underlying them was an artistic or dramatic purpose also his own. Being an original artist, he gave his drama laws and refused to accept the authority of Aristotle and Seneca. He did not obtrude his personality, beliefs, prejudices, likes and dislikes in his plays. He has told us that the end of plays and playing, 'both at the first and now, was

9

and is, to hold as 'twer the Mirrour up to Nature; to show Vertue her owne Feature, Scorne her owne Image, and the verie Age and Bodie of the Time, his forme and pressure.' Shakespeare's gigantic mirror, thus held up to nature, reflects a goodly assembly presenting every phase of Elizabethan life: before us pass kings, queens, nobles and their ladies, cardinals, bishops, priests, knights, pages, patriots, gallants, merchants, soldiers, lovers, rustics, beggars, drunkards, strumpets, fools, clowns, cowards, rogues, villains—but we cannot see even the shadow cast by the holder of the mirror. He was not filled with the bitter indignation that informs such satirists as Juvenal and Jonson; he was not a playwright with a purpose or a mission; he had no wish to reform the world or to force his ideals of life, conduct or art upon his public. We know nothing of his religious beliefs, though we may suspect that he was not the stuff of which martyrs are made. Politics and sociology as we know them did not exist, and, like a sensible man, he left such dryasdust and undramatic topics to our century which is credulous enough to accept and praise dialogues on economics as drama.

⌐Shakespeare was born in an era and world of constant change, in an England that seemed on the verge of destruction. Religion and politics had been inextricably intermingled since the middle of Henry the Eighth's reign, and a rapid succession of nation-wide innovations threatened to end all hope of any permanent stability. The divorce of Catharine of Aragon, the separation of the English Church from communion with Rome, the suppression of the religious orders and the dissolution of the monasteries, the Pilgrimage of Grace, the declaration that the monarch was the supreme head of the English Church, the gradual extinction of the remnant of the feudal aristocracy that survived the Wars of the Roses, the creation of a new nobility, the rise of an official class, the numerous alterations made in religious dogmas and ceremonies, the reaction during the reign of Queen Mary, and the accession of her sister Elizabeth, the daughter of the Reformation, all had happened within less than thirty years. Throughout Elizabeth's reign, religious wars had been devastating France, Germany, the Low Countries, and Ireland; yet England had remained in comparative peace and had steadily prospered. Only three insurrections of any importance had broken out during more than a century; there had been some fighting, but little bloodshed and no civil war or foreign invasions. When Mary died the Tudor dynasty had been on the throne for 73 years; under the strong rule of Henry VII and Henry VIII there had been organised and firmly maintained a system of despotic government such as a Turkish pasha would scarcely have dared to employ in ruling a dependency of the Ottoman Empire. No monarch, of England ever exercised such absolute power as 'good Queen Bess.' Autocracy was in her blood and the very breath of her nostrils. She looked upon her Parliament not as a permanent institution or as a sovereign estate of the realm but as a special assembly which custom compelled her to summon when she had need of money; being a thrifty woman she called it as rarely as she could. Thirteen parliaments met during her reign, and she dissolved each of them after a session of a few weeks. Even in her last parliaments she expressly forbade the speaker to accept bills 'touching matters of state or reformation in causes ecclesiastical,' and thus debates on the Church, the succession to the throne and foreign affairs were strictly tabooed. Members of the House of Commons who disregarded her commands were sent to the Tower till their zeal cooled; Peter Wentworth died there in 1596 after an imprisonment of three years. Freedom of speech she contemptuously conceded to them; this freedom amounted to the privilege of saying 'Aye' or 'No.' She bluntly told the Parliament of 1597-8 that such freedom did not entitle them 'to frame a forme of religion or a state of government as to their idle braynes shall seem meetest.' At the end of the session she vetoed 48 of 91 bills that had passèd both houses. The term 'contrary to law' had no meaning when law came into conflict with her royal prerogative; even when her wisdom felt that she must yield to the general outcry against monopolies, she simultaneously issued a proclamation against such 'as shall seditiously or contemptuously call in question the power or validity of her prerogative royal annexed to her imperial crown.'

Her tyranny was real and exhibited itself even in the ceremony of the court. Paul Hentzner's description is well known:—'Whoever speaks to her it is kneeling; though now and then she raises some one with her hand . . . Wherever she turned her face as she was going along every body fell down on their knees.'[1] He describes the genuflections and prostrations openly practised by those who made ready her table for dinner on every occasion on which they entered or left the room. 'At last came a maiden of great beauty dressed in white silk (we were told she was a countess) accompanied by a matron bearing a tasting knife; who when she had prostrated herself three times in the most graceful manner, approached the table, and rubbed the plates with bread and salt with as much veneration as if the queen had been present.'[2] Elizabeth was always the queen. 'Daily and nightly ceremony, state and formality held sway. It was not the precise and pompous ceremony of a later day; like all else, court ceremonial was still inartificial. But it was none the less real and extreme. When the queen visits a country house its mistress receives her at the threshold " moste humbly on her knees." When the House of Commons visit her at the close of the session they kneel during her long

1. Quoted from Cheyney, *History of England*, vol. I, pp. 16-17.
2. *Ibid.*, p. 17.

address. . . . Another traveller, visiting England in 1585, describes the nobles kneeling on one knee while they conversed with her, and men and women falling on their knees as she passed. The Duke of Stettin who visited her in 1602 records, " At last the queen to show her royal rank ordered some of the noble lords and councillors to approach and they in their stately dress were obliged to remain on their knees all the time the queen addressed them " . . . When (the ten lords of the Order of the Garter) attended morning chapel, where Dr. Bull played and the gentlemen of the chapel sang, each lord on his entrance and departure made three obeisances to the empty seat of the queen.'[3] The rigid exaction of such slavish servility drove self-respecting men of high birth from the court. Thus Naunton says of Peregrine Bertie, ' the brave Lord Willoughby ' of the ballad :— ' had he not slighted the Court, but applyed himself to the Queen, he might have enjoyed a plentifull portion of her grace : And it was his saying, (and it did him no good) That he was none of the Reptilia, intimating, that he could not creep on the ground, and that the Court was not in his Element; for indeed, as he was a great Souldier, so he was of a suitable magnanimity, and could not brook the obsequiousnesse and assiduity of the Court.'[3a] Such of the peers as were descended from the old nobility, the Percies, Nevilles, Cliffords, Devereux, Veres, Ratcliffes and Staffords must have drunk more than their fill of the bitter waters of humiliation, when they were forced to grovel at the feet of the descendant of a Welsh mercenary soldier and a London tradesman to make sport for a petty German princeling. She kept her young nobles in leading strings, and they could not travel or marry without her consent.

She governed through the Privy Council, and its paternal activities took everything said or done or left

3. Cheyney, *History of England*, vol. I, p. 61.
3a. Naunton, *Fragmenta Regalia* (edited by Arber), pp. 37-8.

undone by any man or woman in any part of England to be its province. Certainly at no time in our history has a body of officials exerted such extensive, despotic and arbitrary power over every detail of human life. The Venetian ambassador remarked, ' These lords of the council behave like so many kings.'[4] They broke almost every law and custom of the constitution, put anyone in prison and kept him there at pleasure, without trial or appeal or any redress, ordered prisoners and suspected persons to be tortured, fined and imprisoned juries for returning verdicts contrary to the Council's will, pressed soldiers and sailors for service outside the kingdom, prevented merchants importing or exporting goods, exacted loans under the Privy Seal without paying interest, interfered with elections of members of Parliament and sat with the judges in the Star Chamber to enforce punishment for violating the royal proclamations which they had issued in the queen's name. The Tudor administration was easily alarmed, because it had no standing military force at its disposal to subdue an insurrection, and it punished savagely to conceal its weakness. The queen imposed martial law on London in 1595 on account of a petty riot and ordered the provost-marshal to hang anyone taken in the act without any form of trial; subsequently five apprentices were tried, convicted of high treason and executed. Walshingham and the Cecils controlled an efficient secret service, and any person of local importance who criticised any action or proclamation of the Council ran the risk of being summoned to London. There he might wait for weeks in idleness and continuous apprehension, till the Council was disposed to cite him before them, and he might count himself fortunate if he escaped after making a humble apology and paying a heavy fine. A vigilant eye was kept on the press; only three towns were permitted to print books, and a rigorous censorship

4. Quoted from Cheyney, *History of England*, vol. I, p. 80.

restrained the expression of discontent and criticism of
the government and its actions.

Shakespeare was born and grew up to manhood and
maturity during the reign of the great queen, became
one of the ' Kings Maiesties Servants,' and prospered
by making

> those flights upon the bankes of Thames,
> That so did take Eliza, and our Iames!

He seems not to have known or even thought of any
other form of government than the absolute monarchy
of his own land, and accepted it as well suited to the
times and people. He realised how much the welfare
and life of the State depended on the character of the
ruler whether he was called consul, duke, prince, king
or emperor, and by presenting in his series of English
chronicle plays the miseries, civil wars and misgovernment that followed the usurpation of Henry IV, the long
minority of Henry VI, and the thirty years of struggle
between the rival dynasties, he gave his audiences an
admirably instructive historical background. They could
not but contrast the firm, even if somewhat tyrannical,
rule of the queen who had given England peace at home
for more than forty years and kept the country free
from wars abroad for the first thirty years of her reign.
Shakespeare knew that

> The King-becoming Graces,
> As Iustice, Verity, Temp'rance, Stablenesse,
> Bounty, Perseuerance, Mercy, Lowlinesse,
> Deuotion, Patience, Courage, Fortitude,

have their roots in character not intellect, in conduct not
speech, in wisdom not learning. We may think 'that
Elizabeth was not a pattern of ' Verity,' ' Bounty,'
' Mercy,' ' Lowlinesse,' ' Deuotion ' or ' Patience,' nor
James an exemplar of ' Temp'rance,' ' Stablenesse,'
' Courage ' or ' Fortitude,' but each age has its own
standards and models of conduct and virtue. The poet
prescribes duty, loyalty, obedience and service as ideals

for the subject, but says nothing of his rights, of liberty or freedom. His reading of Plutarch may have convinced him that such political abstractions meant something real to well-born Greeks and Romans; but his Caliban is drunk when he bawls for freedom, and his scheming demagogues or ambitious aristocrats such as Cade, Cassius, Cinna or Sicinius prate of these shadows of a dream merely to mislead their dupes. Being a playwright and not a historian, and therefore less concerned with facts and the development of the English constitution than with character and plot, Shakespeare tells without comment the story dramatised from the chronicles. He may have known that Elizabeth's court nick-name was Richard the Second; of the 33 articles detailing specific acts of misgovernment which Northumberland is so insistent that Richard shall read,

> These Accusations, and these grieuous Crymes,
> Committed by your Person, and your followers,
> Against the State, and Profit of this Land,

the poet tells us nothing, except for an early and rather casual mention of certain illegal methods of raising money which the more prudent Elizabeth did not practise. We may well doubt whether he knew or took the trouble to learn how greatly the character and pretensions of the monarchy had changed since Richard III fell on Bosworth Field.

Sir John Fortescue, the eminent Lancastrian lawyer, in his account of the English Constitution, written c. 1460-1470, declares that

> the maxim of the (Roman) civil law ' what has pleased the prince has the force of law ' has no place in English jurisprudence; the king exists for the sake of the kingdom, not the kingdom for the sake of the king; ' for the preservation of the laws of his subjects, of their persons and goods, he is set up, and for this purpose he has power derived from the people, so that he may not govern his people by any other power '; he cannot change the laws or impose taxes without the consent of the whole nation given in parliament. That parliament, including a senate of more than

three hundred chosen counsellors, represents 'the three estates of the realm.'[5]

Parliament had set up the first Lancastrian king and deposed Richard II partly for breaking the laws which he had sworn to observe, and partly for such rash sayings as 'his laws were in his own mouth and often in his own breast, and he alone could change and frame the laws of the kingdom; and that the life of every liegeman, his lands, tenements, goods and chattels lay at his royal will without sentence of forfeiture; and he had acted upon the saying.'[6] About three-quarters of a century after Fortesque had described the government of England, the obsequious parliament of Henry VIII, representing 'the three estates of the realm,' submissively abandoned its control over legislation by passing a statute giving the king the power of making new laws by proclamation and the right of dispensing with laws already made. A clause of this statute provides:—'That always the king for the time being with the advice of his honourable council may set forth at all times by the authority of this Act his proclamations . . . and that those same shall be obeyed observed and kept as though they were made by Act of Parliament for the time in them limited unless the king's highness dispense with them or any of them under his great seal.'[7]

Elizabeth inherited and habitually used the system of absolutism created by her grandfather and father. She had almost as exalted ideas of her sovereign power as Shakespeare ascribes to Richard II; but her subjects accepted her semi-divinity and practised the passive obedience which Richard preached, because the doctrines of passive obedience and the divine right of kings were two fundamental articles of the Tudor state religion. The members of her House of Commons admitted that her prerogative power enabled her to override any laws

5. Stubbs, *Constitutional History of England* (1880), vol. III, pp. 258-259.
6. Stubbs, *op. cit.*, vol. II, p. 551.
7. *Ibid.*, vol. III, pp. 544-5, n.

B

made by them. Even such an eminent jurist as Coke declared in writing that Parliament was powerless if the Crown chose to exert its full power, and, when he was Speaker, he did not hesitate to obey the queen's command and refused to submit to the House bills on prohibited subjects. We may ask how had the limited monarchy of the Lancastrian kings described by Fortescue developed into what Coke admitted was in reality the absolute monarchy of Elizabeth. For an answer we must go back to the reigns of her father and grandfather. With the almost complete destruction of the feudal aristocracy during the dynastic Wars of the Roses disappeared the rough and variable balance that till then had existed between the king and the three estates. After systematically killing off all the descendants of John of Gaunt that fell into his hands, Edward IV began the creation of a nobility dependent on himself from among the numerous relatives of his wife. Richard III promptly executed them as a preliminary to the secret murder of his nephews; Henry VII persistently depressed the remnants of the old baronage, depriving them of their privileges and enforcing obedience to his laws. He derived his title to the throne from his mother, the heiress of the elder branch of the legitimated Beauforts, and, having neither brother nor sister, left his son his inheritance without any fear of rivalry in his own house. He united the rival Roses by marrying the heiress of Edward IV, and took the additional precaution of imprisoning and subsequently executing the last male of the House of York. When Henry VIII ascended the throne in 1509, he was the first English king for more than a century whose title was accepted by all his subjects. He also had the advantage of not having a brother. He steadily maintained his father's policy of destroying the independence of the feudal baronage, created a new nobility, and governed England personally with the advice and assistance of Ministers whom he appointed and dismissed at pleasure. Like the Turk he bore no rival near his throne. He determined to prevent a disputed succession after his death by exterminating the last scions of the Plantagenet stock; he began by executing the Duke of Buckingham, and, later in his reign, he executed his cousins, the daughter of the Duke of Clarence and her eldest son. The gentry and commons pitied his victims, but approved of the security thus provided for the future peace of the land. 'Bluff King Hal' was for more than twenty years the most popular King of England since the time of Henry V. He was very handsome, fond of outdoor sports, a good scholar, a patron of the arts, profuse in his expenditure, and, like Francis I of France and Charles V, Emperor of Germany, maintained a magnificent court, full of pomp and ceremony.

After the breach with Rome his imperious nature took a tyrannical turn. Scenes of slavish adulation were exhibited at the opening of Parliament; the lords used to rise and bow to Henry whenever the words 'most sacred Majesty' were used. Henry refers to the 'Kingly Power given him by God' in the preamble to an Act of Parliament. His young son was surrounded with abasements and semi-divine reverence; he was served at his table by the highest nobles upon their knees, and even his elder sisters, Mary and Elizabeth, dined at lower tables than their young brother. Elizabeth continued the practice of her father and brother; she was received by her nobles with such bowings and prostrations as seemed to the French and Venetian Ambassadors unworthy of free men. When Henry VIII declared himself supreme head of the English Church, he united in himself, as English Pontiff and King, two titles, hitherto distinct, to the reverence and obedience of his subjects. Not many years had passed before his obsequious clergy, soon to be stripped of almost all their wealth, invented for their self-elected royal semi-divinity a new system of despotic theocracy. A principal article of the new creed was that the King was God's immediate deputy on earth, no longer liable to deposition on account of misrule or disobedience to the Church; obviously the supreme and infallible head of the English Church could not disobey or excommunicate himself. The second new tenet of importance was that the obedience of subjects to the prince was passive and without reservation of any kind, and the allegiance of subjects could not be withheld on any pretext whatsoever. Both these tenets were contrary to the teaching of the Catholic faith. This is set out in a book entitled *De Unitate Ecclesiae,* written by Reginald Pole, Henry's second cousin, early in 1536, and was sent by him to the King. 'What is a king?' the author asked. 'A king exists for the sake of his people; he is an outcome from Nature in labour; an institution for the defence of material and temporal interests. But inasmuch there are interests beyond the temporal, so there is a jurisdiction beyond the king's. The glory of a king is the welfare of his people; and if he knew himself, and knew his office, he would lay his crown and kingdom at the feet of the priesthood, as in a haven and quiet resting-place. To priests it was said, " Ye are gods, and ye are the children of the Most High." Who, then, can doubt that priests are higher in dignity than kings? In human society are three grades—the people—the priesthood, the head and husband of the people—the king, who is the child, the creature, and minister of the other two.'[8] In October, 1536, occurred the great northern rebellion known as the Pilgrimage of Grace, which endangered Henry's throne ; in May of the following year appeared a book, entitled *The Godly and Pious Institution of a Christian Man,* commonly known as the Bishop's Book. Drawn up in convocation three years previously for the direction of the clergy, it was printed by the order of the King; it contains what is, as far as I can discover, the earliest official statement of the new doctrines. In treat-

8. Quoted from Froude's *History of England* (1858), vol. III, pp. 34-35.

ing of the fifth commandment, the authors declare that subjects may not withdraw their allegiance from their Prince upon any pretext whatsoever; it is unlawful 'for the subjects to draw their swords against their sovereign for God has not made subjects their judge. No! He has made the supreme magistrate unaccountable to the people and reserved kings for His own tribunal; all subjects may do is to pray to God that He will turn the heart of their Prince.' Six years afterwards the book was re-issued with certain changes in doctrine, but the passages on divine right and passive obedience were unaltered. Upon the death of King Henry VIII in 1547, a boy of nine years became the Supreme Head of the English Church, and the Council of Regency, acting in his stead, advanced farther on the road to Protestantism. They prohibited the preaching of all sermons except under special licence, and they sent to every parish in the kingdom a book entitled *Certayne Sermons or Homilies, appoynted by the Kynges Maiestie to be declared, and redde by all Persones, Vicars, or Curates, euery Sundaye in their Churches, where they haue cure.'* The tenth homily is 'An exhortation concerning good order and obedience to Rulers and Magistrates,' and fills nine folio pages in the edition of 1640. It is divided into three parts, one to be read on each of three consecutive Sundays, and it briefly expounds such politico-religious doctrines as the divine right of kings, non-resistance, passive obedience, and the wickedness of rebellion. Numerous editions of these official sermons were printed during Edward's reign, but the book was suppressed when Mary became queen and abandoned the title of Supreme Head of the Church. The Homilies were reprinted soon after Elizabeth's accession; in 1563 appeared *The Seconde Tome of Homilies containing XX discourses,'* each of these new sermons being on religious doctrine or morality.

Shakespeare and the Homilies

Rebellion broke out in the north of England in November, 1569, and after causing much alarm throughout the country, was suppressed three months later. Almost immediately afterwards Pope Pius V issued his Bull of Deposition against Elizabeth, excommunicating her and absolving her subjects from their allegiance. Next year Ridolfi plotted the invasion of England; for his share in this the last of England's dukes, the Duke of Norfolk, was executed. The Queen and her Council were seriously alarmed, and instructed the bishops to prepare a new homily on disobedience and wilful rebellion; this new and last addition to the Homilies was printed without a title-page in 1573, and was included in all subsequent editions. With the single exception of the controversial homily on ' Idolatry,' this new homily was by far the longest, extending to 46 folio pages. It is divided into six parts, to each of which is appended a special prayer to be said by the whole congregation; at the conclusion is added ' A thanksgiving for the suppression of the last Rebellion,' to which other references are made in the text. In the preface to this new edition of the first part, published in 1562, we read, ' And when the foresaid Book of Homilies is read over, her Majesties pleasure is, that it be repeated, and read again in such like sort as was before prescribed.'

When Shakespeare was a boy of nearly six years of age he would doubtless see troops being hurried northwards along the two London roads that met at Stratford Bridge. Alderman John Shakespeare would be active in the enlistment of Stratfordian Feebles, Shadows and Warts for the army raised to put down the rebellion of the northern earls. During the following two years, rumours of invasion,

Stuffing the Eares of them with false Reports,

would keep the townsmen on the alert. John Shakespeare, Chief Alderman in 1571, and for the year a Justice

22

of the Peace, would be responsible for the efficiency of
the local militia, its musters, levies, equipment and train-
ing. The poet would be in his tenth year when the new
homily on 'Disobedience and Wilful Rebellion' was
read for the first time in Holy Trinity Church. Its
downrightness, simplicity of language, freedom from
dogma and direct references to events of three years
before were calculated to impress the memory and mind
of an imaginative boy. To forget it or its solemn teachings would be impossible, for on nine Sundays or holy-
days in each year the congregation would hear a portion
of the homily on Obedience or a sixth of that on Disobedience and Wilful Rebellion, and would at the
conclusion of the reading say the prayer for the safety
of the queen and her defence against rebels and traitors.

Such would have been part of the early religious train-
ing of almost all the numerous poets, dramatists,
annalists, and other prose writers that adorned the Elizabethan age, and we can mark the gradual spread and
general acceptance of the doctrine of divine right. Sir
John Cheke, afterwards tutor to Edward VI and secretary to the Council, wrote, as a very young man, a tract
entitled *A Remedy for Sedition, wherein are conteyned
many Thinges concernynge the true and loyall Obey-
sance, that Commens ow vnto their Prince and Souerygne
Lorde the Kynge.* After Ket's rebellion he published
another pamphlet, *The Hurt of Sedicion, how grievous
it is to a Common-wealth.* We do not know the date of
Bishop Bale's anti-Catholic play, *King John,* but it was
probably written during the reign of Edward VI. Here
we find the doctrines of divine right and passive obedience explicitly stated for the first time in drama. Verity
says :—

> For God's sake obey, like as doth you befall;
> For, in his own realm, a king is judge over all
> By God's appointment; and none may him judge again
> But the Lord Himself: in this the Scripture is plain.

Shakespeare and the Homilies

> He that condemneth a king, condemneth God, without doubt;
> He that harmeth a king, to harm God goeth about.
> He that a prince resisteth, doth damn God's ordinance;
> And resisteth God in withdrawing his affiance.
> All subjects offending are under the king's judgment:
> A king is reserved to the Lord omnipotent.
> He is a minister immediate under God,
> Of his righteousness to execute the rod.[9]

The doctrine was spreading in Europe and was held as strongly by the Catholic Mary Queen of Scots as by her Protestant rival Elizabeth. When put upon her trial for her part in Babington's conspiracy, she protested that ' she was a Princess and answerable as such to no earthly tribunal whatever.'[10] ' " Princes anointed," she seemed to think, were not like common mortals, and the word of a Prince, if solemnly given, was an evidence not to be challenged.'[11] After her condemnation to death she was treated by her custodians as degraded from her rank, and she replied:—' She was an anointed Queen. Man could not take her rank from her, and she would die a Queen in spite of them. They had no more right over her, she said, than a highwayman over an honest magistrate, whom he might meet at the corner of a wood. God would avenge her. English Kings had been often murdered, and being of the same blood, it was like enough she would fare no better. They had killed King Richard, and now they might kill her.'[12] Direct allusions to Queen Elizabeth and King James as ' sacred majesty ' or to the ' sacred person ' of royalty are to be found in such prose writers as Lyly, Stubbs, Puttenham, Nashe, Bacon, etc., and in court poetry; they are more numerous in the dramas of Peele, Greene, Marlowe, Shakespeare, Heywood, Fletcher, etc., and in several anonymous plays. Apart from this stock epithet ' sacred.' and the comparison of kings to God, allusions to the doctrines of divine right, passive obedience and the sin of rebellion are infrequent in plays.

9. *Early English Dramatists, Dramatic Writings of John Bale,* pp. 278-9. See also allusions on pp. 234, 237, etc., of this volume.
10, 11, 12. Froude, *History of England* (1870), vol. XII, pp. 282, 285, 310.

Shakespeare's predecessors in our early drama assume
that both Christian and non-Christian princes alike rule
by right divine. Peele in the *Battle of Alcazar*, refers to
the 'sacred name' of Sultan Amurath, whom he elsewhere calls 'the God of earthly kings.' Longshanks in
Edward I, is welcomed on his return from Palestine
'like an earthly God,' and presents John Baliol to the
Scottish nobles as their 'anointed King'; three other
passages speak of his 'sacred person.' The reference in
David and Bethsabe comes from the Bible itself.
Greene's language is similar. In *Alphonsus* Amurack ' the
Great Turk' speaks of Jove as his 'brother;' Fausta, his
wife, addresses her son-in-law Alphonsus as 'sacred
prince,' and Carinus alludes to his son's 'sacred feet.'
The flatterer Ateukin calls James IV 'my God on
earth,' and Dorothea alludes to her husband as 'dear
anointed King.' Marlowe has the same phrases in
Tamburlaine. Bajazeth, the Sultan of Egypt, talks of
his 'sacred arms,' the virgins address the hero as 'sacred
Emperor,' and Zenocrate begs him to save 'his sacred
person free from scathe.' Not one allusion to divine
right is to be found in *Edward II*, which in this respect
contrasts strongly with Shakespeare's *Richard II*. Another reference of a similar character occurs in *Soliman
and Perseda,* in which Amurath calls his brother,

> heauens onely substitute
> And earths commander vnder Mahomet.

This allusion may antedate that found in *The Troublesome Raigne of King John*. The Bastard thus addresses
the peers in revolt:—

> But where fell traitorism hath residence,
> There wants no words to set despite on work.
> I say 'tis shame, and worthy all reproof,
> To wrest such petty wrongs, in terms of right,
> Against a king anointed by the Lord.

> Why, Salsbury, admit the wrongs are true;
> Yet subjects may not take in hand revenge,
> And rob the heavens of their proper power,
> Where sitteth He to whom revenge belongs.[13]

The remarkable fact that each of the three extant plays
on Richard II contains several references to divine right
suggests that the queen's nick-name, Richard the Second,
was well known to the dramatists. They unite in
ascribing to this king an anachronistic belief in the divine
right of kings. The author of the earliest, the anonymous and corrupt *Jack Straw*, in such passages as

> Who are the captains of this rebel rout
> That thus do rise 'gainst their anointed king ?[14]

and

> Your open and unnatural rebellion against your lawful
> Sovereign and anointed prince,[15]

stresses the grave breach of duty and obedience that
rebellion against the Lord's anointed involves. Elsewhere
he terms the rioters 'unnatural rebels' and with monotonous iteration says that they

> unnaturally seek wreak on their lord
> Their true anointed prince, their lawful king.[16]

The court does not permit the boy king to forget his
semi-divinity. The bishop exhorts him to

> rule like God's vice-gerent here on earth,[17]

and his mother speaks of 'my son, their true anointed
king.' Modern critics usually date the anonymous play
on Richard II, discovered in Egerton, MS. 1994, somewhere about 1592-5; two of the longer references to the
divine right of the king closely resemble in language and
thought passages present in Shakespeare's play.

> But hees our Kinge and Gods great deputye,
> And if ye hunt to haue me second ye
> In any rash attempt against his state,
> Afore my God, Ile nere consent vnto it.

13. Furness, *King John*, p. 521, 2nd part. iii. ll. 112-120.
14. *Dodsley* (Hazlitt's edition), vol. 5, p. 390.
15. *Ibid.*, p. 409.
16. *Ibid.*, p. 386.
17. *Ibid.*, p. 391.

> I euer yet was iust and trew to hime,
> And so will still remayne: whats now amiss,
> Our sinnes haue caused; and we must byd heauens will.[18]

These lines are most absurdly put into the mouth of
the restless, intriguing and ambitious Duke of Gloucester,
'plain' Thomas of Woodstock, the political storm-centre
of the period; Shakespeare's *Richard II* opens shortly
after his mysterious death or murder. Richard is
dramatically himself in his boasts and lofty claims:—

> Although we could haue easely surprised,
> Disperst and ouerthrowne your rebell troupes,
> That draw your swords against our sacred person,
> The hyest God's anoynted deputye,
> Breaking your holly oathes to heauen and vs,
> Yett of our mild and princely clemencye
> We haue foreborne.[19]

Several anonymous plays of this period, e.g., *The True
Tragedy of Richard III, A Knack to Know a Knave,
Selimus, Mucedorus, Edward III* and *Sir Thomas More*
allude to the claims of kings, ancient and modern, eastern
or western, to be God's deputies on earth. The three
allusions to 'the sacred presence of a king,' 'sacred
lippes' and 'your sacred selfe,' present in *Edward III*
occur in that part of the play which many critics ascribe
to Shakespeare. Moreover, the decisive argument used
by More in his famous speech to the 'Ill May Day'
rioters (also ascribed to Shakespeare) rests upon their
belief in and acceptance of a theory of government based
upon a kingship whose authority is derived from God.

Shakespeare outdoes every other important dramatist
of his time in the number and variety of the allusions
made to the divine right of the reigning monarch, the
duty of passive obedience, enjoined on subjects by God,
and the misery and chaos resulting from civil war and
rebellion. References to such topics are scattered through
at least twenty plays; the first appears in *I Henry VI*,
the last in *Henry VIII*, his latest play now extant. Though

18. *W. Keller* (edition, 1899, Jahrbuch, XXXV, 3), IV. ii. ll. 143-149.
19. *Ibid.*, V. ii. ll. 100-6.

most frequent in the plays on English history, they are also to be found in comedies of his early and middle period, in the great tragedies and such late romances as *Pericles* and *The Winter's Tale*. ' Sacred ' and ' anointed ' seem to be stock epithets of honour customarily used by Shakespeare of the ruler of a state whether he is styled Emperor, King, prince or duke; the poet dignifies even the ruler's head, breast, blood, state, throne, honour, will and wit, and, in *Richard II,* the handle of his sceptre by describing them as ' sacred.' The participial adjective, ' anointed,' usually keeps the specialized sense of ' consecrated by unction,' and therefore has a more restricted range of usage; the sovereign, king, queen, or majesty is the ' anointed deputy of heaven ' or, in biblical language, ' the Lord's anointed.' In *Love's Labour's Lost* the King of Navarre is addressed rather fantastically by Armado as ' anointed ;' in other plays this epithet is descriptive of the ruler's head, body and flesh. Were thirty or forty allusions of this type all that were present in Shakespeare's plays, he would not, in his language about royalty, exhibit any important difference from his predecessors and contemporaries except in the greater number of such allusions made; even this seeming superiority would be best explained as due to the greater number of his plays now extant. What is peculiar to Shakespeare is that he treats the politico-theological doctrines of divine right, non-resistance, passive obedience and the sin of rebellion, as the accepted and immutable law of almost every land in every age. He has adroitly woven into the fabric of his plays so many and varied references, direct and indirect, to these doctrines, that we may extract from them an excellent digest of the main articles of the factitious political creed of the Tudors concerning the constitution of the body politic in general and the relation of ruler to subject in particular. Shakespeare was a poet and playwright, not a theologian or a politician; neither interest nor zeal compelled

him to dogmatize. Accordingly he does not quote the
words of King David or the sayings of the apostles, and
does not support the prevalent political philosophy with a
battalion of texts chosen from the Scriptures, as do the
authors of the homilies on *Obedience* and *Disobedience
and Wilful Rebellion.*

These two homilies put into the form of sermons a
series of simple lessons on the fundamental principles of
Tudor politics, in which were expounded the logical and
theological bases of the constitution of the Tudor Church
and State in language simple, forceful and at times
eloquent. The various themes were developed in orderly
sequence, and were designed to teach congregations the
duties of docile subjects, and thus keep the people (in
unquestioning obedience. I give below a short summary
of the non-theological portions, and then set out at some
length a number of comparative passages chosen from
the plays of Shakespeare and the two homilies respectively.

Order is Heaven's first law in the universe, in this
world of ours, in nature, and in human society. To
everything, animate or inanimate, God has assigned a set
place. The maintenance of order, so essential to the
continuity of national life or even its existence, rests upon
the orderly interdependence of the various ranks into
which He has divided the people of every nation. Unless
law and order prevail, chaos must result, civilized man
would sink into the savage, and might would be right.
God has ordained Kings and Rulers to govern communities for the common benefit of all. The principal duty
of the subject is obedience unlimited; the king's authority may be proved both from the Scriptures and from
the teaching and examples of the Apostles, to be derived
directly from God. The titles given in the Scriptures
to Kings are a proof that God has bestowed on them
power over their subjects; since this power is God's gift,
man cannot take it away. If a king be wicked and prove

a scourge to his people, the only remedy is patient endurance—till his death. Disobedience to a king is disobedience to God; rebellion against God's deputy is rebellion against God. The crimes of a wicked king must be left to God to punish; He defends kings, just and unjust, and punishes the sin of rebellion with plagues, famine and civil war. A king is called a god on earth in the Scriptures.

Rebellion is always wrong; subjects may not sit in judgment upon their sovereign, and may not depose or kill him. Rebellion is not a good method of obtaining the redress of grievances, as the evils arising from it far exceed the worst evils due to the worst government. It is the greatest sin in the black book of human iniquity, and includes all the worst crimes, especially robbery, perjury and murder. Breaking an oath of allegiance to a prince is breaking an oath sworn to God. Miseries of every kind afflict a land in which rebellion breaks out; disease, pestilence, famine and all the horrors of civil war are inevitable, and are followed by destruction of liberty and the captivity, slavery or slaughter of both rebels and obedient subjects. Robbery and murder keep company with rebellion and treason. God punishes rebels with exemplary severity; even if we judge rebellion from the standpoint of worldly success, it is always and almost everywhere a failure, and the rebels, their families and friends, are ruined and destroyed. History records the ill success of rebellions and the extinction of many great and noble houses, of dukes, marquises, earls, barons and others who have taken part in insurrections against their princes. The usual pretexts offered for rebellion, such as changes in religion, redress of grievances, and the need of reforming the state, are insufficient reasons for committing such a crime against God, king, and country. The rebel-leaders are 'restless-ambitious' men; their followers mostly wastrels, spendthrifts, ruined men and criminals. Reform is the euphemism of the rebel for the robberies and murders which he intends to commit. The Devil is the true captain of rebels, and to his machinations and promptings rebellion is usually due.

The tenth homily of the first series entitled ' An Exhortation Concerning Good Order and Obedience to Rulers and Magistrates ' begins thus:—

> Almighty God hath created and appointed all things in heaven, earth and waters, in a most excellent and perfect Order. In heaven he hath appointed distinct and several orders and states of Archangels and Angels: In earth he hath assigned and appointed Kings, Princes, with other Governours under them in all good and necessary order. The water above is kept, and raineth down in due time and season. The Sun, Moon, Starrs, Rain-bow, Thunder. Lightning, Clouds, and all the Birds of the Ayr do keep their order. . . . All the parts of the whole year, as Winter, Summer, Moneths, Nights and Dayes, continue in their order: All kinds of Fishes in the Sea, Rivers and Waters, with all Fountains, Springs, yea, the Seas themselves keep their comely course and order: . . . every degree of people in their vocation, calling and office, hath appointed to them their duty and order: some are in high degree, some in low, some Kings and Princes, some inferiours and subjects, Priests and Lay-men, Masters and Servants, Fathers and Children, Husbands and Wives, Rich and Poor, and every one hath need of other: so that in all things is to be loved and praised the goodly order of God, without the which no House, no City, no Common-wealth can continue, and endure or last.[20]

The above themes are Tudor commonplaces. Shakespeare's passionate love of order produced poetry not preachments; he viewed the events in the world around him with a poet's eye, and gave even topical allusions an imaginative setting.

For five years, 1594-8, bad season followed bad season; the refrain of Feste's song, ' The rain it raineth every day,' was almost literally true, if we may believe Stow and Camden. The results were high prices, a scarcity of food amounting to famine, and much turbulence and discontent. The poet in alluding to these calamities in

20. *Certain Sermons or Homilies* (1640), p. 69.

A Midsummer Night's Dream, turns them to admirable dramatic account by ascribing these unusual reversals of the order of Nature to the quarrels between Oberon and Titania.

> Therefore the Windes, piping to vs in vaine,
> As in reuenge, haue suck'd vp from the sea
> Contagious fogges: Which falling in the Land,
> Hath euerie petty River made so proud,
> That they haue ouer-borne their Continents.
> .   .   .   .
> The humane mortals want their winter heere,
> No night is now with hymne or caroll blest;
> Therefore the Moone (the gouernesse of floods)
> Pale in her anger, washes all the aire;
> That Rheumaticke diseases doe abound.
> And through this distemperature, we see
> The seasons alter; hoared headed frosts
> Fall in the fresh lap of the crimson Rose,
> And on old Hyems chinne and Icie crowne,
> An odorous Chaplet of sweet Sommer buds
> Is as in mockry set. The Spring, the Sommer,
> The childing Autumne, angry Winter change
> Their wonted Liueries, and the mazed world,
> By their increase, now knowes not which is which.[21]

Here Shakespeare describes the 'progeny of euills' that afflict mankind when Nature becomes orderless; in *Henry V* the Archbishop forgets to preach, and points his moral of the necessity of Order with his tale of the 'Hony Bees' and their 'King.' Exeter gives his Grace a chance of expatiating on

> The Act of Order to a peopled Kingdome.

> EXETER. For Gouernment, though high, and low, and lower,
> Put into parts, doth keepe in one consent,
> Congreeing in a full and natural close,
> Like Musicke.
> CANT.   Therefore doth heauen diuide
> The state of man in diuers functions,
> Setting endeuour in continual motion:
> To which is fixed as an ayme or butt,
> Obedience: for so worke the Hony Bees,
> Creatures that by a rule in Nature teach
> The Act of Order to a peopled Kingdome.

21. *Midsummer Night's Dream,* II. i. ll. 88-92; ll. 101-114.

They haue a King, and Officers of sorts,
Where some like Magistrates correct at home:
Others, like Merchants venter Trade abroad:
Others, like Souldiers armed in their stings,
Make boote vpon the Summers Veluet buddes:
Which pillage, they with merry march bring home
To the Tent-royal of their Emperor:
Who busied in his Maiesties surueyes
The singing Masons building roofes of Gold,
The ciuil Citizens kneading vp the hony;
The poore Mechanicke Porters, crowding in
Their heauy burthens at his narrow gate:
The sad-ey'd Iustice with his surly humme,
Deliuering ore to Executors pale
The lazie yawning Drone.[22]

With the extract from the Homily we may also compare the great speech of Ulysses in the third scene of *Troilus and Cressida*.

Perhaps the homily gave a hint to Shakespeare which his generalising mind and poetic imagination developed into this magnificent recognition of a general Law of Order that governs alike the Universe, nature and that moral and political animal, man.

The Heauens themselues, the Planets, and this Center,
Obserue degree, priority, and place,
Insisture, course, proportion, season, forme,
Office, and custome, in all line of Order:
And therefore is the glorious Planet Sol
In noble eminence, enthron'd and sphear'd
Amid'st the other, whose med'cinable eye
Corrects the ill Aspects of Planets euill,
And postes like the Command'ment of a King
Sans checke, to good and bad . . .
                              O, when Degree is shak'd,
(Which is the Ladder to all high designes)
The enterprize is sicke. How could Communities,
Degrees in Schooles, and Brother-hoods in Cities,
Peacefull Commerce from diuidable shores,
The primogenitiue, and due of Byrth,
Prerogatiue of Age, Crownes, Scepters, Lawrels,
(But by Degree) stand in Authentique place?[23]

The homily is concerned with civilised society as it existed

22. *Henry V*, I. ii. ll. 180-204.
23. *Troilus and Cressida*, I. iii. ll. 85-94, 101-8.

c

then in Europe or had existed in the past, and declares that without order man would sink in the scale and revert to brute savagery.

> For where there is no right order, there reigneth all abuse, carnal liberty, enormity, sinn, and Babylonical confusion. Take away Kings, Princes, Rulers, Magistrates, Judges, and such estates of Gods order, no man shall ride or go by the high way unrobbed, no man shall sleep in his own house or bed unkilled, no man shall keep his wife, children and possession in quietness, all things shall be common, and there must needs follow all mischief, and utter destruction both of souls, bodies, goods and Common-wealths.[24]

Shakespeare has several important passages referring to the ruin that invariably accompanies widespread disorder. The wild outburst of 'crafty-sick' Northumberland when he learns that Hotspur, whom he has forsaken, is dead is a fine touch of characterisation. Grief and perhaps remorse for the death of his son, rage and disappointment at the failure of the conspiracy, and craven fears for his own safety overmaster his habit of prudence, and in revengeful wrath he would involve all the world in his own impending ruin if wishes could prevail.

> Let Heauen kisse Earth; now let not Natures hand
> Keepe the wilde Flood confin'd: Let Order dye,
> And let the world no longer be a stage
> To feed Contention in a ling'ring Act:
> But let one spirit of the First-borne Caine
> Reigne in all bosomes, that each heart being set
> On bloody Courses, the rude Scene may end,
> And darknesse be the burier of the dead.[25]

The mature wisdom of Ulysses traces the subversion of order in a community when irreverence leads to insubordination, insubordination to 'neglection of degree' and finally to 'Chaos when Degree is suffocate.'

> Take but Degree away, vn-tune that string,
> And hearke what Discord followes: each thing meetes
> In meere oppugnancie. The bounded Waters,
> Should lift their bosomes higher then the Shores,
> And make a soppe of all this solid Globe;

24. *Homilies*, pp. 69-70.
25. *2 Henry IV*, I. i. ll. 153-160.

> Strength should be Lord of imbecility,
> And the rude Sonne should strike his Father dead:
> Force should be right, or rather, right and wrong,
> (Betweene whose endlesse iarre, Iustice recides)
> Should loose her names, and so should Iustice too.
> Then euery thing includes it selfe in Power,
> Power into Will, Will into Appetite,
> And Appetite (an vniuersall Wolfe
> So doubly seconded with Will, and Power)
> Must make perforce an vniuersall prey,
> And last, eate vp himselfe.[26]

Patrician pride, an ungovernable temper, and measure-less contempt for the plebeians combine to make the political wisdom of Coriolanus valueless to the Rome that he loves:—

> This double worship,
> Whereon part do's disdaine with cause, the other
> Insult without all reason: where Gentry, Title, wisedom
> Cannot conclude, but by the yea and no
> Of generall Ignorance, it must omit
> Reall Necessities, and giue way the while
> To vnstable Slightnesse. Purpose so barr'd, it followes,
> Nothing is done to purpose.[27]

Professor R. W. Chambers has shown that More's magnificent speech to the Ill May Day rioters has the right Shakespearean ring, and that the only parallels to the thought and its expression are to be found in *Troilus and Cressida* and *Coriolanus*. The rebels have demanded the forcible expulsion of foreign merchants from London, and More develops his arguments against the adoption of such a policy.

> Graunt them remoued, and graunt that this your noyce
> Hath chidd downe all the maiestie of Ingland:
> Ymagin that you see the wretched straingers,
> Their babyes at their backes and their poor lugage,
> Plodding tooth ports and costes for transportacion,
> And that you sytt as Kinges in your desyres,
> Aucthoryty quyte sylenct by your braule,
> And you in ruff of your opynions clothd;

26. *Troilus and Cressida,* I. iii. ll. 109-124.
27. *Coriolanus,* III. i. ll. 142-149.

> What had you gott? I'le tell you: you had taught
> How insolence and strong hand shoold preuayle,
> How ordere shoold be quelld; and by this patterne
> Not on of you shoold lyue an aged man,
> For other ruffians, as their fancies wrought,
> With sealf same hand, sealf reasons, and sealf right,
> Woold shark on you, and men lyke rauenous fishes
> Woold feed on on another.[28]

This passage comes from the scene of the play, which many critics attribute to Shakespeare.

The homilist then proceeds to prove from numerous passages of the Scriptures that

> by the infallible, and undeceivable Word of God, Kings, and other supreme, and higher officers are ordained of God.[29]

This doctrine is repeated shortly afterwards:—

> We must refer all judgment to God, to Kings and Rulers, Judges under them, which be God's officers to execute justice, and by plain words of Scripture, have their authority, and use of the sword granted from God.[30]

We find in the poet's plays some direct and many indirect allusions to this fundamental article of Tudor state-craft that the monarch is the divinely appointed representative of God upon earth. In *King John,* Cardinal Pandulph, immediately on his entrance, greets the Kings of England and France with the words,

> Haile you annointed deputies of heauen.[31]

King John challenges the right of the pope to interfere in English affairs by asking the Cardinal

> What earthie name to Interrogatories
> Can tast the free breath of a sacred King?[32]

He bids the legate tell the pope

> (But) as we, vnder heauen, are supreame head,
> So vnder him that great supremacy
> Where we doe reigne, we will alone vphold
> Without th' assistance of a mortall hand.[33]

---

28. *Sir Thomas More*, II. iv. 92-107 (*The Shakespeare Apocrypha*, 1908).
29. *Homilies*, p. 70.
30. *Homilies*, p. 71.
31, 32, 33. *King John*, III. i. 136, ll. 147-8, 155-8.

Earlier in the play, he announces to Philip of France his resolve to maintain his rights, peacefully if possible,

> If not, bleede France, and peace ascend to heauen,
> Whiles we Gods wrathfull agent doe correct
> Their proud contempt that beats his peace to heauen.[34]

Richard II is the main Shakespearean storehouse of passages relating to divine right.   The loyal Bishop of Carlisle fittingly reminds King Richard that he may rely upon God's help,

> Feare not my Lord, that Power that made you King
> Hath power to keepe you King, in spight of all.[35]

We may expect that the royal saint, King Henry the Sixth, will modestly recognise his own semi-divinity,

> And therefore by his maiestie I sweare,
> Whose farre-vnworthie Deputie I am,
> He shall not breathe infection in this ayre,
> But three dayes longer, on the paine of death.[36]

But we may gasp in wonder at the claim of the royal criminal, Richard the Third, to this God-ordained sacrosanctity.

> A flourish Trumpets, strike Alarum Drummes :
> Let not the Heauens heare these Tell-tale women
> Raile on the Lords Annointed.   Strike I say.[37]

Sir Thomas More comes much nearer to the words of the homily when he tells the rioters,

> For to the King God hath his offyce lent
> Of dread, of iustyce, power and commaund,
> Hath bid him rule, and willd you to obay.[38]

The logical corollary of the above doctrine is the paramount duty of obedience to authority; this is thus explicitly formulated by the homilist.

> Let us learn of Saint Paul the chosen vessel of God, that all persons having souls (he excepteth none, nor exempteth none, neither Priest, Apostle, nor Prophet, saith S. Chrysostom)

34. *Ibid.*, II. ll. 86-8.
35. *Richard II*, III. ii. ll. 27-8.
36. *2 Henry VI*, III. ii. ll. 285-8.
37. *Richard III*, IV. iv. ll. 148-150.
38. *Sir Thomas More*, II. iv. ll. 122-4.

do owe of bounden duty, and even in conscience, obedience, submission and subjection to the high powers, which be set in authority by God, for as much as they be Gods Lieutenants, Gods Presidents, Gods Officers, Gods Commissioners, Gods Judges, ordained of God himself, of whom only they have all their power, and all their authority. And the same S. Paul threateneth no less pain, than everlasting damnation to all disobedient persons, to all resisters against this general and common authority, for as much as they resist not man but God, nor mans device, and invention, but Gods wisedom, Gods Order, Power, and Authority.[39]

In the homily on Wilful Rebellion the author declares,

'It is evident that Obedience is the principal vertue of all vertues, and indeed the very root of all vertues, and the cause of all felicity.[40]

Shakespeare's noble characters not only themselves obey, but insist on obedience to authority in others. The loyal Sir Walter Blunt, whose devotion to his master, Henry IV, leads to his death, declines to exchange courtesies and compliments with Hotspur, and stands against him ' like an Enemie '

So long as out of Limit, and true Rule,
You stand against Anoynted Maiestie.[41]

Bates tells the disguised king on the night before the battle of Agincourt,

Wee know enough, if wee know wee are the Kings Subiects: if his Cause be wrong, our obedience to the King wipes the Cryme of it out of vs.[42]

The king settles the argument with the Tudor sentiment,

Euery Subiects Dutie is the Kings, but euery
Subiects Soule is his owne.[43]

The nobles of King John before their revolt breathe passive obedience even to the whims of the king. He has been crowned a second time contrary to their advice, and they reluctantly acquiesce. Pembroke replies to the king's ' Heare once againe we sit ' with,

39. *Homilies*, p. 71.
40. *Ibid.*, pp. 275-6.
41. *1 Henry IV*, IV. iii. ll. 39-40.
42. *Henry V*, IV. i. ll. 123-6.
43. *Henry V*, IV. i. ll. 165-6.

> This once again (but that your Highnes pleas'd)
> Was once superfluous: you were Crown'd before,
> And that high Royalty was nere pluck'd off:
> The faiths of men, nere stained with reuolt:
> Fond expectation troubled not the Land
> With any long'd-for-change, or better State.[44]

Pembroke doubts the wisdom of the king's action, prefacing his objection, however, with the words,

> But that your Royall pleasure must be done.[45]

Salisbury is much more explicit in his humble submission.

> To this effect, before you were new crown'd
> We breath'd our Councell: but it pleas'd your Highnes
> To ouer-beare it, and we are all well pleas'd,
> Since all, and euery part of what we would
> Doth make a stand, at what your Highnesse will.[46]

Macbeth's reply to King Duncan's warm thanks is in the true spirit of the homilies.

> The seruice, and the loyaltie I owe,
> In doing it, payes it selfe.
> Your Highnesse part, is to receiue our Duties:
> And our Duties are to your Throne, and State,
> Children, and Seruants; which doe but what they should,
> By doing euery thing safe toward your Loue
> And Honor.[47]

When Richard the Second's uncle, the regent York, learns of his nephew Bolingbroke's unauthorised return from banishment, he wavers between loyalty to the king and his sense of justice, and does nothing:—

> Both are my kinsmen,
> Th' one is my Soueraigne, whom both my oath
> And dutie bids defend: th' other againe
> Is my kinsman, whom the King hath wrong'd,
> Whom conscience, and my kindred bids to right.[48]

To the list of titles given to kings in the passages cited above from the homilies may be added those of

44. *King John*, IV. i. ll. 3-8.
45. *Ibid.*, IV. i. l. 17.
46. *Ibid.*, IV. i. ll. 35-9.
47. *Macbeth*, I. iv. ll. 22-27.
48. *Richard II*, II. ii. ll. 111-14.

God's 'Lieutenant,' 'Vicegerent,' and 'Minister' found later; Shakespeare easily outdoes the homilist in the number and variety of such titles. Gaunt refers to his nephew, King Richard, as God's 'Minister' and

> Gods substitute
> His Deputy annointed in his sight.[49]

The Bishop of Carlisle, speaking in parliament, terms Richard,

> the figure of Gods Maiestie,
> His Captaine, Steward, Deputie elect.[50]

Prince John of Lancaster, the sober-blooded son of the usurper Bolingbroke, reproaches Archbishop Scroop thus :—

> You haue tane vp
> Vnder the counterfeited Zeale of God,
> The Subiects of his Substitute, my Father,
> And both against the Peace of Heauen, and him,
> Haue here vp-swarmed them.[51]

The reference in *2 Henry VI* has already been quoted. Shakespeare does not use the word 'Lieutenant' in this connection, but prefers 'Captain;' in addition to the passage in Carlisle's speech, Richmond in his prayer on the night before the battle of Bosworth Field, says

> O thou, whose Captaine I account my selfe,
> Looke on my Forces with a gracious eye.[52]

The Homilies frequently refer to kings as 'God's Ministers' or 'God's Officers;' Shakespeare uses the first phrase only once, Gaunt referring to his nephew Richard as 'God's Minister,' and the second phrase twice. A muddled recollection of this appellation, as used in the homilies of the king, must have flitted through Hostess Quickly's mind when she upbraids Falstaff and Bardolph for their resistance to the officers of the sheriff :—

> O thou Hony-suckle villaine, wilt thou kill Gods officers, and the Kings ?[53]

49. *Ibid.*, I. ii. ll. 37-41.
50. *Ibid.*, IV. i. ll. 125-7.
51. *2 Henry IV*, IV. ii. ll. 26-30.
52. *Richard III*, V. iii. ll. 99-100.
53. *2 Henry IV*, II. i. ll. 46-7.

Don Armado's affected letter to King Ferdinand of Navarre begins,

> Great Deputie, the Welkins Vicegerent, the sole dominator of Nauar.[54]

King John calls himself 'Gods wrathfull agent,' and Richard the Second speaks of 'My master, God omnipotent.'

The homilist lays his flattery on with a trowel, and does not hesitate to call kings gods on earth.

> As the name of a King is very often attributed and given unto God in the holy Scriptures; so doth God himself in the same Scriptures sometime vouchsafe to communicate his Name with earthly Princes, terming them gods; doubtless for that similitude of government which they have, or should have, not unlike unto God their King.[55]

The poet makes several allusions to this claim to be Gods on earth. Henry the Seventh, himself the grandson of a Welsh mercenary soldier, the ancestor of our English dynasty of semi-divine monarchs, ends his first speech to his followers with the following couplet,

> True Hope is swift, and flyes with Swallowes wings,
> Kings it makes Gods, and meaner creatures Kings.[56]

Armado in his letter calls King Ferdinand of Navarre 'my soules earths God.' The Duchess of York, after begging a pardon for her stepson, Rutland, from Henry IV, flatteringly addresses the newly self-elected usurping king,

> A God on earth thou art.[57]

Hamlet's uncle, King Claudius, quickly 'assumes the god'; when Laertes breaks into the king's presence, Claudius retains his calmness.

> Let him go Gertrude: Do not feare our person:
> There's such Diuinity doth hedge a King,
> That Treason can but peepe to what it would,
> Acts little of his will.[58]

54. *Love's Labour's Lost*, I, i, ll. 214-5.
55. *Homilies*, p. 278.
56. *Richard III*, V. ii. ll. 23-4.
57. *Richard II*, V. iii. 1. 𝒆𝒕. 136
58. *Hamlet*, IV. v. ll. 118-121.

41

In *Pericles* two such references occur; the first, 'Kings are earths gods' in the first scene of the play, the second in the last scene.

> The gods can haue no mortal officer
> More like a god than you.[59]

The doctrines of passive obedience and non-resistance are the logical consequences of deriving the king's authority directly from God. The homily emphatically insists

> That Kings, Queens, and other Princes . . . are ordained of God, and to be obeyed, and honoured of their subjects: that such subjects, as are disobedient or rebellious against their Princes, disobey God and procure their own damnation.[60]

> God defendeth them (Princes) against their enemies, and destroyeth their enemies horribly.[61]

Richard the Second is depicted as the dupe of his own credulity, in that he relies on a miracle to put down the rebellion of Bolingbroke:—

> For euery man that Bullingbrooke hath prest,
> To lift shrewd Steele against our Golden Crowne
> God for his Richard hath in heauenly pay
> A glorious Angell: then if Angels fight,
> Weake men must fall, for Heauen still guards the right.[62]

Richard looks upon revolt against him as a sin in the sight of God:—

> Reuolt our Subiects? That we cannot mend,
> They breake their Faith to God, as well as vs.[63]

When 'young Laertes, in a Riotous head' overpowers the royal guards and forces his way into the presence of the king, the latter asks him,

> What is the cause Laertes,
> That thy Rebellion lookes so Gyant-like?

On learning that his father is dead, his son renounces his vows of allegiance and declares that he will risk the

59. *Pericles*, V. iii. ll. 62-3.
60. *Homilies*, p. 277.
61. *Ibid.*, pp. 276-7.
62. *Richard II*, III. ii. ll. 58-62.
63. *Ibid.*, III. ii. ll. 100-101.

penalty of eternal damnation denounced against rebels
in order to be revenged on his father's murderer.

> How came he dead? Ile not be Iuggel'd with.
> To hell Allegeance: Vowes, to the blackest diuell.
> Conscience and Grace, to the profoundest Pit.
> I dare Damnation: to this point I stand,
> That both the worlds I giue to negligence,
> Let come what comes: onely Ile be reueng'd
> Most throughly for my Father.[64]

Sir Thomas More bluntly tells the rioters that rebellion
against the king is a sin involving their eternal damnation.

>   tis a sinn
> Which oft thappostle did forewarne vs of,
> Vrging obedience to authority;
> And twere no error, yf I told you all
> You wer in armes gainst your (God himself)
> ALL. Marry, God forbid that!
> MOO. Nay, certainly you are;
> For to the King, God hath his offyce lent
> Of dread, of iustyce, power and commaund,
> Hath bid him rule, and willd you to obay;
> And to add ampler maiestie to this,
> He hath not only lent the King his figure,
> His throne and sword, but gyuen him his owne name,
> Calls him a god on earth. What do you, then,
> Rysing gainst him that God himsealf enstalls,
> But ryse gainst God? What do you to your sowles
> In doing this?[65]

The homilies teach that subjects have duties but no
rights except the right of paying taxes and of enduring
oppression in patience and without a murmur. The
preacher expounds at great length the many lessons to
be drawn from the story of David's dealings with King
Saul. He puts a supposititious case that 'men desirous
of rebellion' ask David a series of questions on the right
of subjects to

> rise, and rebel against a Prince, hated of God, and Gods
> enemy, and therefore not like to prosper either in war, or
> peace, but to be hurtful, and pernicious to the Common-
> wealth.[66]

64. *Hamlet*, IV. v. ll. 116-7, 126-132.
65. *Sir Thomas More* (*Shakespeare's Apocrypha*, 1908), II. iv. ll. 115-131.
66. *Homilies*, p. 287.

To each of these questions David returns an unqualified
' No ' for answer; the last but one of these questions
runs :

Are not they (say some) lusty, and couragious Captains,
valiant men of stomach, and good mens bodies that do venture
by force to kill, and depose their King, being a naughty
Prince, and their mortal enemy? They may be as lusty, and
couragious as they list, yet, saith godly David, they can be
no good, nor godly men that do so: for I not only have
rebuked, but also commanded him to be slain as a wicked
man, which slew King Saul mine enemy, though he . . .
desired that man to slay him.[67]

What answer, think you, would he make to those that demand,
whether they (being naughty, and unkind subjects) may not,
to the great hazard of the life of many thousands, and the
utter danger of the state of the Common-wealth, and whole
Realm, assemble a sort of Rebels, either to depose, to put in
fear, or to destroy their natural, and loving Prince, enemy to
none, good to all, even to them the worst of all other; the
maintainer of perpetual peace, quietness and security?[68]

The answer to the last question is given as a marginal
note, ' An unnatural and wicked question.'

Richard II is the Shakespearean storehouse of
passages relating to deposition; the king declares :—

Not all the Water in the rough rude Sea
Can wash the Balme from an anoynted King;
The breath of worldly men cannot depose
The Deputie elected by the Lord.[69]

The King is trapped in Flint Castle, and when that
' haught insulting man,' Northumberland, fails to bend
his knee in the royal presence, Richard's cup of wrath
overflows :—

We thought our selfe thy lawfull King :
And if we be, how dare thy ioynts forget
To pay their awfull dutie to our presence?
If we be not, shew vs the Hand of God,
That hath dismiss'd vs from our Stewardship,
For well wee know, no Hand of Blood and Bone
Can gripe the sacred Handle of our Scepter,
Vnlesse he doe prophane, steale, or vsurpe.[70]

67. *Ibid.*, pp. 287-8.
68. *Homilies*, pp. 287-8.
69. *Richard II*, III. ii. ll. 54-7.
70. *Ibid.*, III. iii. ll. 74-81.

The Bishop of Carlisle boldly calls the usurping Bolingbroke 'a foule Traytor,' and denies the right of subjects
to sit in judgment on their sovereign.

> Would God, that any in this Noble Presence
> Were enough Noble, to be vpright Iudge
> Of Noble Richard: then true Noblenesse would
> Learne him forbearance from so foule a Wrong.
> What Subiect can giue Sentence on his King?
> And who sits here, that is not Richards Subiect?
> Theeues are not iudg'd, but they are by to heare,
> Although apparant guilt be seene in them:
> And shall the figure of Gods Maiestie,
> His Captaine, Steward, Deputie elect,
> Anoynted, Crown'd, planted many yeeres,
> Be iudg'd by subiect, and inferior breathe,
> And he himselfe not present? Oh, forbid it, God.[71]

Shakespeare has delineated two characters, each of
whom is tempted to murder a king. Sir Pierce Exton
clutches at temptation when it comes his way, and after
murdering Richard, his thoughts prepare us for his
reception by the tempter who profits by the crime :—

> Oh would the deed were good.
> For now the diuell, that told me I did well,
> Sayes, that this deede is chronicled in hell.[72]

In contrast we have the conduct of Camillo, who has
been forced by the threats of his jealous master, King
Leontes, to consent to murder his master's friend and
guest, King Polixenes.

> To doe this deed,
> Promotion followes: If I could find example
> Of thousand's that had struck anoynted Kings,
> And flourish'd after, Il'd not do't: But since
> Nor Brasse, nor Stone, nor Parchment beares not one,
> Let Villanie it selfe forswear't.[73]

When the penitent Leontes, for many years wifeless and
childless in consequence of his crimes, sees for the first
time Prince Florizel, the son of his injured friend

71. *1 Richard II*, IV. i. ll. 115-129.
72. *2 Ibid.*, V. v. ll. 114-6.
73. *The Winter's Tale*, I. ii. ll. 356-361.

Polixenes, he renews his sorrow and confesses his sin against God in plotting the murder of a king.

> You have a holy Father,
> A gracefull Gentleman, against whose person
> (So sacred as it is) I haue done sinne,
> For which, the Heauens (taking angry note)
> Haue left me Issue-lesse.[74]

The men 'desirous of rebellion' having received from 'Godly David' no other answers than 'No' to all their questions, ask him in despair,

> What shall we then do to an evil, to an unkind Prince, an enemy to us, hated of God, hurtful to the Common-wealth: Lay no violent hand upon him, saith good David, but let him live until God appoint, and work his end, either by natural death, or in war by lawful enemies, not by traiterous subjects.[75]

In the early homily on *Obedience,* the king is referred to as

> A person reserved and kept (for his office sake) only to Gods punishment and judgement.[76]

For subjects the only remedy is patience:—

> We must in such case patiently suffer all wrongs and injuries, referring the judgment of our cause only to God.[77]

John of Gaunt accepts the view that the punishment of a wicked king lies in God's hands alone. His answer to his bereaved sister-in-law, the Duchess of Gloucester, who urges him to revenge the murder of his brother (here attributed to the king) breathes the resigned docility of the most perfect passive obedience.

> Alas, the part I had in Woodstocks blood
> Doth more solicite me then your exclaimes,
> To stirre agaipst the Butchers of his life.
> But since correction lyeth in those hands
> Which made the fault that we cannot correct,
> Put we our quarrel to the will of heauen,
> Who when they see the houres ripe on earth,
> Will raigne hot vengeance on offenders heads.[78]

74. *Ibid.,* V. i. ll. 170-4.
75. *Homilies,* pp. 287-8.
76. *Homilies,* p. 74.
77. *Ibid.,* p. 75.
78. *Richard II,* I. ii. ll. 1-8.

The duchess urges the ties of brotherhood and self-preservation as motives for action, but Gaunt takes his stand on the duty of non-resistance imposed by God on subjects and refuses to avenge Gloster's murder.

> Gods is the quarrel: for Gods substitute,
> His Deputy annointed in his sight,
> Hath caus'd his death, the which if wrongfully
> Let Heauen reuenge: for I may neuer lift
> An angry arme against his Minister.[79]

The conduct of the weak and vacillating Duke of York, appointed regent of England during Richard's absence in Ireland, typifies the difficulties that confronted a moderately loyal subject in times of revolution. When Bolingbroke first returned to England from banishment, York told him bluntly that he and his allies were rebels and traitors; a little later York so sharply reproves Northumberland for discourteously omitting Richard's title that the politic Bolingbroke, afraid that his powerful supporter may be offended, interposes with

> Mistake not (Vnckle) further then you should.

The regent resents what from its tone and brevity seems to be a command and retorts with dignity,

> Take not (good Cousin) further then you should.
> Least you mistake the Heauens are ouer our heads.

This rather cryptic suggestion that God is in his heaven and rebels must beware his wrath is answered with covert irony by Bolingbroke,

> I know it (Vnckle) and oppose not my selfe
> Against their will.[80]

When success has turned rebellion into revolution, and the rebel Bolingbroke has become ' an anointed king ' by deposing the undeposable ' figure of Gods Maiestie,' York makes an admirable speech in which he describes to his ·duchess the entry into London of the triumphant victor and his victim. He concludes it with the sage

79. *Ibid.*, I. ii. ll. 37-41.
80. *Richard II*, III. iii. ll. 15-19.

reflections that God knows best and that a subject combines duty and safety who obeys the king on the throne.

> But heauen hath a hand in these euents,
> To whose high will we bound our calme contents.
> To Bullingbrooke, are we sworne Subiects now,
> Whose State, and Honor, I for aye allow.[81]

The homilist vigorously condemns 'that most detestable Vice of Rebellion' as an abominable sin against God and man.

> How horrible a sin against God, and man Rebellion is, cannot possibly be expressed according unto the greatness thereof. For he that nameth Rebellion, nameth not a singular or one only sin, as is theft, robbery, murther and such like; but he nameth the whole puddle, and sink of all sins against God, and man, against his Prince, his Country, his Country-men, his parents, his children, his kinsfolks, his friends, and against all men universally; all sins, I say, against God, and all men heaped together nameth he, that nameth Rebellion.[82]

Though Shakespeare's plays are not politico-religious pamphlets, rebels and rebellion get nothing but hard words from his noble characters. When Bolingbroke returns from exile without permission, his uncle York, the regent, declines to accept his nephew's homage and greetings, declaring 'I am no Traytors Vnckle,' and when the smooth-spoken Bolingbroke asks

> My gracious Vnckle, let me know my Fault,
> On what Condition stands it, and wherein?

York tells him,

> Euen in Condition of the worst degree,
> In grosse Rebellion, and detested Treason.[83]

That plain, blunt man, Henry the Fifth, inferentially and with the modest humility so becoming in a king, compares himself to God in the concluding words of his denunciation of the conspirator, Lord Scroope,

> I will weepe for thee.
> For this reuolt of thine, me thinkes is like
> Another fall of Man.[84]

81. *Richard II*, V. ii. ll. 37-40.
82. *Homilies*, p. 292.
83. *Richard II*, II. iii. ll. 108-9.
84. *Henry V*, II. ii. ll. 140-2.

Rebellion against Henry reminds him of Man's first disobedience to God. Worcester, wilfully misreporting the offers made by the king to the rebels on the eve of the battle of Shrewsbury, tells Hotspur that

> He cals vs Rebels, Traitors, and will scourge
> With haughty armes, this hatefull name in vs.[85]

Falstaff rebukes the servant of the Chief Justice, whom he pretends to take for a beggar,

> Do not the Rebels need Soldiers? Though it be a shame to be on any side but one, it is worse shame to begge, then to be on the worst side, were it worse then the name of Rebellion can tell how to make it.[86]

Westmoreland makes it a bitter reproach to the Archbishop that he dresses

> The oughly forme
> Of base, and bloodie Insurrection,
> With your faire Honors.[87]

and he demands of him the reason

> That you should seale this lawlesse bloody Booke
> Of forged Rebellion, with a Seale diuine,
> And consecrate Commotions bitter edge.[88]

The homilist is at pains to prove that rebels break all the ten commandments. He refers to

> the dishonour done by Rebels unto God's holy Name, by their breaking of their oath made unto their Prince, with the attestation of Gods Name, and calling his Majesty to witness . . .
> . . . Rebels by breach of their faith given, and the oath made to their Prince, be guilty of most damnable perjury. It is wonderful to see what false colours, and fained causes, by slanderous lies made upon their Prince, and the Counsellors, Rebels will devise to cloak their rebellion withal.[89]

Shakespeare's historical plays teem with attacks made by various characters upon perjury, oath-breaking and

85. *1 Henry IV*, V. ii. ll. 40-1.
86. *2 Henry IV*, I. ii. ll. 70-2.
87. *2 Henry IV*, IV. i. ll. 39-41.
88. *2 Henry IV*, IV. i. ll. 90-2.
89. *Homilies*, pp. 292-3.

D

breaches of the oath of allegiance. Richard puts the broad issue simply in lines already quoted :—

> Reuolt our Subiects? That we cannot mend,
> They break their Faith to God, as well as vs.[90]

In that part of the deposition scene in which he formally abdicates, he first releases from their oaths of allegiance those who have been faithful to him,

> With mine owne Breathe release all dutious Oathes,

and a little afterwards prays,

> God pardon all Oathes that are broke to mee,
> God keepe all Vowes unbroke are made to thee.[91]

Subsequently the deposed king bitterly rebukes Northumberland for his disloyalty and treachery. He has asked the king to read

> These Accusations, and these grieuous Crymes,
> Committed by your Person, and your followers,
> Against the State, and Profit of this Land:
> That by confessing them, the Soules of men
> May deeme, that you are worthily depos'd.

The king replies

> Gentle Northumberland,
> If thy Offences were vpon Record,
> Would it not shame thee, in so faire a troupe,
> To read a Lecture of them? If thou would'st,
> There should'st thou finde one heynous Article,
> Contayning the deposing of a King,
> And cracking the strong Warrant of an Oath,
> Mark'd with a Blot, damn'd in the Booke of Heauen.[92]

When Salisbury renounces his allegiance to Henry VI, the king asks him,

> Hast thou not sworne Allegeance vnto me?

And when Salisbury replies ' I have,' the king asks,

> Canst thou dispense with heauen for such an oath?[93]

Unlike the homilist, Shakespeare holds no brief for authority. Even in his dramatic nonage he was the im-

90. *Richard II*, III. ii. ll. 100-101.
91. *Richard II*, IV. i. ll. 210, 215-6.
92. *Ibid.*, IV. i. ll. 223-227, 229-236.
93. *2 Henry VI*, V. i. ll. 179-181.

personal and impartial dramatist, and thus he took care
that the subject, born into a state of passive obedience,
had a chance of explaining his point of view.   Two
gamekeepers have arrested the fugitive ex-King Henry
the Sixth during the reign of Edward IV; the following
dialogue ensues :—

HUM. You are the king King Edward hath depos'd :
　　　And we his subiects, sworne in all Allegeance,
　　　Will apprehend you, as his Enemie.
KING. But did you neuer sweare, and breake an Oath.
HUM. No, neuer such an Oath, nor will not now.
KING. Where did you dwell when I was K. of England?
HUM. Heere in this Country, where we now remaine.
KING. I was annointed King at nine monthes old,
　　　My Father, and my Grandfather were Kings :
　　　And you were sworne true Subiects vnto me :
　　　And tell me then, haue you not broke your Oathes?
SIN. No, for we were Subiects, but while you wer king.
KING. Why? Am I dead? Do I not breath a Man?
　　　Ah simple men, you know not what you sweare.[94]

Shakespeare agrees with the homilist that

thefts, robberies, and murthers, which of all sins are most
loathed of most men, are in no men so much, nor so per-
niciously, as in rebels . . . Rebels are the cause of infinite
robberies, and murthers of great multitudes.[95]

Shakespeare's earliest study of the mob in rebellion
is found in *2 Henry VI*.   Cade begins with the murder
of the clerk of Chatham; after the death of the two
Staffords he drags their bodies at his horse's heels,
breaks open the gaols and frees the prisoners, kills one
of his own followers for addressing him as ' Jack Cade '
instead of ' Lord Mortimer,' murders Lord Say and his
son-in-law, carries their heads on poles, orders his men
to burn London bridge, and pull down the Inns of Court,
and prepares to sack the city.   The messenger announces
to the king,

All Schollers, Lawyers, Courtiers, Gentlemen,
They call false Catterpillers, and intend their death.[96]

94. *3 Henry VI*, III. i. ll. 69-93.
95. *Homilies*, p. 293.
96. *2 Henry VI*, IV. iv. ll. 36-7.

Clifford effectively disposes of Cade's pretensions to
leadership of the Commons by showing that his policy
means the robbery and murder of his countrymen:—

> Alas, he hath no home, no place to flye too:
> Nor knowes he how to liue, but by the spoile,
> Vnlesse by robbing of your Friends, and vs.[97]

King Henry V, denouncing the plot of Cambridge,
Scrope, and Grey against his life, declares

> Treason, and murther, euer kept together,
> As two yoake diuels sworne to eythers purpose,[98]

The homilist graphically describes

> the mischief and wickedness, when the Subjects unnatur-
> ally do rebel against their Prince, whose honour and life
> they should defend, though it were with the loss of their
> own lives: Countrymen to disturb the publick peace, and
> quietness of their Country, for defence of whose quietness they
> should spend their lives: the brother to seek, and often to
> work the death of his brother, the son of his father, the
> father to seek or procure the death of his sons being at man's
> age, and by their faults to disinherit their innocent children,
> and kinsmen their heirs for ever . . . Instead of all quiet-
> ness, joy and felicity, which do follow blessed peace, and due
> obedience, to bring in all trouble, sorrow, disquietness of
> minds, and bodies, and all mischief, and calamity, to turn all
> good order upside down, to bring all good laws in contempt,
> and to tread them under feet, to oppress all vertue, and
> honesty, and all vertuous, and honest persons, and to set
> all vice and wickedness; and all vicious, and wicked men at
> liberty to work their wicked wills, . . . to weaken, to over-
> throw, and to consume the strength of the Realm, their
> natural Country.[99]

Carlisle's fine speech of protest against the deposition
of Richard concludes with a prophecy of the woes to
come upon England during the Wars of the Roses.

> And if you Crowne him, let me prophecie,
> The blood of English shall manure the ground,
> And future Ages groane for his foule Act.

97. *Ibid.*, IV, viii. ll. 36-8.
98. *Henry V*, II. ii. ll. 105-6.
99. *Homilies*, pp. 295-6.

> Peace shall goe sleepe with Turkes and Infidels,
> And in this Seat of Peace, tumultuous Warres
> Shall Kinne with Kinne, and Kinde with Kinde confound,
> Disorder, Horror, Feare, and Mutinie
> Shall here inhabite, and this Land be call'd
> The field of Golgotha, and dead mens Sculls.
> Oh, if you reare this House, against this House
> It will the wofullest Diuision proue,
> That euer fell vpon this cursed Earth.
> Preuent it, resist it, and let it not be so,
> Lest Child, Childs Children cry against you, Woe.[100]

With this speech we may compare Antony's outbursts of indignant anger when the assassins of his friend and master leave the stage. Few critics have noticed that Shakespeare represents the murder of Caesar, the ruler of Rome, as a calamity and crime equal to, if not transcending in its consequences, the deposition and murder of King Richard.

> Woe to the hand that shed this costly Blood.
> Ouer thy wounds, now do I Prophesie,
>
> .   .   .   .
>
> A Curse shall light vpon the limbes of men;
> Domesticke Fury, and fierce Ciuill strife,
> Shall cumber all the parts of Italy:
> Blood and destruction shall be so in vse,
> And dreadfull Obiects so familiar,
> That Mothers shall but smile, when they behold,
> Their Infants quartered with the hands of Warre:
> All pitty choak'd with custome of fell deeds.[101]

A stage direction after the conclusion of the king's long speech in *3 Henry VI* (III. v. l. 54) recalls the language of the homily on the unnatural and savage family murders characteristic of civil war.

> Alarum. Enter a Sonne that hath kill'd his Father, at one doore; and a Father that hath kill'd his Sonne at another doore.

A son enters first, hoping that

> This man whom hand to hand I slew in fight,
> May be possessed with some store of Crownes.[102]

100. *Richard II*, IV. i. ll. 136-149.
101. *Julius Caesar*, III. i. ll. 259-270.
102. *3 Henry VI*, II. v. ll. 56-7.

He discovers that he has killed his father and weepingly implores pardon of God. The king, overhearing his outcries of sorrow, exclaims

> O pitteous spectacle! O bloody Times!
> Whiles Lyons Warre, and battaile for their Dennes,
> Poore harmlesse Lambes abide their enmity.[103]

The folio version has another stage direction,

> Enter Father, bearing of his Sonne.

He addresses his dead enemy, so far unknown to him,

> Giue me thy Gold, if thou hast any Gold:
> For I haue bought it with an hundred blowes.[104]

He discovers that the dead man 'is mine onely Sonne' and cries,

> O pitty God, this miserable Age!
> What stragems? how fell? how Butcherly?
> Erreoneous, mutinous, and vnnaturall,
> This deadly quarrell daily doth beget?
> O Boy! thy Father gaue thee life too soone,
> And hath bereft of thy life too late.[105]

The gentle king has supped too full of horrors:—

> Wo aboue wo: greefe, more then common greefe,
> O that my death would stay these ruthfull deeds:
> O, pitty, pitty, gentle heauen pitty.[106]

Thus even in his earliest plays Shakespeare shows his audience how rebellion never fails, in the words of the homily, ' to bring in all trouble, sorrow, disquietness of minds, and bodies, and all mischief and calamity.' He exhibits on the stage Jack Cade and his

> Rebellious Hinds, the filth and scum of Kent,

in the act of turning 'all good order upside down.' The homilist asserts that the rebels set

> all vicious and wicked men at liberty to work their wicked wills;

103. *Ibid.*, II. v. ll. 73-5.
104. *Ibid.*, II. v. ll. 80-1.
105. *Ibid.*, II. v. ll. 88-93.
106. *Ibid.*, II. v. ll. 94-6.

Jack Cade agrees to

> breake open the Gaoles, and let out the Prisoners.[107]

The homilist graphically describes the ruin and destruction that follow in the train of civil war and rebellion:—

> So finally, to make their Country, thus by their mischief weakned, ready to be a prey, and spoil to all outward enemies that will invade it, to the utter, and perpetual captivity, slavery and destruction of all their country-men, their children, their friends, their kinsfolks left alive, whom by their wicked Rebellion they procure to be delivered into the hands of the foraign enemies, as much as in them doth lie[108]

Henry the Fifth uses very much the same language in his summary of the crimes contemplated by the conspirators who had plotted against his life.

> You haue conspir'd against Our Royall person,
> Ioyn'd with an enemy proclaim'd, and from his Coffers,
> Receyu'd the Golden Earnest of Our death:
> Wherein you would haue sold your King to slaughter,
> His Princes, and his Peeres to seruitude,
> His Subiects to oppression, and contempt,
> And his whole Kingdome into desolation.[109]

The Elizabethans were devil-ridden. Industrious devil-mongers had compiled what they believed was a complete census of demons and devils, and had named, ranked and classified them according to their usual occupations and residence. They peopled inter-stellar and sub-mundane space with regiments and legions of fiends, minor and major. In several passages of his discourse the preacher declares that the devil is ' the grand Captain, and Father of Rebels,' and he concludes the opening paragraph of the homily on *Disobedience and Wilful Rebellion* with the assertion that

> The first authour of which rebellion, the root of all vices, and mother of all mischiefs, was Lucifer, . . . who by rebelling against the Majesty of God, of the brightest and most glorious Angel, is become the blackest and most foul fiend, and Devil.[110]

107. *2 Henry VI*, IV. iii. ll. 14-15.
108. *Homilies*, p. 296.
109. *Henry V*, II. ii. ll. 167-173.
110. *Homilies*, p. 276.

The preacher certainly left his audience in no doubt about
the company that rebels keep.

> Where most Rebellions and Rebels be, there is the express
> similitude of Hell, and the Rebels themselves are the very
> figures of fiends and devils, and their Captain the ungracious
> pattern of Lucifer, and Sathan, the prince of darkness; of
> whose Rebellion as they be followers, so shall they be of his
> damnation in hell undoubtedly be partakers.[111]

Later he speaks of rebels as 'those wicked imps of the
devil.' Shakespeare in *1 Henry VI* alludes to the unholy
alliance of traitors with the powers of evil. Talbot,
Bedford and Burgundy are planning to retake Orleans,
in which the rebellious French led by the Dauphin are
celebrating their recent victory.

> TALB. Embrace we then this opportunitie,
> As fitting best to quittance their deceite,
> Contriu'd by Art, and balefull Sorcerie.
> BED. Coward of France, how much he wrongs his fame,
> Dispairing of his owne armes fortitude,
> To ioyne with Witches, and the helpe of Hell.
> BUR. Traitors haue neuer other company.[112]

Perhaps the remembrance of the frequent allusions made
in the homilies to the devil as the 'Father of Rebels'
suggested to Shakespeare the thought that conspiracy and
treason are due to the promptings and subtlety of the
devil. Speaking to Lord Scroope Henry says:—

> But whatsoeuer cunning fiend it was
> That wrought vpon thee so preposterously,
> Hath got the voyce in hell for excellence:
> And other diuels that suggest by treasons,
> Do botch and bungle vp damnation,
> With patches, colours, and with formes being fetcht
> From glist'ring semblances of piety:
> But he that temper'd thee, bad thee stand vp,
> Gaue thee no instance why thou shouldst do treason,
> Vnlesse to dub thee with the name of Traitor.
> If that same Daemon that hath gull'd thee thus,
> Should with his Lyon-gate walke the whole world,
> He might return to vastie Tartar backe,
> And tell the Legions, I can neuer win
> A soule so easie as that Englishmans.[113]

111. *Homilies*, pp. 296-7.
112. *1 Henry VI*, II. i. ll. 13-19.
113. *Henry V*, II. ii. ll. 111-125.

The homilist was wise in his generation. He knew that his Biblical thunderbolts often missed their mark, and that threats of God's wrath and future punishment would not, and did not, deter discontented subjects from rebellion. Accordingly he descended to the lower and more worldly ground of profit and loss, and suggested that rebellion was not worth while because it did not pay; the experience of centuries proved that it had always been unsuccessful.

> As the holy Scriptures do show, so doth daily experience prove, that the counsels, conspiracies, and attempts of Rebels, never took effect, neither came to good, but to a most horrible end . . . God never yet prospered the subjects being Rebels against their natural soveraign, were they never so great or noble, so many, so stout, so witty, and politick, but always they came by the overthrow, and to a shameful end.[114]

Shakespeare repeatedly emphasises the ill success of conspiracies and rebellions. After the battle of Shrewsbury Henry IV greets the captured Earl of Worcester with the words,

> Thus euer did Rebellion finde Rebuke.[115]

Another such allusion occurs in the Induction to *2 Henry IV*,

> Why is Rumour heere?
> I run before King Harries victory,
> Who in a bloodie field by Shrewsburie,
> Hath beaten downe yong Hotspurre, and his Troopes,
> Quenching the flame of bold Rebellion,
> Euen with the Rebels blood.[116]

Riding post-haste from that ' bloodie field,' Travers is outridden by a gentleman,

> I did demand what Newes from Shrewsbury:
> He told me, that Rebellion had ill lucke,
> And that yong Harry Percies Spurre was cold.[117]

The poet has most admirably described how the word

114. *Homilies*, pp. 300-301.
115. *1 Henry IV*, V. iv. l. 1.
116. *2 Henry IV*, Ind., ll. 22-7.
117. *2 Henry IV*, I. i. ll. 40-2.

'Rebellion' dashed the fighting spirit of Hotspur's troops :—

> My Lord (your Sonne) had onely but the Corpes,
> But shadowes, and the shewes of men to fight.
> For that same word (Rebellion) did diuide
> The action of their bodies, from their soules,
> And they did fight with queasinesse, constrain'd
> As men drinke Potions ; that their Weapons only
> Seem'd on our side : but for their Spirits and Soules,
> This word (Rebellion) it had froze them vp,
> As Fish are in a pond.[118]

King Richard's rather fanciful warnings to Northumberland that the vengeance of God will fall upon such disloyal subjects as he, is remarkable.

> Yet know, my master, God Omnipotent,
> Is mustring in his Clouds, on our behalfe,
> Armies of Pestilence, and they shall strike
> Your Children yet vnborne, and vnbegot,
> That lift your Vassal Hands against my Head.[119]

The thought may be a reminiscence of a passage in the homily on *Wilful Rebellion* :—

> Some of the children of Israel, being murmurers against their Magistrates appointed over them by God, were stricken with foul leprosie : many were burnt up with fire suddenly sent from the Lord : sometime a great sort of thousands were consumed with the pestilence.[120]

The homilist invites the members of his congregation

> (To) turn over, and read the Histories of all Nations, look over the Chronicles of our own Country, call to mind so many Rebellions of old time, and some yet fresh in memory, ye shall not find that God ever prospered any Rebellion against their natural and lawful Prince, but contrariwise that the Rebels were overthrown and slain, and such as were taken prisoners, dreadfully executed.[121]

Prince John of Lancaster having by a gross breach of faith captured the rebel leaders, tells them that he will keep his promise to redress their grievances,

118. *Ibid.*, I. i. ll. 191-200.
119. *Richard II*, III. iii. ll. 85-90.
120. *Homilies*, p. 299.
121. *Ibid.*, p. 301.

> But for you (Rebels) looke to taste the due
> Meet for Rebellion, and such Acts as yours,
>
> . . . .
>
> Some guard these Traitors to the Block of Death,
> Treason's true Bed, and yeelder vp of Breath.[122]

Usurpers draw upon themselves the wrath of God, and time inevitably works their downfall.

> For though Vsurpers sway the rule a while,
> Yet Heau'ns are iust, and Time suppresseth Wrongs.[123]

Camillo echoes the thought of the above passage quoted from the homilies in the soliloquy spoken after Leontes has left him.

> If I could find example
> Of thousand's that had struck anoynted Kings,
> And flourish'd after, Il'd not do't: But since
> Nor Brasse, nor Stone, nor Parchment beares not one,
> Let Villanie it selfe forswear't.[124]

The fate of rebels is figured in Iden's treatment of the body of Cade.

> Hence will I dragge thee headlong by the heeles
> Vnto a dunghill, which shall be thy graue,
> And there cut off thy most vngracious head,
> Which I will beare in triumph to the King,
> Leauing thy trunke for Crowes to feed vpon.[125]

Every theatre-goer would realise that the cycle of English history plays presented in the theatres exemplified the truth of the following passage:—

> Consider the great and noble families of Dukes, Marquesses, Earles, and other Lords, whose names ye shall read in our Chronicles, now clean extinguished and gone; and seek out the causes of the decay, you shall find, that not lack of issue, and heirs male, hath so much wrought that decay and waste of noble bloods and houses, as hath Rebellions.[126]

Shakespeare had witnessed during his short life the attainder, execution or exile of the representatives of such ancient and famous houses as those of Neville, Percy, Dacre, Brooke, Devereux and Howard as the

122. *2 Henry IV*, IV. ii. ll. 116-123.
123. *3 Henry VI*, III. iii. ll. 76-77.
124. *The Winter's Tale*, I. ii. ll. 357-361.
125. *2 Henry VI*, IV. x. ll. 78-82.
126. *Homilies*, p. 301.

price paid for taking part in conspiracies and rebellions. Audiences that saw the stage deaths of such illustrious rebels as Hotspur and Warwick on the field of battle, and of the Buckinghams, father and son, on the scaffold, would remember that Elizabeth had executed a Percy for rebellion in 1572 and that his successor, imprisoned in the Tower for conspiracy, had committed suicide in 1585; the last Earl of Westmoreland had died abroad in great poverty about the same time, and the last of the Staffords, the descendant of two lines of kings, was living in abject squalor.

The preacher contrasts ' the Queen's most honourable Counsellors' and rebels. Whosoever

> Considereth the persons, state and condition of the Rebels themselves, the reformers, as they take upon them, of the present Government, he shall find that the most rash and hair-brained men, the greatest unthrifts, that have most lewdly wasted their own goods and lands, those that are over the ears in debt, and such as for their thefts, robberies and murthers, dare not in any well governed Common-wealth, where good Laws are in force, shew their faces, such as are of the most lewd and wicked behaviour, and life, and all such as will not, or cannot live in peace, are alwayes most ready to move Rebellion, or take part with Rebels.[127]

> As for envy, wrath, murther, and desire of blood, and covetousness of other mens goods, lands and livings, they are the inseparable accidents of all Rebels, and peculiar properties that do usually stir up wicked men to Rebellion. Now such as by riotousness, gluttony, drunkenness, excess of apparel, and unthrifty games, have wasted their own goods unthriftily, the same are most apt unto, and most desirous of rebellion, whereby they trust to come by other men's goods unlawfully, and violently.[128]

Shakespeare puts similar language into the mouths of such of his characters as are rulers. In reply to Worcester's indictment of his treatment of the Percies, King Henry replies:—

> These things indeede you haue articulated,
> Proclaim'd at Market Crosses, read in Churches,
> To face the Garment of Rebellion
> With some fine colour, that may please the eye
> Of fickle Changelings, and poor Discontents,

127. *Homilies*, pp. 302-3.
128. *Ibid.*, p. 294.

> Which gape, and rub the Elbow at the newes
> Of hurly burly Innouation:
> And neuer yet did Insurrection want
> Such water-colours, to impaint his cause:
> Nor moody Beggars, staruing for a time
> Of pell-mell hauocke, and confusion.[129]

Westmoreland bluntly reproves the Archbishop of York, Mowbray and Hastings for associating themselves with the ' rude and rascal commons ' in rebellion against the king :—

> If that Rebellion
> Came like it selfe, in base and abiect Routs,
> Led on by bloodie Youth, guarded with Rags
> And countenanc'd by Boyes and Beggerie:
> I say, if damn'd Commotion so appeare,
> In his true, natiue, and most proper shape,
> You (Reverend Father, and these Noble Lords)
> Had not beene here, to dresse the ougly forme
> Of base, and bloodie Insurrection,
> With your faire Honors.[130]

Sir Humphrey Stafford is as blunt but not very tactful in his speech offering pardon to Cade's followers :—

> Rebellious Hinds, the filth and scum of Kent,
> Mark'd for the Gallowes: Lay your Weapons downe,
> Home to your Cottages: forsake this Groome.[131]

The same description of the rebel army is given by the messenger that brings the news of Stafford's defeat and death to the court.

> His army is a ragged multitude
> Of Hindes and Pezants, rude and mercilesse.[132]

The homilist describes the sinister alliance of religion and rebellion at great length.

> Not only great multitudes of the rude, and rascal Commons:
> but sometime also men of great wit, nobility and authority,
> have moved Rebellions against their lawful Princes . . .
> they pretend sundry causes, as the redress of the Common-
> wealth . . . or reformation of Religion . . . they have made
> a great shew of holy meaning by beginning their Rebellions

129. *1 Henry IV*, V. i. ll. 72-82.
130. *2 Henry IV*, IV. i. ll. 32-41.
131. *2 Henry VI*, IV. ii. ll. 115-7.
132. *Ibid., IV*, iv. ll. 32-3.

with a counterfeit service of God . . . they display, and
bear about Ensigns, and Banners, which are acceptable unto
the rude ignorant common people, great multitudes of whom
by such false pretences and shews, they do deceive and draw
unto them.[133]

He refers to banners having 'the Image of the Plough
painted therein, with God speed the Plough written
under in great letters'; to banners bearing 'the picture
of the five wounds painted' by 'some lewd painter.'
Others 'do bear the Image of the Cross painted in a
rag.' To all persons he gives the advice,

let no good, and godly subject, upon any hope of victory or
good success, follow such Standerd-Bearers of Rebellion.[134]

The passage in which Shakespeare has described the part
played by Archbishop Scroop in the rebellion against
Henry IV owes very little to Holinshed. It was omitted
in the quartos and appeared for the first time in the
Folio of 1623. The part omitted below has been
previously quoted :—

The gentle Arch-bishop of Yorke is vp
With well appointed Powres: he is a man
Who with a double Surety bindes his Followers.

.　　.　　.　　.　　.　　.　　.　　.　　.

　　　　　But now the Bishop
Turnes Insurrection to Religion,
Suppos'd sincere, and holy in his Thoughts:
He's followed both with Body, and with Minde:
And doth enlarge his Rising, with the blood
Of faire King Richard, scrap'd from Pomfret stones,
Deriues from Heauen his Quarrell, and his Cause:
Tels them, he doth bestride a bleeding Land,
Gasping for life, vnder great Bullingbrooke,
And more, and lesse, do flocke to foillow him.[135]

Wise enough to say and to know that

An habitation giddy, and vnsure
Hath he that buildeth on the vulgar heart.[136]

the rebel prelate decided to trust the untrustworthy

133. *Homilies*, p. 301.
134. *Ibid.*, p. 303.
135. *2 Henry IV*, I. i. ll. 189-191, 200-209.
136. *Ibid.*, I, iii, ll. 89-90.

' fond many ' for success in his rebellion.   Westmoreland
asks him for the reason

> That you should seale this lawlesse bloody Booke
> Of forged Rebellion, with a Seale diuine
> And consecrate Commotion's bitter edge.[137]

The text of the play is mutilated at this point; it would
seem that the Archbishop replied that he was in arms to
redress the grievances of the Commonwealth; Westmoreland brusquely brushes this explanation aside :—

> There is no neede of any such redresse :
> Or if there were, it not belongs to you.[138]

The Tudor scheme of things had no place for members
of the church militant; the homilist quotes many texts to
prove that

> Our .Saviour Christ himself, and his Apostle Saint Paul,
> Saint Peter, with others, were unto the Magistrates, and
> higher powers, which ruled at their being upon the earth, both
> obedient themselves, and did also diligently, and earnestly
> exhort all other Christians to the like obedience unto their
> Princes, and Governors; whereby it is evident that men of
> the Clergy, and Ecclesiastical Ministers, as their successors,
> ought both themselves specially, and before others, to be
> obedient unto their Princes, and also to exhort all others
> unto the same.[139]

Prince John sternly rebukes the aged Prelate, Archbishop
Scroop, for turning himself into

> an Iron man
> Chearing a rowt of Rebels with your Drumme,
> Turning the Word, to Sword; and Life to death.[140]

He charges him with abusing the ' Countenance of the
King,' using religion as a cloak for rebellion, and mis-
leading his spiritual subjects.

137. *Ibid.*, IV, i, ll. 91-3.
138. *2 Henry IV*, IV. i. ll. 97-8.
139. *Homilies*, p. 308.
140. *2 Henry IV*, IV. ii. ll. 8-10.

> Who hath not heard it spoken,
> How deepe you were within the Bookes of God?
> To vs, the speaker in his Parliament;
> To vs, th' imagine Voyce of God him selfe:
> The very Opener, and Intelligencer,
> Betweene the Grace, the Sanctities of Heauen,
> And our dull workings. O, who shall beleeue,
> But you mis-vse the reuerence of your Place,
> Employ the Countenance, and Grace of Heauen,
> As a false Fauorite doth his Princes Name,
> In deedes dis-honourable? You haue tane vp,
> Vnder the counterfeited Zeale of God
> The Subiects of his Substitute, my Father,
> And both against the Peace of Heauen, and him
> Haue here vp-swarmed them.[141]

The Archbishop cuts a very sorry figure. He has no answer to the prince's scathing indictment except that he is in arms because

> The Time (mis-order'd) doth in common sence
> Crowd vs, and crush vs, to this monstrous Forme,
> To hold our safetie vp.[142]

The homilist comments caustically on the catchword, 'reformation,' so popular in his day.

> Surely that which they falsely call reformation is indeed not only a defacing or a deformation. but also an utter destruction of all Common-wealth, as would well appear, might the Rebels have their wills; and doth right well, and too well, appear by their doing in such places of the Country where Rebels do rout, where though they tarry but a very little while, they make such reformation, that they destroy all places, and undo all men where they come, that the child yet unborn may rue it, and shall many years hereafter curse him.[143]

What the preacher describes, the dramatist shows in action. Jack Cade has the demagogue's penchant for popular cries and prefaces an attractive programme of reform with the self-praise that recommends a leader to the mob:—

> Be braue then, for your Captaine is Braue, and Vowes Reformation. There shall be in England, seuen halfe peny Loaues sold for a peny: the three hoop'd pot, shall

141. *2 Henry IV*, IV. ii. ll. 16-30.
142. *Ibid.*, IV. ii. ll. 33-35.
143. *Homilies*, p. 303.

haue ten hoopes, and I wil make it Fellony to drink small
Beere. All the Realme shall be in Common, and in
Cheapside shall my Palfrey go to grasse: and when I
am King, as King I will be.

ALL. God saue your Maiesty.

CADE. I thanke you good people.[144]

Cade's practice of 'Reformation' corresponds exactly to
the description given by the homilist. He agrees at once
to a suggestion made by Dicke Butcher,

The first thing we do, let's kill all the Lawyers.[145]

A messenger hurries to report to the king and court.

Jack Cade hath gotten London-bridge.
The Citizens flye and forsake their houses:
The Rascall people, thirsting after prey,
Ioyne with the Traitor, and they ioyntly sweare
To spoyle the City, and your Royall Court.[146]

He orders his 'rabblement' to pull down, burn,
destroy:—

But first, go and set London Bridge on fire,
And if you can, burne down the Tower too.[147]

So sirs: now go some and pull down the Sauoy:
Others to'th Innes of Court, downe with them all.[148]

He purifies Law and Legislation with fire:—

Away, burne all the Records of the Realme, my
mouth shall be the Parliament of England.[149]

His final order epitomizes mob rule:—

Kill and knocke downe, throw them into Thames.[150]

The less brutalized Roman mob depicted in *Julius Caesar*
is as instinctively destructive as Cade's rabble, once
Antony has stirred up its passions. The leaders shout in
unison 'Go fetch fire,' 'Plucke downe Benches,' 'Plucke
down Formes, Windowes, anything,' and the pack is in
full cry. They meet Cinna the poet, mistake him for
Cinna the conspirator, unthinkingly tear him to pieces,
and disappear from the play, shrieking 'Burne all.'

The last quotation from the Homilies contains a
sentence, 'The child yet unborn may rue it,' which seems

144-150. *2 Henry VI*, IV. ii. ll. 60-68; l. 72; iv. ll. 49-53; vi. ll. 13-15;
vii. ll. 1-2; 11-13; viii. l. 2.

E

to have fixed itself in the poet's memory.

Richard II uses it in the passage already quoted about God's mustering armies of pestilence; later in the play, Carlisle says at the end of the deposition 'scene,'

> The Woes to come, the Children yet vnborne,
> Shall feele this day as sharpe to them as Thorne.[151]

So also Henry the Fifth, resenting the insulting message sent by the Dauphin, uses almost the very words of the homily,

> And some are yet vngotten and vnborne,
> That shal haue cause to curse the Dolphin's scorne.[152]

' The principal and most usual causes' of rebellion, says the homilist, are ambition and ignorance.

> As these are the two chief causes of Rebellion: So are there specially two sorts of men in whom these vices do raign, by whom the Devil, the authour of all evil, doth chiefly stir up all disobedience, and Rebellion.
> The restless ambitious, having once determined by one means or other to atchieve to their intended purpose, when they cannot by lawful, and peaceable means clime so high as they do desire, they attempt the same by force, and violence: wherein when they cannot prevail against the ordinary authority, and power of lawful Princes, and Governours themselves alone, they do seek the aid, and help of the ignorant multitude, abusing them to their wicked purpose.[153]

Hotspur explains to Blunt how Bolingbroke, the ' poore vnminded Out-law, sneaking home,' grew into popularity and royal authority with the help of the Earl of Northumberland and the other Percies:—

> And now (forsooth) takes on him to reforme
> Some certaine Edicts, and some strait Decrees,
> That lay too heauie on the Common-wealth;
> Cryes out vpon abuses, seemes to weepe
> Ouer his Countries Wrongs: and by this Face,
> This seeming Brow of Iustice, did he winne
> The hearts of all that hee did angle for.[154]

Richard II also describes how Bolingbroke sought popularity:—

151. *Richard II,* IV. i. ll. 321-2.
152. *Henry V,* I. ii. ll. 287-8.
153. *Homilies,* p. 307.
154. *1 Henry IV,* IV. iii. ll. 78-84.

Our selfe and Bushy: heere Bagot and Greene
Obseru'd his Courtship to the common people:
How he did seeme to diue into their hearts,
With humble, and familiar courtesie,
What reuerence he did throw away on slaues.[155]

Bolingbroke instructs his son in the practice of hypocrisy:—

And then I stole all Courtesie from Heauen,
And drest my selfe in such Humilitie,
That I did plucke Allegeance from mens hearts,
Lowd Showts and Salutations from their mouthes,
Euen in the presence of the Crowned King.[156]

The number and variety of the passages quoted from the many plays of Shakespeare, in which he makes definite allusions to such topics as the divine right of the sovereign, the duty of passive obedience imposed on the subject, the sin of wilful rebellion and other less important but collateral articles of the Tudor politico-religious creed give, in my opinion, very strong support to my contention that Shakespeare derived these ideas either directly or indirectly from the homilies. The homilist, it is true, is uncompromisingly rigid in his claim that subjects must slavishly obey a wicked or worthless prince and passively endure intolerable tyranny; but dogma does not make for moderation or wisdom. The homilies on Obedience and against Wilful Rebellion were as much part of the State religion as those on Prayer, the Sacraments, the Resurrection and the Peril of Idolatry. Shakespeare's 'anointed' kings are invariably described as sacrosanct and above the law; yet his wise princes get what obedience they can and know that they will be obeyed only as long as they keep a firm grip on their royal power. While the poet treats the rebellion even of princes of royal blood against such incapable kings as Richard II and Henry VI as a sin, and describes Bolingbroke, his son, and his grandson as each in his turn conscience-plagued, he is never at odds with the facts of history or of life. In his plays the usurper of capacity

155. *Richard II*, I. iv. ll. 22-26.
156. *1 Henry IV*, III. ii. ll. 50-54.

may have his moments of remorse, but he assumes with the crown the semi-divinity attached to the kingly office, and is entitled to the unquestioning obedience of his subjects. Thus Shakespeare has no sympathy for the fate of rebels such as Hotspur or Archbishop Scroop, and counts political principles, even if bolstered up with the sanction of religion, of little consequence in comparison with the continuance of good government and internal peace.

If we wish to trace to its source this theory of the government of England, we discover that neither John nor Richard II, nor any of their successors up to the time of Henry VII based their ample, if legally undefined, prerogative on any immediate delegation of power from God, that Halle, Holinshed and Stowe contain no mention of it in their chronicles, that only meagre references to certain portions of it appear in the plays of Shakespeare's predecessors and contemporaries, and that it is unknown to the lawyers or to the few writers on politics or the English Constitution prior to 1598. Shakespeare did not invent it; the spinning and weaving of a score or more of scattered texts from the Scriptures into a logical politico-religious creed was work fitter for a theologian than a popular dramatist.

My first contention is that the ascription to John, Richard II, or any of their nobles of a belief in the doctrine of the divine right of kings is historically false. Richard II may have had more exalted notions of the almost illimitable power inherent in the regal prerogative than perhaps any English king up to Henry VIII, but in 1398-9 there were too many nobles of the blood royal alive to permit him to claim much more than his true feudal position of being *primus inter pares*. Lawyers as a class were just rising into prominence, and were certain to prove determined opponents of a system of absolutism based upon a divine sanction and designed to put the king's pleasure above the law. Except for two incidental remarks Holinshed says nothing from which

we could deduce that any widespread belief in the divine
right of kings existed in the fourteenth or fifteenth centuries. After the deposition of Richard II the Commons
proposed 'that the causes of his deposing might be published through the realm for satisfieing of the people:
which demand was granted.'[157] The Bishop of Carlisle
stoutly opposed this, asking them, 'will ye proceed to
the iudgment of an anointed king, having neither his
answer nor excuse.'[158] This reference to the spiritual
character of a part of the coronation service would seem
to his audience little more than a rhetorical flourish such
as might be expected from a bishop. If we may believe
an almost contemporary annalist, Richard agreed to
abdicate his regal functions but refused to say

> With mine owne Teares I wash away my Balme.[159]

Bishop Stubbs states:—' It was known at the time that
Richard, when he was further pressed to renounce all
the honours and dignity pertaining to a king, refused to
renounce the spiritual honour of the royal character
impressed upon him or his unction.'[160] But this Latin
chronicle was almost certainly not known to Shakespeare.
This refusal may not be unconnected with the story told
by Holinshed of the extravagant flattery used by Sir
John Bushy, one of Richard's favourites, in addressing
the king:—

> Sir John Bushie, in all his talke, when he proponed any
> matter vnto the king, did not attribute to him titles of
> honour, due and accustomed but inuented vnused termes, and
> such strange names as were rather agreeable to the diuine
> maiestie of God, then to any earthlie potentate. The prince,
> being desirous inough of all honour, and more ambitious then
> was requisite, seemed to like well of his speech, and gaue good
> eare to his talke.[161]

Perhaps other such stories of Richard were current in
the days of Elizabeth, and these may have been the basis
of the notion found in three extant plays on the reign

157. *Holinshed's Chronicle as Used in Shakespeare's Plays* (1927), p. 43.
158. *Ibid.*, p. 43.
159. *Richard II*, IV. i. 1. 207.
160. Stubbs, *Constitutional History* (1880), vol. III. p. 14.
161. *Holinshed, op. cit.*, p. 51.

of Richard that he believed in his own divine right to rule and in the duty of passive obedience on the part of his subjects. If *Richard II* was the only play of Shakespeare in which such a doctrine appeared, we might justifiably assert that the poet introduced it into his plot to subserve some definite dramatic purpose. Such allusions are found, however, in over twenty of his plays, and consequently we cannot attach overmuch significance to the large number in *Richard II,* especially as a very large number of references to the analogous doctrine of the sin of wilful rebellion is to be found in the two plays on Henry IV. The parliamentary proceedings against Richard are described with much particularity by Holinshed, but nowhere does he state or even hint that the deposed king had based his system of government on divine right. Sir John Fortescue, in his treatises on the laws of England, makes it clear that the system of absolutism by which Richard attempted to govern England during the last year of his reign was unknown to the law and a breach of the coronation oath. Further, he does not even mention Richard's belief in his own divine right to rule, which is so prominent in Shakespeare's play. We cannot explain why the Elizabethan dramatists credited Richard with this obsession; history does not lend it any support.

My second contention is that Shakespeare did not find the theory of divine right or any of its implications in his source-books. Neither Halle nor Holinshed refer to it in their chronicles for the excellent reason that the majority of the annalists from whom these writers borrowed their facts wrote before the theologians of Henry VIII had revealed to his subjects their discovery of that monarch's divinity. At the time of the breach with the Pope Halle was a man of mature years, and, though an enthusiastic admirer of King Henry, probably accepted his royal master's newly-assumed semi-divinity for political rather than religious reasons. The extract previously quoted from Holinshed concerning Bushy's flattery of Richard II suggests that this author did not think such extravagant language, as Carlisle and Gaunt use in speaking of the king, seemly or reverent.

In the third place I think it very improbable that Shakespeare derived this doctrine from current political literature; practically nothing was written in England on politics during the sixteenth century. Buchanan and James VI in Scotland, Bellarmine and Suarez in France, and Mariana in Spain indulged in abstract speculations on government and the limits of kingly power; each of these authors came to conclusions in exact agreement with the dogmas upon which his own form of religion was based. All except King James wrote in Latin; the royal dissertation on *The trve Lawe of free Monarchies: or the reciprock and mutval Dutie betwixt a free King and his Naturall Subiectes* first appeared anonymously in Edinburgh in 1598, and was reprinted in Edinburgh and London five years afterwards. Shakespeare could not have borrowed from this. Apart from More's *Utopia,* Cheke's two pamphlets on Sedition, an English translation of Fortescue's book on the laws of England, and Sir Thomas Smith's *The Maner of Gouernment or Policie of the Realme of England,* political philosophy written in English was a blank. Four books of Hooker's *Ecclesiastical Politie* appeared in 1594, and the tenth section of the first book states views on the origin and functions of government which, except for a sentence or two, might have come from the pen of Locke or Rousseau. Hooker jettisons texts of Scripture and the authority of the Fathers, and develops his argument from first principles, supporting them with quotations from Plato, Aristotle and Cicero. He denies to the Prince the right of making laws except with the consent of his people:—

> By the Natural Law whereunto he (God) hath made all subiect, the lawfull power of making Lawes, to command whole Politike Societies of men, belongeth so properly vnto the same intire Societies, that for any Prince or Potentate, of what kind soeuer vpon earth, to exercise the same of himselfe, and

not eyther by expresse Commission immediately and personally receiued from God, or else by authoritie deriued at the
first from their consent vpon whose persons they impose
Lawes, it is no better then meere tyrannie. Lawes they are
not therefore which publike approbation hath not made so.[162]

Verplanck has drawn attention to a certain similarity in
thought between the speech of Ulysses on order and the
third section of Book One of the *Ecclesiastical Politie*
treating of the Law of Nature; Shakespeare may have
read it but he certainly did not take his politics from
Hooker.

Finally, I do not think that Shakespeare borrowed his
notions of divine right either from his predecessors in
the English drama or from the old plays which, according
to a doubtful literary tradition, he remodelled during his
years of apprenticeship to play-writing. We may divide
known dramatists of this period into two main groups.
The first consists of those who wrote plays before 1594,
the second of those who wrote plays after that date. The
earlier group includes Lyly, Peele, Greene, Kyd, Marlowe, Wilson, Lodge, Munday, Shakespeare, and perhaps
Heywood; in addition there may have been almost as
many others whose names we do not know. Nearly every
one of these dramatists introduces into one or more
of his plays direct or indirect allusions to the theory
of divine right. The adjectives 'sacred' or 'anointed'
seem to have been stock or ornamental epithets applied
to kings, queens, princes, emperors, sultans, etc., as titles
of reverence; their frequent recurrence at times reminds
us of such repetitive epithets as 'cloud-gathering,'
'ox-eyed,' 'gray-eyed,' 'wary-wise,' etc. in Homer, or
'pius' and 'fidus' in Virgil. Most of the references to
the more important portions of the theory of divine right,
e.g., to the unlimited power of the monarch, the duty of
obedience, and the sin of rebellion are to be found only
in certain anonymous plays such as *The Troublesome
Raigne of King John, Jack Straw, The Knack to Know
a Knave, 1 Richard II, Edward III,* and above all *Sir*

162. Hooker, *Of the Lawes of Ecclesiastical Politie* (1622), book I, p. 28.

Thomas More. The climax of the first part of the last-
named play is the impressive and dramatic speech of
More in which he denounces the rioters for the sin of
rebellion:—

> What do you, then,
> Rysing gainst him that God himself enstalls,
> But ryse gainst God? what do you to your sowles
> In doing this?[163]

Once again I shall remark that all the references made to
divine right in *Edward III* and *Sir Thomas More* occur
in those parts only of these two plays which many competent critics have attributed to Shakespeare on grounds
of vocabulary, style, treatment of subject-matter and
dramatic quality. These plays were probably written
during the two or three years which saw the production
of *King John, Richard II* and *Henry IV,* the plays
containing the most numerous references to this theory.
The reasonable inference that may be drawn from these
facts is that Shakespeare and all the other dramatists
drew their allusions to the doctrines associated with the
divine right of kings from a common source. This source
was the *Book of Homilies*; with it and its teachings all
would be necessarily acquainted from early boyhood.
Attendance at church service was compulsory, and all
church-goers would hear read once a year the two
homilies on *Obedience* and *Disobedience and Wilful
Rebellion.*

The second group of dramatists consists of men who
began playwriting after 1594-5, and includes Chapman,
Heywood, Dekker, Jonson, Marston, Day, Middleton,
Webster, Tourneur, Beaumont and Fletcher, and others
of less importance; to these must be added Lyly, Munday,
Shakespeare and a few other survivors of the earlier
group. With the exception of Heywood, Shakespeare
and Fletcher, they rarely refer to divine right and the
doctrines associated with it. Heywood almost to the end
carries on the tradition inherited from his predecessors;
but we must turn to *The Maid's Tragedy* and *Valen-*

163. *Sir Thomas More* (Brooke's *The Shakespeare Apocrypha*), II. iv. ll. 128-
131.

tinian to re-discover the more than ultra-royalism characteristic of Carlisle and John of Gaunt. Coleridge's censure on Fletcher, 'the most servile *jure divino* royalist,' is well deserved:—

> It is a real trial of charity to read this scene (Act I, sc. 3 of *Valentinian*) with tolerable temper towards Fletcher. So very slavish—so reptile—are the feelings and sentiments represented as duties. And yet remember he was a bishop's son, and the duty to God was the supposed basis.164

We may wonder why Shakespeare escaped this critic's lash for the same offence. The difference is important and characteristic of the two authors. Shakespeare, being on the side of authority, seems to have accepted, in a semi-philosophic spirit, the divine right of kings as a fundamental principle of the system of government that he knew best. The king, good or bad, is sacrosanct. He then exhibits the deposition and subsequent murder of Richard II, who believes in and proclaims his own semi-divinity; the king's faults are political, arising, in the main, from a tyrannical abuse of the legitimate royal prerogative. Fletcher also accepts the principle of divine right, and stresses the duty of passive obedience. Valentinian, like Richard, is ruled by favourites and flatterers; he ravishes the wife of his noblest and most powerful subject, who is induced to endure submissively this unpardonable wrong and deep dishonour, because he must not lift his hand against the Lord's anointed. Fletcher degrades the very principle which he desires to support, by thus casting over royal lust the mantle of sanctity.

I have said that Shakespeare borrowed the doctrines of the divine right of kings, passive obedience and the sin of rebellion from the homilies. He deliberately inserted in *King John* and *King Lear* references to these doctrines which are not present in the old plays used by him as raw material. In preparing *2 Henry VI* and *3 Henry VI* for representation, the play-adapter probably struck out all such allusions from the acting versions;

164. Coleridge, *Literary Remains* (1836), vol. II, p. 308.

not a line remains in *The True Tragedy* of King Henry's speeches on the sin of oath-breaking and the duty of allegiance imposed on subjects. The actors had the last word in deciding what they would speak on the stage; the poet continued to write as much as he pleased, and we find a far greater number of allusions to divine right in *Richard II* and *Henry IV*. They occur in comedies, histories, and tragedies written during every stage of his career. Why did the poet give so much prominence to doctrines favoured by authority and to a system of government which, a quarter of a century after his death, led to a prolonged civil war and the temporary downfall of the Stuart dynasty? Did he believe in the doctrine of the divine right of kings? Any answer to such questions must be a guess, but he probably thought the principle itself and the system of government based upon it not unsuited to the people of his times. This doctrine was very much alive in Germany prior to the Great European War, and still lingers in Japan; it is as logically defensible as the modern worship of a majority. Selfishness and environment usually determine a man's political opinions. The London companies of actors owed their legal existence, and every actor his livelihood, to the favour of the sovereign and the court. By taking the larger companies into their service, the powerful nobles who were members of the Privy Council saved our early stage from extinction. When the plague broke out in the city or the turbulent apprentices made a riot, the city fathers and the Puritan preachers invariably put the blame upon the theatres and petitioned the Council to close them. Shakespeare had excellent reasons for his belief in authority and his dislike of mobs. If he was a resident of London from 1588 to 1595 he must have been an eye-witness of four serious riots, and, as a result, found that for some weeks after each of these disturbances, his occupation was gone. He would not have been human if he had not preferred strict order sternly enforced by the Tudor theocratic tyranny to spasmodic licence and turbulence. Our first of poets had an eye to the main chance, yet apart from thoughts of his own welfare he must have perceived the vast importance both of the personal character of the sovereign and of the stability of the government to the happiness and prosperity of the people. A real sanctity surrounded the prince as the centre and symbol of the life of the state. This was the teaching of the homilies, heard so often in his youth, and thus religion would add its weighty sanction to the sage experience and reflection of manhood. Religious controversy rather than political speculation occupied the best minds of that age. Shakespeare had but a small portion of the ponderous classical learning characteristic of the age of folios, and thus was without that bias in favour of the heroes, institutions and political thought of antiquity which marks and at times mars the Roman plays of Jonson and Chapman. He had read enough of Plutarch to know that the murder of Julius Caesar plunged the Roman world into chaos and calamity, and he had enough philosophy to realize that political murder is always a crime and, what is worse, a blunder. He does not permit us to forget that the assassin Brutus killed his friend and benefactor, the ruler of Rome, not because he was a tyrant but lest he might prove himself a tyrant. Admiration of tyrannicide as practised in Rome and Greece, and the intense ferocity of religious hatreds during the last twenty-five years of the sixteenth century had convinced zealots and statesmen that assassination was not merely justifiable but highly meritorious, provided that they could select the victims. William the Silent, Henry III of France, the Duc de Guise, and later Henry IV were murdered at the instigation of political or national enemies. Elizabeth had often been in serious danger. Five major plots at least had been discovered, each aimed at her life. Perhaps in his insistence on the doctrine of divine right, with its corollary the sacro-sanctity of the queen, Shakespeare was trying to do the State some service.

76

PLAY ABRIDGMENT—PART I

THE LENGTH OF ELIZABETHAN AND JACOBEAN PLAYS

SO many contradictory opinions have recently been expressed on the normal length of the unabridged Elizabethan play written for the public stage that it seems worth while to state the facts. The modern opinion that this length was about 3,000 lines springs from an unwarranted extension to all plays of a result obtained by Fleay[1] for 29 plays of Shakespeare. He used the Globe edition, which gives higher totals than any other edition that I have seen. Arithmetic was not Fleay's forte; his own figures prove that the average should have been 3,053 lines. Sir E. K. Chambers[2] has taken the trouble of re-counting these figures, and excluded six 'abnormal' plays; he finds that the average length of the thirty-one 'normal' plays is 2,920 lines. Fleay's average for the thirty-seven plays is 2,860 lines; Sir E. K. Chambers makes it 2,864. These two results are extraordinarily close together considering that Fleay made errors varying from 20 to 900 lines in the various totals of no less than seventeen plays. My own figures, based on the text of the Cambridge edition of 1863-1866, make the average for the thirty-seven plays 2,751 lines a play. Fleay's totals have been quoted by authors for nearly sixty years; recent critics have accepted Fleay's 'proof' that normal, unabridged plays of Shakespeare average 3,000 lines in length, and have added, without any further appeal to figures, a corollary that normal Elizabethan plays average 3,000 lines in length. Professor J. D. Wilson[3] has no doubts.

1. *Shakespeare Manual* (1878), p. 259.
2. *William Shakespeare* (1930), vol. ii, pp. 398-405.
3. *The Hamlet Transcript* (1918), p. 38.

Shakespeare and the Homilies

Something about 3,000 lines seems to have been the normal length of a drama to which an Elizabethan audience was accustomed.

He repeats this in the New Shakespeare[4]:

> The normal length of a play for the London stage in Elizabethan days was about 3,000 lines; the received text of *The Two Gentlemen* contains some 2,380 lines. After what has just been said it should not be difficult to believe that at least 600 lines of the original have disappeared.

Hence alarums and excursions in pursuit of the missing lines. Dr. W. W. Greg[5] is more conservative and suggests that 2,400 to 2,500 lines ' would be a moderately long play.' Mr. G. B. Harrison,[6] in his introduction to a reprint of the first quarto of *Hamlet,* says:

> Q 1 contains 2,143 lines, and the addition of a quarter would make the length of the original play about 2,780 lines; the average length of an Elizabethan play being about 2,800-3,000 lines.

Professor L. L. Schücking[7] has his doubts whether acting versions ever exceeded 2,600 lines. The most recent references appear in Sir E. K. Chambers's *William Shakespeare.*[8] In discussing abridgments, he says,

> Court entertainments often lasted for three hours, and a full length play of 3,000 lines would not require more.

The doctors disagree, as is usual, but, by their leave, an average is not a matter of opinion but of arithmetic; the material for finding the correct answer to the question, How long was the unabridged Elizabethan play, has always been ready to our hand. If we are prepared to count the total number of lines in all the plays written for the public stage during the years 1590-1616 we shall have the correct average. As my custom had always been to add up the lines of every play as I read it, I was led to make a complete tally of the lines in all the plays acted on the public stage during the years when Shakespeare was associated with the theatre. I have counted the number of lines in 233 plays, which include all but

4. *The Two Gentlemen of Verona* (1921), p. 81.
5. *Two Elizabethan Stage Abridgements,* p. 310n.
6. Bodley Head Quartos, *Hamlet* (1923), p. xxvi.
7. *Times Literary Supplement,* September 22, 1930.
8. *William Shakespeare* (1930), vol. i. pp. 214-15.

two of the extant plays known to have been written for or acted on the public stage during the years 1590-1616. I have used the list of plays arranged in chronological order by Sir E. K. Chambers.[9] Two plays have been omitted because they are not in the Melbourne Public Library. Latin plays, English translations of classical and French plays, University and the so-called ' Closet ' plays have been excluded, as have been all plays printed after 1616 unless we have evidence sufficient to prove that they were written or acted not later than that year.

Something must be said on the method of counting which has been adopted. A uniform edition of all Elizabethan and Jacobean plays does not exist, and is a desideratum; consequently the totals of lines obtained for the plays of one dramatist are too frequently not comparable with the totals obtained for the plays of another. If we use Fairholt's edition of Lyly's plays *Endimion* runs to 2,407 lines, which in Bond's edition are reduced to 2,082 lines. The difference of 325 lines for this short play might easily exceed 600 lines for two texts of such a Gargantuan prose play as *Bartholomew Fair*. Two editors of a play in blank verse usually agree closely in the totals recorded; there will always be room for small differences amounting to a few lines. Consistency in totals is ensured if we count as one line the two, three or more parts into which it may be broken in dialogue. My own totals for the plays in verse which are printed in facsimile of the original editions differ considerably from those obtained by the editors; it is their practice to count as a line whatever had been printed as a line in the first quartos, and they thus add to their totals the scene and stage directions. The length of *Macbeth* in the first folio is 2,396 lines, which the Cambridge editors reduce to 2,084 lines; Mr. Lucas's recent edition of the *Duchess of Malfi* runs to 3,316 lines; counting full metrical lines only, I make the total 3,037 lines.

More than one-half of the extant plays written by

9. *The Elizabethan Stage*, vol. iv, Appendix L, pp. 379-97, and Appendix N, pp. 404-406.

Shakespeare's contemporaries are in verse or contain very little prose; and thus for purposes of counting we are independent of the edition in which the text is printed. Furthermore, short tests have shown that the average word-content of an Elizabethan blank-verse line varies very little whoever may be the author, and that a line may be taken to contain as an average almost exactly eight words. The difficulty of standardising the length of the plays of Shakespeare in which much prose is present recurs and is intensified in any attempt to do the same for the plays of his contemporaries. Counting is tedious drudgery; too much of it is 'tolerable and not to be endured,' and would overtax the proverbial patience of the Chinese. Fortunately, results accurate enough for the purpose of this investigation are obtainable without any excessive labour. I have shown elsewhere[9a] that, on the average, 100 lines of prose in the Cambridge edition (1863-1866) of Shakespeare's plays contain 818 words, and consequently we may assert, without falling into any serious error, that the average prose line of this edition has the same word-content as the line of blank verse. We may thus give a semi-quantitative meaning to the statement that *The Merry Wives* contains 2,634 lines, implying that these lines, prose or verse, average eight words to the line. The 'full' prose line of the Cambridge text as it appears in long and continuous passages of prose speech averages very nearly eleven words a line. After making a considerable number of short tests, I found that if the 'full' prose lines of the text of any dramatist's plays average eleven words to the line I could safely infer that the average word-content of his prose line—dialogue and long speech—would come out a little more than eight words to the line. I have used, therefore, when I could find them, editions of dramatists in which the 'full' prose line averaged as closely as possible eleven words to the line. The range of choice in the editions of the old dramatists

9a. *Review of English Studies*, viii, 29, January, 1932.

varies considerably; where several editions are available I have chosen the one in which the prose text approximates most nearly to the conditions stated above. Of many plays, however, only one or two editions exist, and I have been compelled to admit to my lists totals comparatively too great or too small.

I give in Table I a list of the editions used, the number of the plays included, and the value in words of the full prose line of each edition.

I have divided the 201 plays included in the table into three groups. The first contains 107 plays; the totals for these require little or no adjustment if the editions named are used. The second group of fifty plays consists of plays in which the 'full' prose line averages less than eleven words to the line. The totals for each of these plays will be, in a comparative sense, too high, and will raise the average length of all the plays. As a rough measure of the consequent increase it may be noted that the average length of the thirty-three plays of Shakespeare which contain prose is 2,759 lines in the Cambridge text—eleven words to the 'full' prose line, and 2,885 lines in the Globe text—'full' prose line of nine words; the difference amounts to 126 lines a play. Most of the texts of plays in the second group average ten words to the 'full' prose line, and this difference of 126 lines a play should probably be halved. The third group is the smallest, and contains the plays in which the 'full' prose line exceeds eleven words; in this group the totals will be, comparatively, too low, and tend to decrease the average length of all the plays. The increase in average length due to the second group will be cancelled in part by the decrease due to the third group. My results are perhaps a little too high —but not, according to my estimate, more than twenty lines a play.

It is not suggested that a solution has been found for all the troublesome problems involved in an attempt to make comparable the totals obtained for plays of different

F

Shakespeare and the Homilies

TABLE I

Average Number of Words in Full Prose Line

Group.	Name of dramatist.	Number of plays.	Edition or editors.	Average number of words.
1.	Shakespeare	37	Clark and Wright	11
	Jonson	3	Herford and Simpson	11
	Jonson	8	Various editions	11
	Chapman	12	Parrott	11
	Various authors	15	Dodsley (1780)	11
	Marlowe	7	Bullen	$10\frac{2}{3}$
	Peele	3	Bullen	$10\frac{2}{3}$
	Marston	9	Bullen	$10\frac{2}{3}$
	Middleton	13	Bullen	$10\frac{2}{3}$
2.	Day	5	Bullen	$9\frac{1}{3}$
	Heywood	13	Pearson's reprint	10
	Dekker	11.	Pearson's reprint	10
	Various authors	10	Hazlitt's Dodsley	10
	Various authors	5	Mermaid series	$10\frac{1}{2}$
	Various authors	6	Bullen	$9\frac{3}{4}$
3.	Greene	6	Collins	$11\frac{1}{3}$
	Lyly	3	Bond	12
	Webster	3	Lucas	$11\frac{1}{4}$
	Beaumont and Fletcher	17	Waller	12
	Various authors	15	Malone Society re-prints	$12\frac{1}{2}$

authors which are printed in a variety of editions; all that is claimed is that a definite and almost quantitative meaning has been given to the phrase ‘a line of dramatic prose,’ and that the length of any play may therefore be directly compared with the average length of Shakespeare's plays, as computed on the text of the Cambridge edition (1863-1866). The average length of plays given below is approximately correct, and is certainly not understated. In the following table are included all plays intended for the London stage which were printed or are known to have been acted within the limits of the periods indicated at the head of each column.

82

TABLE II

PLAYS ARRANGED ACCORDING TO THEIR LENGTHS FOR VARIOUS GROUPS OF YEARS

Number of lines.	Number of Plays acted or written during						
	I. 1590 to 1594.	II. 1594 to 1603.	III. 1590 to 1603.	IV. 1603 to 1616.	V. 1594 to 1616.	VI. 1590 to 1616.	VII.[10] 1590 to 1616.
Over 3,400	1	4	5	3	7	8	0
3,200–3,400	0	0	0	5	5	5	0
3,000–3,200	1	4	5	11	15	16	7
Totals above 3,000	2	8	10	19	27	29	7
2,800–3,000	1	8	9	11	19	20	15
2,600–2,800	4	16	20	21	37	41	35
2,500–2,600	4	4	8	14	18	22	15
2,400–2,500	4	5	9	11	16	20	19
2,300–2,400	2	0	2	12	12	14	13
2,200–2,300	2	0	2	10	10	12	11
2,000–2,200	5	8	13	14	22	27	23
1,800–2,000	7	2	9	5	7	14	14
1,600–1,700	6	5	11	3	8	14	13
Below 1,600	11	2	13	7	9	20	20
Totals under 3,000	46	50	96	108	158	204	178
Totals ..	48	58	106	127	185	233	185
Corrupt or abridged ..	12	2	14	4	6	18	18
Sound Texts ..	36	56	92	123	179	215	167

A glance at the above table is sufficient to disprove finally and completely the oft-repeated assertion that the normal length of the Elizabethan or Jacobean play was about 3,000 lines. Not at any period, neither before the plague of 1592-1593 nor between 1594 and the death of Elizabeth nor between the accession of James and the death of Shakespeare did more than a negligible percentage of plays written for the London stage exceed 3,000 lines. Not one-eighth of extant plays reach the normal

10. VII = Total plays excluding Shakespeare's and Jonson's.

length postulated by recent critics. Up to 1603 Shakespeare and Jonson contributed all but one of these outsize dramas, and from 1590-1616 twenty-two out of a total of twenty-nine. At least forty dramatists shared in the 185 plays not written by Shakespeare or Jonson; seven plays only exceed 3,000 lines, or less than 4 per cent.[11] The supply of these Gargantuan dramas ceased almost immediately after the death of Shakespeare, and the almost simultaneous retirement of Jonson from active practice as a playwright; after 1616 such plays ceased to be written. The three-thousand-line play came in with Shakespeare and went out with him, yet it is not his 'normal' play; if he has eleven plays above, he has twenty-six below this limit.

We have now to find the average length of the Elizabethan play. For this purpose we may use the figures given in the table, in the final row giving the totals of 'Sound Texts,' picking out a point in each column above which the number of plays is as nearly as possible equal to the number of plays below. The length of the middle play of each column will be approximately the average length of all the plays in the column. The following are the adjusted results.

TABLE III

MEAN LENGTH OF PLAYS AT DIFFERENT PERIODS

Column.	Period.	Number of plays.	Mean length.
I.	1590–1594	36	2,250
II.	1594–1603	56	2,650
III.	1590–1603	92	2,500
IV.	1603–1616	123	2,520
V.	1594–1616	185	2,560
VI.	1590–1616	215	2,515
VII.[12]	1590–1616	167	2,440

11. My list credits Dekker with two plays, *The Honest Whore*, Parts I and II, each about 3,000 lines. The count was made on the texts of Pearson's edition, in which the full prose line averages about ten words. About one-half of each play is in prose, and I estimate that on the amount of prose present at least 100 lines should be deducted from the total of each play, if it is to be made strictly comparable with those obtained from the Cambridge text of Shakespeare's plays.
12. Excludes the plays of Shakespeare and Jonson.

Elizabethan and Jacobean Plays

TABLE IV

Period.	Number of plays.	Total lines.	Average per play.	Estimated average.
1590–1594	48	98,617	2,054	2,000
	12 (corrupt)	17,752	1,479	
	36	80,865	2,246	2,250
	5 (Shakespeare's)	14,002	2,800	
	31	66,863	2,157	
1594–1603	58	150,029	2,588	2,650
	2 (corrupt)	2,913	1,457	
	56	147,116	2,627	2,650
	4 (Jonson's)	15,592	3,898	
	52	131,524	2,529	
	19 (Shakespeare's)	51,353	2,703	
	33	80,171	2,429	
1590–1603	106	248,646	2,347	2,433
	14 (corrupt)	20,665	1,476	
	92	227,981	2,478	2,500
	4 (Jonson's)	15,592	3,898	
	88	212,389	2,414	
	24 (Shakespeare's)	65,352	2,723	
	64	147,037	2,297	
1603–1616	127	315,732	2,486	2,507
	4 (corrupt)	5,160	1,290	
	123	310,572	2,525	2,520
	7 (Jonson's)	23,793	3,399	
	116	286,779	2,472	
	13 (Shakespeare's)	36,443	2,803	
	103	250,336	2,430	
1594–1616	185	465,666	2,517	2,545
	6 (corrupt)	8,073	1,345	
	179	457,593	2,556	2,560
	11 (Jonson's)	39,385	3,580	
	168	418,208	2,490	
	32 (Shakespeare's)	87,804	2,744	
	136	330,404	2,429	
1590–1616	233	564,383	2,422	2,475
	18 (corrupt)	25,824	1,435	
	215	538,559	2,505	2,515
	11 (Jonson's)	39,385	3,580	
	204	499,174	2,447	
	37 (Shakespeare's)	101,803	2,751	
	167	397,371	2,379	

The results of Table III are approximate; for greater accuracy more detail is necessary. Before computing averages it was necessary to remove from the list corrupt plays or abridgments of longer non-extant plays. Most of these are anonymous and came to the press after the disastrous plague years of 1592-1594; usually they are short, but we must keep in mind that carefully edited plays, such as *Sophonisba* (1,611 lines), *The Conspiracy of Byron* (2,058 lines), *Blurt Master Constable* (2,054 lines), *The Shoemaker's Holiday* (2,136 lines), *A Woman Killed with Kindness* (2,028 lines), *Humour Out of Breath* (1,897 lines), and many others not much longer were written at a time when the average length of plays was at its highest. We are not justified in asserting that a play is necessarily corrupt or abridged because it is hundreds of lines shorter than other plays written by the same author. Corruption, too, may increase rather than decrease the length of a play—the *Doctor Faustus* of 1616 adds over 700 lines, most of them poor stuff, to the corrupt abridgment printed in 1604. The sub-divided table (Table IV) gives the calculated average length for each group of plays included in the same period as in the preceding table. In each divisional table the estimated average given in Table III and the computed average are placed together for purpose of comparison.

After 1616 the average length of plays fell steadily till it was about 2,250 lines, and very few plays varied very much from the average. Thus Shirley during the last ten years before the closing of the theatres in 1642 wrote twenty-three plays that averaged about 2,230 lines; not one of these exceeded 2,500 lines in length.

These tables must convince any reader that at no time during the thirty years 1587-1616 did the average length of plays much exceed 2,500 lines. Though much less than a half of the plays acted at the Rose, the Theatre and the Curtain prior to the plague of 1592-1594 have come down to us, we may accept without distrust 2,250 lines as the normal length of a play at that period. Shakespeare undoubtedly originated the practice of writing plays too long to be completely acted. When the theatres re-opened in June, 1594, Greene, Marlowe, and perhaps Kyd, were dead, Peele and Lodge had probably ceased to write for the stage, and a new generation of dramatists began work; among the dramatists writing between 1594 and 1603 were Heywood, Munday, Chettle, Chapman, Drayton, Jonson, Porter, Day, Dekker, Hathaway, Haughton, Webster, Marston and Middleton, though some of these, perhaps, may have been connected with the stage before the plague. It was during the following decade, 1594-1603, that the average length of plays reached its highest, viz., 2,627 lines; yet a little investigation shows that there was no real rise. The contribution made by Jonson and Shakespeare to the total of fifty-six plays amounts to more than two-fifths; Jonson's four printed plays average 3,900 lines, and add nearly 100 lines to the average length of the whole. Another cause of the rise was the great vogue of the rambling and episodic play on English history, of which thirteen belong to this period; these average 2,839 lines a-piece. If we exclude these and the four prodigious plays of Jonson, the average length of the remaining thirty-nine plays, which include fifteen of Shakespeare's, falls to 2,439 lines, a result in excellent agreement with that for the succeeding period 1603-1616. If we use the term 'Elizabethan play' in its strict sense and consider the plays of the period 1587-1603, we find that, after excluding the four plays of Jonson and twenty-one plays on subjects taken from English history from the total of ninety-two plays with sound texts, the average length of the remaining sixty-seven is 2,282 lines. This result agrees well with the average of 2,297 lines for all plays written by authors other than Jonson and Shakespeare during the last fourteen years of the Queen's reign.

Shakespeare and the Homilies

For the period 1603-1616, the great age of our poetic drama, the average length of all plays with sound texts drops from 2,627 to 2,525 lines; if, however, we omit the plays of Jonson and Shakespeare the average length of plays for the whole period 1594-1616 remains unchanged—a fact that by itself is a striking and convincing proof that the conditions of play production and stage representation did not change much during the whole of Shakespeare's dramatic career. More than thirty dramatists contributed one or more plays to a total of 136 plays; this number is enough to give us a satisfactory basis for a reliable average. Many of these dramas were carefully edited by their authors, and we may confidently rely upon a result to which so many contribute their mites. Jonson in this, as in his artistic attitude, stands apart from his contemporaries. His plays average over 800 lines a play more than those of Shakespeare and exceed the general average by 1,150 lines; he seems to have regarded length as a merit. Just as we must exclude abridgments and corrupt plays because they contain less than the authors wrote and thus reduce the average, so we must exclude the plays of one who deliberately wrote far more than could be acted, and then made considerable additions to over-long plays prior to printing them.

A summary of the results for the years 1594-1616 is worth making. Thirty-three known authors contributed 179 plays in all. Jonson wrote eleven of these, averaging 3,580 lines a play, Shakespeare thirty-two, averaging 2,744 lines. The remaining thirty-one dramatists provided 136 plays that average 2,430 lines. Which of these three ought we to accept as the normal length of plays written for the public stage? Shakespeare's? Jonson's? or that of the thirty-one dramatists? There can be but one answer—the thirty-one authors determine the rule, the two are the exception; accordingly we may say that

the normal length of a play in the days of Shakespeare
was about 2,430 lines.

In confirmation of this important result I add a list
giving the average length of 144 plays with sound texts
written by fifteen of the principal dramatists and acted
on the public stage during the years 1590-1616; any
corrupt or abridged play is omitted. By the side of the
author's name is placed the name of the editor of the
edition used.

TABLE V

GIVING THE AVERAGE LENGTH OF PLAYS BY CERTAIN DRAMATISTS

Name of author.	Name of editor.	Number of plays.	Average length in lines.
Peele	Bullen	2	2,325
Greene	Collins	4	2,197
Kyd	Boas	2	2,318
Marlowe	Bullen	5	2,302
Shakespeare	Clark and Wright	37	2,751
Chapman	Parrott	12	2,405
Middleton	Bullen	13	2,487
Jonson	Herford and Simpson⎱ Various editors ⎰	11	3,580
Marston	Bullen	9	2,211
Dekker	Pearson's reprint	11	2,777
Beaumont and⎱ Fletcher ⎰	Bullen⎱ Waller⎰	17	2,580
Day	Bullen	5	2,350
Heywood	Pearson's reprint	13	2,511
Webster	Lucas	3	2,688
		144	2,626

Dissecting these figures we have—

144	plays contain	378,109	lines;	average	2,626	lines.
11	„ (Jonson's) contain	39,385	„	„	3,580	„
133	„ contain	338,724	„	„	2,547	„
37	„ (Shakespeare's) contain	101,803	„	„	2,751	„
96	„ contain	236,921	„	„	2,468	„

This average of 2,468 lines is significant, because it proves that thirteen very important dramatists thought a play somewhat below 2,500 lines quite long enough for any London theatre. Many, if not the majority, of these ninety-six plays were carefully edited by their authors, and we may be certain that we have all that they wrote, and probably more than was spoken by the actors in certain plays. This average agrees very well with that for the 136 plays written by authors other than Shakespeare and Jonson during the years 1594-1616. If we include Shakespeare's plays the average length for 133 plays does not exceed 2,550 lines, or 450 lines less than the modern 'normal length' postulated by Professor J. D. Wilson and others.

Some critics may suggest that the Chamberlain-King's men may have staged longer plays than other companies; it is therefore worth while finding the average length of the plays acted at each important London theatre during the period 1594-1616. I have accepted the repertory assigned to each company by Sir E. K. Chambers,[13] and have taken into account 175 plays, a number which includes some written and acted before the re-organization of 1594. Not more than one-eighth of all the plays known to have been acted during this period are omitted; most of these are rather short.

1. THE CHAMBERLAIN-KING'S MEN

72 plays contain		191,216 lines;	average	2,656 lines.
3 „ (corrupt or short) contain		3,261 „	„	1,087 „
69 „ contain		187,955 „	„	2,724 „
7 „ (Jonson's) contain		24,053 „	„	3,436 „
62 „ „ „		163,902 „	„	2,644 „
37 „ (Shakespeare's) contain		101,803 „	„	2,751 „
25 „ „ „		62,099 „	„	2,484 „

13. *The Elizabethan Stage*, vol. iv, Appendix L, pp. 379-97, and Appendix N, pp. 404-406.

Though this total of seventy-two plays is more than double the number that survives of the repertory of the Admiral-Prince's men, probably twice as many have been lost. More than half of their extant plays are Shakespeare's. Burbage and his partner produced no less than twenty-one of the twenty-nine surviving plays that contain over 3,000 lines each; eleven are by Shakespeare, and seven by Jonson. Their contribution of forty-four plays out of a total of seventy-two swamps and obscures the far lower figures of at least seven, and perhaps a dozen authors represented in the remaining twenty-five plays. For the years 1594-1603 the Admiral's men produced a play about every fortnight; even if we suppose that the audiences of the Curtain, Globe and Blackfriars were not quite so fond of novelty as those who patronized the Rose and the Fortune, we probably under-estimate in suggesting that Shakespeare's fellows produced a new play every five or six weeks. On this scale of production they would have bought quite 200 plays during this period, and the extant seventy-two plays would represent about a third of their repertoire. Who wrote the missing plays? For an answer read the record of Chettle's work in Henslowe's diary;[14] he had a hand in forty-eight plays, and his name does not appear on the title-page of one! The average of 2,484 lines for twenty-five plays written by dramatists other than Jonson and Shakespeare is in excellent agreement with the 2,468 lines obtained for ninety-six plays above in Table V; it indicates that plays provided for the public by Shakespeare's ' fellows ' averaged about 2,500 lines. This average is supported by the fact that the additions made to *The Malcontent* ' to entertaine a little more time, and to abridge the not received custome of musicke in our theater,' increase it to 2,531 lines in length.

14. Chambers, *Elizabethan Stage,* vol. ii, pp. 264-67.

II. THE ADMIRAL-PRINCE'S MEN

If we may judge from Henslowe's records for the nine years, 1594-1603, the thirty-two plays attributed to this company represent not an eighth part of those acted by them during the twenty-two years, 1594-1616. How tight a grip Henslowe and the actors kept upon their plays may be realized from the fact that from 1606 to 1616 three only came to the press. The following are the figures:

32 plays contain		78,397 lines; average 2,450 lines.
4 „ (corrupt) contain	5,804 „	„ 1,451 „
28 „ contain	72,593 „	„ 2,592 „

This average agrees well enough with that of 2,644 lines for the sixty-two plays of the King's, and is about 100 lines a play higher than that of plays written by authors other than Shakespeare and Jonson. Two of Dekker's plays and one of Porter's exceed 3,000 lines, but the totals for these and twelve other plays were computed from texts in which the full prose line contains ten words and are too high.

III. THE WORCESTER-ANNE'S MEN

This company seems to have made its first London appearance in 1601, and was taken under Queen Anne's patronage early in the new reign. Heywood was their principal playwright during this period, and accounts for more than half of the extant twenty-two plays; two or three of these are doubtful attributions.

22 plays contain		52,533 lines; average 2,388 lines.
2 „ (corrupt) contain	2,934 „	„ 1,467 „
20 „ contain	49,599 „	„ 2,480 „

This average is substantially the same as that of plays produced by the King's men, if we omit the work of Shakespeare and Jonson. Only one play exceeds 3,000 lines.

IV. The Children of St. Paul's

Twenty printed plays belonging to the repertoire of this boys' company for the years 1599-1606 are extant.

20 plays contain	45,970 lines;	average 2,299 lines.
1 play (short) contains	1,217 „	„ —
19 plays contain	44,753 „	„ 2,355 „

This is the lowest average for any of the five theatres, and is due almost entirely to the unusually short plays written by Marston. Although no play equals 3,000 lines in length nine, or practically one-half, exceed 2,500 lines. The dramatists include Dekker, Marston, Middleton, Beaumont, Chapman, Webster, and probably others; we may certainly rely on the soundness of the texts.

V. The Children of the Chapel and of the Queen's Revels

This important company of boy actors seems to have been acting off and on from 1600 to 1614; almost every dramatist of importance except Dekker, Webster and Shakespeare contributed plays to their repertory, the list of authors, including Jonson, Day, Marston, Chapman, Middleton, Beaumont, Fletcher, Daniel and Field. Jonson jeeringly says, ' The ghosts of some three or foure playes, departed a dozen years since, have bin seene walking on youre stage heere '; which suggests that new versions of old plays were also upon the acting list.

29 plays contain	74,347 lines;	average 2,564 lines.
3 „ (Jonson's) contain	11,493 „	„ 3,831 „
26 „ contain	62,854 „	„ 2,417 „

The average of 2,417 lines a play is a little higher than that of the plays produced by the Children of St. Paul's, and is substantially the same as the average for all plays other than those of Shakespeare and Jonson during the years 1594-1616. Three plays are over 3,000 lines—all

Jonson's, and thirteen exceed 2,500 lines. The textual soundness of most of these plays cannot be successfully challenged.

On combining the figures for all the companies our results are as below:

Plays.	Total lines.	Average lines per play.
175	442,463	2,528
10 (corrupt or abridged) ..	13,216	1,322
165	429,247	2,601
11 (Jonson's)	39,385	3,580
154	389,862	2,532
37 (Shakespeare's)	101,803	2,751
117	288,059	2,462

We have now established certain facts that apply to all extant plays with sound texts written or acted during the years 1594-1616.

1. Plays of 3,000 lines and upwards were very rarely written, except by Jonson or Shakespeare, and amount in all to less than one-eighth of the total number.

2. Jonson's plays are abnormally long, averaging nearly 3,580 lines, and must be excluded from the count if we are to obtain a correct average.

3. This average for all plays (except Jonson's), written or acted during this period, is 2,490 lines.

4. The average length of all plays written by fourteen important dramatists (excluding Jonson) during these years is 2,547 lines, or only 57 lines higher than the general average for all plays.

5. The average length of all the plays (except Jonson's) produced by the five most important companies at the principal London theatres equals 2,532 lines.

6. The high average length of Shakespeare's plays is largely due to the presence of ten plays on English history; if these are deducted the average length of his remaining twenty-seven plays equals 2,671 lines.

We may arrive at the normal length of 2,500 lines in yet another way. Let us exclude from our list as super-normal eight plays over 3,400 lines and twenty plays under 1,600 lines as subnormal. There will remain 205 plays ranging between 3,400 and 1,600 lines; of these 103 are above and 102 below 2,500 lines, the mean of the highest and the lowest. This is exactly the result that we should expect to get if we asked forty-one authors to write five plays a-piece, stipulating that they must not exceed 3,400 lines, or write less than 1,600 lines. On the other hand, if we gave our authors to understand that audiences were accustomed to plays of about 3,000 lines in length, they would certainly write almost as many plays above the standard as below it.

PLAY ABRIDGMENT—PART II

THE TIME ALLOTTED FOR REPESENTATION OF ELIZABETHAN AND JACOBEAN PLAYS

HAVING fixed the normal length of the Elizabethan and Jacobean play at about 2,500 lines, we are now in a position to discuss certain consequences. The length of the acting version of a play will depend chiefly upon the time allotted for the stage representation; minor factors likely to affect it would be the rate at which the actors spoke their lines, the presence or absence of dumb-shows and processions, the number of songs and of dances, and the amount of stage 'business.' Up to 1594 we have no definite statement from any one except professed opponents of plays and actors concerning the time taken for the representation of a play in a London theatre. Such clerical thunder as that of Fenton, North-brooke and Whetstone, all of whom talk in a general way of 'two or three houres,' belongs to a period of stage history of which very little is known. Perhaps the earliest definite reference after 1587 occurs in *Martins Months Minde* (August, 1589).

> Martin . . . calling his sonnes . . . said . . . I perceiue that euerie stage plaier, if he play the foole but two houres together, hath somewhat for his labour: and, I . . . nothing.[1]

Such allusions have little more than corroborative value. The first piece of evidence is to be found in an official letter written on October 8, 1594, by Henry Lord Hunsdon, Lord Chamberlain, to the Lord Mayor, in which he states that

> my nowe companie of Players haue vndertaken to me that, where heretofore they began not their Plaies til towardes fower a clock, they will now begin at two, and haue don betwene fower and fiue, and will nott vse anie Drumes or trumpettes att all for the callinge of peopell together.[2]

1. Quoted from Chambers, *Elizabethan Stage*, vol. iv, p. 230.
2. *Ibid.*, p. 316.

This document makes provision for a playing time of less than three hours, commencing at two o'clock. The undertaking given by the players to have the performance over before 5 o'clock was to meet the objection of the city fathers that the theatres kept their sons, apprentices and servants out till late at night. This letter fixes the hour of commencement for the company of which Shakespeare remained a member for the rest of his dramatic career; a later allusion (cited below), made by Platter, suggests that all the London companies found it convenient to begin at the same hour. We have no evidence that any change in this hour of commencement at the public theatres was made for many years.

Shakespeare is the earliest playwright who made a practice of alluding in his plays to actors and acting, the stage, and theatrical customs and technicalities; he is the first, also, to state the time allotted to the performance of a play. The reference in the prologue to the surreptitious quarto of *Romeo and Juliet* (1597) to

the two howres traffique of our Stage

fixes the amount of time allotted to the representation of the play, but may exclude the time given to music and the inevitable jig. The quarto runs to 2,215 lines and the version could be acted in a little less than two hours. The prologue is defective, and probably is a ' report ' of the correct version found in the second quarto. We may assume, therefore, that it was spoken on the stage, and dates back to the first performance of the play. The same phrase occurs in the ' good ' quarto of 1599, which contains 2,989 lines and would need more than two hours and a half for complete representation. Shakespeare, it would seem, wrote a play of nearly 3,000 lines, though he knew that out of it his ' fellows ' would carve a two-hour play. Platter, a German who visited England towards the end of 1599, gives us some valuable contem-

G

porary evidence on London theatrical performances. He
says :—

> Thus every day at two o'clock in the afternoon in the city of
> London two and sometimes three comedies are performed at
> separate places.   At the end of the comedy they danced
> according to their custom with extreme elegance.   Two in
> men's clothes and two in women's gave this performance, in
> wonderful combination with each other.[3]

The allusion is probably to the jig; evidently the hour of
commencement suggested by Lord Hunsdon had been
adopted by all companies.   The next allusion to the time
allotted to the performance of a play by Shakespeare's
' fellows ' is found in *The Alchemist* (1610).   Jonson
begins his prologue in his most aggressive style:

> Fortune, that fauours Fooles, these two short howers
> We wish away; both for your sakes, and ours,
> Iudging Spectators.

The play contains 3,066 lines, and would require not
' two short howers ' but about two hours and forty
minutes for complete representation.   The use of the
phrase ' two short howers ' by such a precisian as Jonson
has much significance.   Allusions of this kind became
more frequent.   *Henry VIII* is usually assigned to 1613,
and though the prologue may not be Shakespeare's, we
have no reason to suspect that it belongs to a revival of
the play.   It runs:

> Those that come to see
> Onely a show or two, and so agree
> The Play may passe: If they be still, and willing,
> Ile undertake may see away their shilling
> Richly in two short houres.

Two hours and a half would scarcely be long enough
to ' see away ' the 2,807 lines of *Henry VIII,* a play full
of ceremonies and processions.   Similar remarks apply
to the allusion found in the prologue to the *Two Noble
Kinsmen* (c. 1613) acted at Blackfriars.   The author
of the prologue, probably Fletcher, deprecates any
comparison with Chaucer, yet promises the audience,

3. Chambers, *Elizabethan Stage*, vol. ii, p. 365.

Time Allotted for Representation

We know nothing of the stage history of Middleton's *Mayor of Quinborough,* which the title-page declares was played at Blackfriars (and therefore after 1609) by his Majesty's Servants. The presenter, 'Raynulph, Monk of Chester,' says in the prologue:

> If all my powers,
> Can win the grace of two poor hours,
> Well apaid I go to rest.

The length of the play (2,249 lines) would permit of its being acted without any abridgment in 'two poor hours.'

The above allusions constitute all the evidence that we have on the time allotted for acting a play by the Chamberlain-King's Men from 1597 to about 1616. Prologues and epilogues to plays may have been, and often were, written years after the plays in which they appear; but the references in the prologues to *Romeo and Juliet* and *The Alchemist* are found in the first quartos of these plays, and must be accepted as decisive of this question as far as this company is concerned. Four professional dramatists, each having a long and intimate knowledge of the stage and play production, one of them a professional actor, a second an ex-actor, concur in the statement that the duration of a stage performance was two hours. Jonson and Shakespeare, who between them wrote three-fourths of all the plays over 3,000 lines in length, both speak of 'two short hours' as the time allotted for the representation of plays that could not even be read aloud in the time by any one, unless he raced along without a moment's interruption at the extraordinary speed of 200 words a minute. Fletcher and Middleton give us valuable evidence in corroboration of the statements made by the older poets.

In the *Whore of Babylon* (2,550 lines), printed in 1607, but written about 1605 and acted at the Fortune by

99

the Prince's servants, Dekker writes with the grace of
his happier moods:

> So, winged Time that long agoe flew hence
> You must fetch backe, with all those golden yeares
> He stole, and here imagine still hee stands,
> Thrusting his silver locke into your hands.
> There hold it but two howres, It shall from Graues
> Raize vp the dead.

This allusion suggests that plays produced at the Fortune occupied about the same time in representation as
at the Globe; it also serves to bridge the gap between the
allusion in *Romeo and Juliet* and that in *The Alchemist.*
The play could be acted in a little less than two hours
and a quarter.

Dekker made a second allusion to the time devoted to
the performance of a play in the epilogue to his queer
and queerly named drama, *If It be not Good, The Deuil
is in It,* which was acted by the Queen's Servants at
the Red Bull, probably in 1611:

> Hereby is meant
> If for so many nones, and midnights spent
> To reape three howres of mirth, our haruest-seede
> Lyes still and rot.

This is the only dated reference to a three-hour performance prior to 1616. The play runs to 2,700 lines
and could be acted without any abridgment in two hours
and twenty minutes; perhaps second-class theatres such
as The Red Bull gave longer performances in order to
attract an audience. Heywood's *Apology for Actors,*
probably written c. 1607, came out the same year (1612),
and to it Christopher Beeston (like Heywood, one of
Queen Anne's Servants) contributed a few lines of
commendatory verse which conclude:

> Two hours well spent, and all their pastimes done,
> What's good I follow, and what's bad I shun.

Yet probably Heywood and Beeston both had parts in
Dekker's play for the performance of which the author
asks three hours. Beeston's verses are written in the

character of a spectator rather than in that of an actor, and refer to what was certainly the usual duration of performances at London theatres. It is difficult to reconcile the 'three hours' of which Dekker speaks with what Heywood says a year or two later in his epilogue to *The Iron Age, Part II* (c. 1613), which was almost certainly acted by the Queen's Servants. Ulysses, almost the only character left alive at the end of the play, thus deprecates the displeasure of the audience:

> If you thinke he hath done your patience wrong
> (In teadious sceanes) by keeping you so long,
> Much matter in few words, hee bad me say,
> Are hard to expresse, that lengthned out his Play.

This apology for the length of a play that does not exceed 2,300 lines and could be acted in two hours is little less than absurd if the company usually gave three hours to the performance.

During their short career as public entertainers the Children of St. Paul's did not devote much more than two hours to the performance of both play and music. William Percy[4] in 'a note to the Master of Children of Powles,' says of his own plays:

> Memorandum, that if any of the fine and formost of these Pastorals and Comoedyes conteyned in this volume shall but ouereach in length (the children not to begin before foure, after prayers, and the gates of Powles shutting at six) the tyme of supper, that then in tyme and place conuenient, you do let passe some of the songs, and make the consort the shorter; for I suppose these plaies be somewhat too long for that place. Howsoeuer, on your own experience, and at your best direction, be it.

The Cuck-Queanes contains 2,139 lines and could easily be played in a little less than two hours if the actors 'let passe some of the songs.' Perhaps plays grew longer and the 'consort' shorter, for the average length of the company's plays was 2,355 lines; perhaps, too, the plays tended to 'ouereach in length the time of supper.' St.

---

4. Chambers, *Elizabethan Stage*, vol. ii, p. 21.

Paul's had several side-gates available for the use of church dignitaries, and these may have been opened for the audience if the performance lasted after six o'clock.

Percy's statement is confirmed by Middleton in his induction to *Michaelmas Term* (c. 1606).

> But, gentlemen, to spread myself open unto you, in cheaper terms I salute you; for ours have but sixpenny fees all the year long; yet we despatch you in two hours without demur; your suits hang not long here after candles be lighted.

Michaelmas Term is 2,581 lines in length and would take two hours and a quarter for complete representation; seven other plays belonging to this boys' company are longer.

Another allusion crops up in *Ram Alley*, acted by the Children of the King's Revels about 1607-1608 at White-friars. The noble author does not claim a ready wit if we are to take this couplet at face value:

> Thus two hours have brought to end,
> What many tedious hours have penn'd.

The play is of about average length (2,472 lines) and would require a few minutes over two hours to act.

The same theatre saw early in 1613 the production by some London prentices of Robert Tailor's short and shorter-lived play, *The Hog Hath Lost his Pearl* (1,951 lines). In the epilogue, which was not spoken because the sheriff arrested the actors before the play ended, the author said, with the mock-modesty customary in such after-speeches:

> For this, our author saith, if 't prove distasteful,
> He only grieves you spent two hours so wasteful.

The following passage in the Induction to *Bartholomew Fair* shows Jonson's usual preciseness of detail:

> It is couenanted and agreed, by and betweene the parties abouesaid, and the said Spectators and Hearers, aswell the curious and enuious, as the fauoring and iudicious, as also the grounded Iudgements and vnderstandings, doe for themselues seuerally Couenant, and agree to remaine in the places, their money or friends haue put them in, with patience, for the

space of two houres and an halfe, and somewhat more. In which time the Author promiseth to present them by vs, with a new sufficient Play called Bartholomew Fayre.

This prodigious play of 4,344 prose lines was produced at the Hope by the Princess Elizabeth's Servants, and could not be acted in less than three and a half to four hours. The date of Beaumont and Fletcher's *Four Plays in One* is uncertain; critics, however, agree that Beaumont wrote two of the four, and the play cannot therefore be later than 1616. One of the ' Spectators of the Play at the celebration of their nuptials,' says:

Besides, Signior, we will censure, not only the King in the Play here, that Reigns his two hours; but the King himself, that is to rule his life time.

The play is 2,345 lines in length and may have been produced by one of the boys' companies.

The above are all the allusions that can be proved to belong to plays written within the years 1594-1616. Dekker is the only dramatist who alludes to a three-hour playing period in the prologue or epilogue to a play. The words found in the *Raven's Almanack* (1608),

Hee shall be glad to play three houres for two pence to the basest stinkard in London, whose breth is stronger than Garlicke, and able to poison all the 12-penny roomes.'

are a spark of that ever-smouldering dislike of actors which we discover in his pamphlets and plays. The context suggests that ' three houres ' is in direct antithesis to ' two pence '; Dekker wishes his harsh taskmasters, the actor-sharers, the maximum of work for the minimum of pay in the most unsavoury surroundings. Other allusions after 1616 occur in the plays of Heywood, Fletcher, D'Avenant and Shirley; one of Fletcher's references in *Love's Pilgrimage* is worth quoting because it expresses the ideal of actor and audience:

This night
No mighty matter, nor no light,
We must intreat you look for: A good tale,
Told in two hours, we will not fail
If we be perfect, to rehearse ye.

103

The evidence may be briefly summarized.

1. Shakespeare, Jonson, Fletcher, Beaumont, Percy, Middleton, Barry, Tailor, Beeston, and Dekker all speak of 'two hours' as the time spent in the representation of a play. Shakespeare and Beeston were actors and Jonson was an ex-actor. Dekker also speaks of a three-hour playing period, and Jonson of 'somewhat more' than two hours and a half.

2. Dated references to the two-hour play begin in 1597 (repeated in 1599) and continue at intervals in 1601, 1605, 1606, 1607, 1610, 1612, 1613. Others are of uncertain date. The two allusions to a playing time of more than two hours occur in 1611 and 1614.

3. The Chamberlain-King's Men, Admiral-Prince's Men, Children of St. Paul's, and Children of the King's Revels produced two-hour plays. The evidence for the Queen Anne's Men is contradictory; Beeston the actor speaks of 'two hours,' Dekker of 'three hours.'

4. The theatres in which two-hour plays prevailed were the Theatre, Globe, Fortune, Rose, Blackfriars, and Whitefriars. The Red Bull was the home of Queen Anne's Men from about 1606; it did not bear a good name.

Conclusions on this as on any other subject must be based on the facts available and on reasonable inferences deduced from them. Shakespeare, Jonson, Fletcher, Middleton, Beeston and the rest use plain words in expressing themselves; if they wrote 'two hours' we have no option but to think that they meant exactly what they said. They knew—and their knowledge must be better than our guesses—that the actors usually allotted about two hours for the representation of a play, and they used the simplest words in saying so. After the passage of more than three hundred years some modern critics assert or imply that in the days of King James 'two hours' had not its literal sense in such passages, and must be understood as a conventional or semi-technical term used by actors and playwrights for a period of time not less than two hours and not quite three. The most venturesome critic, however, has so far hesitated to suggest that when Jonson speaks of 'two short howers' he really means

160 minutes, the time necessary to play *The Alchemist* without abridgment. He is certainly definite enough in covenanting that he shall have 'two houres and an halfe, and somewhat more' to present his colossal *Bartholomew Fair*. The use of such significant phrases as 'two poor hours,' 'two short hours,' 'these two hours,' suggests that the actors associated with Shakespeare maintained the two-hour limit with some rigidity; now and again, perhaps, a popular play might run on for an extra ten or fifteen minutes. Wherever 'two hours' appears in verse, 'three hours' would suit sense and metre just as well; a few minutes over two hours would suffice for the representation of the play of average length, *i.e.,* of 2,500 lines. We are not, in my opinion, entitled to disregard facts in order to be able 'to frolic in conjecture,' as Dr. Johnson puts it. Prior to 1614 at least a dozen allusions were made by ten very important dramatists and actors connected with the principal companies and theatres to the prevalent custom of allotting two hours to the representation of a play. Only one dramatist speaks of a three-hour playing time; beyond this statement there is not a scrap of evidence in favour of any other than two-hour plays. I prefer to take the words of Shakespeare, Jonson, Middleton and the rest in their literal sense, because each one of these poets could always find the right words for anything that he wished to say.

One of the reasons why the actors would keep rather strictly to the limit of two hours for the performance of the play was the necessity of finding time for the jig that concluded each day's entertainment. This popular song and dance 'turn' had probably won its place as a permanent item of the afternoon's programme in every public theatre long before Shakespeare began his London career; even in the days of Charles 1, Shirley and Glapthorne bewail the popular love of a jig. We do not know how long it lasted, but, if we may judge from the sneering dislike expressed by some dramatists, the time taken up by this artistically worthless after-piece resulted in considerable abridgment of plays. Even in a tragedy the clown would speak more than was set down for him; after the play was over, a low comedian, such as Kemp, who wrote his own jigs, probably took possession of the stage for as long as he pleased. Even a long play such as 2 *Henry IV* ended with a jig. 'If my Tongue,' says the speaker of the epilogue, probably Will Kemp, 'cannot entreat you to acquit me; will you command me to vse my Legges?' Evidently the jig was a matter of course, or the groundlings called for it, for at the end he says, 'My Tongue is wearie; when my Legs are so, I will bid you good night.' Outside of the music for the jig, we have little evidence that there was any but incidental music at the public theatres. Jonson gave a stage direction in *Sejanus* for a chorus of musicians to play between the acts, but did he get it? If he did, the music failed to calm 'the people's beastly rage.' At the private theatres music had an important place in the programme, because the boy actors were trained choristers; as a result less time would be available for the play.

A brief summary of the facts so far established in this and the previous essay may be of advantage.

1. The average length of 168 extant plays written by more than thirty dramatists for the various London companies of actors during the years 1594 to 1616 was 2,490 lines. Jonson's plays are excluded from this total.

2. The average length of the plays acted by the five principal London companies of actors differed a little from this average of 2,490 lines, but in no instance did the increase or decrease amount to more than 160 lines.

3. The hour of commencement observed at the unroofed or public theatres probably remained fixed at 2 o'clock during the years named.

4. The time allotted by the actors of each of the chief London companies for the performance of a play was about two hours; this probably did not include the time required for the jig or music.

To make quite clear the undoubted dependence of

106

the average length (2,490 lines) of extant plays on the time allotment of two hours for representation, we must estimate as accurately as we can the number of lines which an Elizabethan company could act in two hours under the existing stage conditions.

No one would attempt to maintain that in 'two short hours' Burbage and his 'fellows' spoke either the 2,989 lines of *Romeo and Juliet* or the 3,066 lines of *The Alchemist*; such feats of rapid utterance would mean continuous and unbroken 'patter' or gabble, spoken by every member of the cast, at the extraordinary rate of more than 200 words a minute. Let any one read aloud or recite without any action, but with clear enunciation of each letter, syllable and word, three or four hundred lines of blank verse chosen from any play of this period. He will discover as a mean result of a dozen such tests that twenty-two lines of blank verse require a full minute for utterance; this is equivalent to a speech-rate of 176 words a minute. This pace is considerably faster than that of most public speakers and demands for its successful accomplishment that the words shall be spoken, as Shakespeare says, 'trippingly on the tongue' and not 'mouthed' as is too often the practice of our modern reciters. A trifle over twenty-one lines of prose such as we have in the Cambridge text of Shakespeare means the same number of words a minute. Speaking without the slightest pause at this pace one could read through *Romeo and Juliet* in two hours and sixteen minutes; *The Alchemist* would take three minutes more. As over a quarter of *Hamlet* is in prose, its 3,762 lines would involve continuous reading for nearly three hours. The rate of twenty-two lines a minute equals 1,320 lines an hour or 2,640 lines in two hours. The Elizabethan actors earned their living, however, by acting, not reading, plays. They were the best actors of their time; and good acting on their stage must have meant precisely the same as it has always meant on every other stage in every century, plenty of bustling action and vigorous elocution rather than unbroken monotony of continuous speech. No Elizabethan company ever acted a play of 2,640 lines in two hours. Entrances, exits, changes of scene, processions, dumb-shows, by-play, sword and buckler fights, rapier and dagger duels, cudgel bouts, stage battles and brawls, incidental music and songs, clowning and the consequent laughter, and all the multifarious bits of stage ' business '—everything in fact that distinguishes a well-acted play from reading the same play aloud in the silence of the study—combine to eat up the minutes and to reduce the number of lines that can be acted in two hours. Thus the first scene of *Romeo and Juliet* contains 236 lines, and, if the reader maintains the rate of 22 lines a minute, will take 10¾ minutes to read through. Let us, however, look upon this scene with the eye of the actor, and we cannot fail to notice how full it is of incidents and how many opportunities it gives the players for effective stage ' business,' which, quite apart from the speeches, take, in the aggregate, an appreciable amount of time. The play opens with the quarrel of the Capulets with the Montagues; they would not merely speak their lines but act them. Sampson and Gregory enter and are cracking their rather tiresome jokes as they move about the stage, when they perceive Abram and Balthazar approaching. Fierce stares of defiance, scowls, biting of thumbs, fingering scabbards, half-drawing of swords, nudges and looks around punctuate and draw out the dialogue and precede the drawing of swords and actual fighting. Benvolio is standing apart, and must draw his sword and cover some twenty feet before he can try to beat down the weapons of the four combatants—a rather risky and time-taking action. The appearance of Tybalt compels a slight pause; he must come to the centre of the stage, draw his rapier, attract the attention of Benvolio, and be busy fighting before the three or four citizens appear with their clubs or partisans. Their entrance and efforts to stop the fray would take much more time than the six or seven seconds requisite for shouting out the two lines spoken by the first officer. Cudgel play, sword and buckler fights, and duels with rapier and dagger were not the ludicrous make-believe that passes for a fight on the modern stage, but vigorous scientific contests played by skilful swordsmen and cudgel-players before keenly interested spectators who knew every point of the fencer's art. The brawl would be at its height when the entrances of old Capulet held back by his wife and of his enemy Montague held back by his wife would introduce some serio-comic relief. Fourteen characters are on the stage by this time, when a flourish on the trumpet announces the entry of Prince Escalus to suppress the riot. His entry ' with his traine ' of six or eight armed guards dressed in uniform formed one of those processions which were a notable feature of the Elizabethan stage. They would busy themselves in separating the combatants before the Prince began his speech. The departure of the Prince, Capulet and his wife, and the guards by one door, and of Tybalt, the citizens and the rival partisans at the other door would not be as instantaneous as the simple stage ' Exeunt ' might suggest, and would be diversified and lengthened with the black looks, savage grimaces and subdued muttering threats of the brawlers. The remainder of the scene is rather wanting in action, but I think at least two minutes would be spent in the actions and ' business ' described above, apart from nearly eleven minutes required for the speeches. Several subsequent scenes, notably the fifth, eleventh, nineteenth and twenty-second require plenty of lively action to make them go well on the stage. Actors are never backward in taking full advantage of good opportunities for by-play, and may be relied on to make their exits and entrances as effective and noticeable as possible. We may be sure that Kemp,

Pope and Singer would not come on or leave the stage without some gag or quip designed to raise a laugh. Kemp played 'Peter,' and probably made a 'fat' part for himself out of the few lines written for him by the poet. His wooden face, vacant stare, silly grimaces, clownish walk and actions, and the laughter that greeted almost every word of the favourite comedian would probably lengthen the scenes in which he appeared by as much as five minutes. Changes of scene were made very rapidly, but each involves the exit of one set of characters, and the entrance of another, and if we allow three minutes for the twenty-two changes of scene in *Romeo and Juliet,* the allowance would not be excessive. There is little incidental music in this play, but songs that can be read over in less than a minute take three or four minutes to sing. After adding together the time lost in making numerous changes of scene and that spent in action and stage 'business' of all kinds, I think that we must deduct from the customary two hours not less than fifteen minutes for time spent otherwise than in speaking the author's lines. Accordingly, if the actors maintained throughout the rather high average rate of 176 words a minute, they would get through about 2,300 lines in the 105 minutes available for recitation. This I fix as the maximum length of the acting version of a play that was intended not to exceed two hours in the acting; 100 lines may be added for each addition of five minutes to the playing-time.

The position of the Elizabethan stage almost in the centre of the theatre probably permitted the actors to speak a little more rapidly than they speak in our time. An average rate of 176 words a minute—which one actor might make 200 words, and another reduce to 150 words —is high enough to cover all possibility of such variation; it is certainly faster than the average rate of speaking prevalent on the modern stage. Exception may be taken to the deduction of as much as fifteen minutes from the playing time on account of the time lost in various ways; there is plenty of room for difference of opinion on this matter. Even if we reduce the time devoted to music, action, stage ' business,' etc., to ten minutes, the maximum length of the two-hour play will not exceed 2,420 lines: this agrees very well with the average length (2,447 lines) of all plays with sound texts acted between 1590 and 1616—this latter average excludes Jonson's plays but includes Shakespeare's. Though I am convinced that the length of the acting version of a play intended to take not more than two hours in representation did not exceed 2,300 lines, I am adopting 2,400 lines as the maximum length in order that my conclusions may meet with a more general acceptance.

It will be noticed that the average length (2,490 lines) of 168 extant printed plays acted between 1594 and 1616 exceeds by 90 lines the 2,400 lines fixed as the maximum length of the two-hour play; nearly five minutes more would be required to act these ninety lines. The discrepancy is apparent rather than real, as very few plays would be staged without more or less abridgment. Sir E. K. Chambers says,

> We know that cutting was a theatrical practice, since authors themselves have told us so . . . Probably *Hamlet* was always too long for performance as a whole.[5]

It was—by about 1,350 lines. The average length of the acting version cannot be even approximately known, and any suggested total must be little better than a guess; it was almost certainly below 2,400 lines. If we assume that all plays under 2,400 lines were staged without any abridgment, and that those exceeding this length were cut down to normal size, the average length of acting versions would be about 2,290 lines.. If we do not insist on rigid adherence to the two-hour limit, and if we suppose that all plays containing 2,700 lines or less were acted without any cuts, and that

5. William Shakespeare, vol. i, p. 229.

all longer plays were reduced to 2,700 lines, the average length of acting versions would be slightly under 2,380 lines. Consequently Shakespeare and other dramatists could write, without any real error, of 'the two howres traffique of our Stage.'

I now propose to discuss briefly certain objections likely to be raised to my conclusions by critics who may interpret the facts differently. They may quite reasonably contend that, just as the actors would occasionally spend less time on the play if it was short, so they would probably extend the two hours considerably if they thought that a longer play was likely to draw good houses. Obviously, too, other adjustments involving some increase or decrease in the usual playing-time might be made during rehearsal or after the first production. Good reasons can be advanced, however, in support of the statement that in theatres open to the sky the whole performance—play, jig, and incidental music—could not have lasted during the winter months more than two hours and a half. In the first place, we must keep in mind that the visibility inside the tall, unroofed public theatres must often have been very bad, especially on dull winter days. Webster tells us that *The White Devil* was a failure,

> since it was acted in so dull a time of Winter, presented in so open and blacke a Theater, that it wanted . . . a full and vnderstanding Auditory.

The action of this play requires the use of 'the place behind the stage,' which on a dull day would be full of shadows. From almost the beginning of November to the end of February London is in darkness, except for artificial light, before five o'clock in the afternoon, and on cloudy or foggy days there is little light but rather darkness visible from half-past four. Playing in the winter would frequently be almost impracticable even earlier, and as two o'clock was the time of commencement, only on clear, sunny days would so much as two hours and a half

112

be available for play, jig and music. The actor-managers could not rely with certainty on getting more than two and a quarter hours of daylight after two o'clock on every day during the winter months, and I take this two and a quarter hours to have been the customary duration of the entertainments provided by them at the public theatres. Alleyn, Burbage, Heminge and Shakespeare did not each amass a competency by making the success of their business depend on the results of a daily gamble on the state of the weather, and they would be the better able to keep faith with their patrons if they provided a programme of such a length that it could always be completed before dusk whatever the time of the year or state of the sky. If the groundlings called for a jig, they got it even though the play lost ten minutes as a consequence; undoubtedly the managers would refuse to take the risk of irritating the turbulent pit by omitting this popular after-piece or playing it in semi-darkness merely to gratify the vanity of some prolix poet.

In the second place, the company found it necessary and profitable to consult the convenience of their public. All the public theatres were outside the boundary of the city, and most theatre-goers came from it or the suburbs either through the fields or across the river by bridge or boat. Most of the patrons of the theatres on the Bankside were rowed across the Thames and back again by the watermen. Crossing the Thames near London Bridge might take nearly fifteen minutes, if a fresh wind was blowing and the tide was running strongly. Consequently such spectators as returned home by water would find it necessary to leave the theatre a little before half-past four on winter days if they desired to reach the opposite bank of the river before dark. In the petition of the Queen's Players to the Privy Council and the answer of the Corporation of London (c. 1584), the second of the missing articles forwarded with the petition evidently

113

referred to the difficulties of producing plays in winter. The reply of the Corporation is:

> If in winter the dark do cary inconuenience, and the short time of day after euening prayer do leaue them no leysure, and fowlenesse of season do hinder the passage into the feldes to playes, the remedie is ill conceyued to bring them into London, but the true remedie is to leaue of that vnnecessarie expense of time, whereunto God himself geueth so many impediments.[6]

Among the counter 'remedies' suggested by the Mayor and Corporation is:

> That no playeing be in the dark, nor continue any such time but as any of the auditorie may returne to their dwellings in London before sonne set, or at least before it be dark.

The arrangement made by Lord Hunsdon with the Mayor and Corporation ten years afterwards practically accepted the above condition that there should be no playing in the dark. A better feeling gradually grew up between the theatre owners and the civic authorities; probably the 'two-hour' limit for plays was originally imposed and steadily maintained by the various companies of actors as a matter of business, to prevent any breach of the contract made on their behalf by the Lord Chamberlain. Burbage and some of the older men knew from experience how difficult it was to carry on a theatrical enterprise successfully if they were to be always up against the vigorous and persistent opposition of the city fathers. If the theatres closed early enough to enable the audience to reach their homes before dark and in time for supper, even bigoted puritans could not justly complain that the theatres led their sons, apprentices and servants into evil ways and kept them out till late at night.

Thirdly, we have not the slightest evidence that artificial lighting was used in the public theatres, at least up to 1616. We read of torches, tapers and lamps, but, as Sir E. K. Chambers says, they were used 'to give the illusion of scenic darkness.' Attempts to light with smoky torches and guttering candles the wooden galleries and

6. Chambers, *Elizabethan Stage*, vol. iv, pp. 301-2.

114

narrow rooms of a theatre open to the sky and exposed to every gust of wind would have been costly and dangerous. Prior to 1594, however, some system of illuminating the stage in the winter months must have existed, if performances did not commence before four o'clock in the afternoon. The absence of any allusion to such a picturesque sight as an illuminated stage is remarkable considering how much of what we know comes from incidental remarks of the dramatists. By starting two hours earlier the actors could do without artificial light and its cost and risks, provided the performance was over in daylight.

Sir E. K. Chambers hazards a suggestion that ' Perhaps the shorter plays were chosen for the shorter days, or the jig was omitted.'[7] A careful examination of the acting list of the Admiral's Men for two years (1594-1596) does not disclose any evidence in favour of such a seasonal variation of programme. Five plays of Marlowe's, viz. *Tamburlaine, Parts I* and *II, Faustus, The Jew of Malta* and the *Massacre at Paris,* only one of which exceeds 2,400 lines in length, were played at any time during the year, as was also a very short play, *A Knack to Know an Honest Man* (1,684 lines); so, too, were *The French Comedy, The Wise Men of Chester, Caesar and Pompey, French Doctor, Pythagoras, Chinon of England,* as well as other lost plays of unknown length. If the actors made special abridgments of long plays for the winter season, we have no evidence of their existence. Such long plays as *Sir John Oldcastle* (2,898 lines), *Fortunatus* (2,914 lines), *The Two Angry Women of Abingdon* (3,098 lines), *The White Devil* (3,013 lines) and *Patient Grissel* (2,715 lines) were written and staged for the first time during the winter months. On the other hand, comparatively short plays, such as *The Gentle Craft* (2,136 lines), *All Fools* (2,213 lines) and *The Knack to Know*

7. *Elizabethan Stage,* vol. ii, p. 345.

a Knave (1,851 lines) were first acted in the summer months. The length of a new play seems to have been, in the opinion of the actors, a matter of very little importance; excessive length was a fault easily corrected in the acting version. The actors did not produce the long plays in the summer months and reserve the shorter plays for the winter season. The authors did not consciously vary the number of lines in their plays with the season of the year. Thus Dekker wrote the 2,136 lines of *The Gentle Craft* in the early summer, and a few months later the 2,914 lines of *Fortunatus,* which was first acted in the depth of winter. The evidence is rather scanty, but it tells against this suggestion of Sir E. K. Chambers, and against a later one which he has put in a slightly different form; he says,

> It is just possible that conditions of lighting tied the London public theatres themselves to shorter performances in the winter than in the summer, and that this may be one explanation of abridgment.[8]

Undoubtedly the long summer days gave the actors an opportunity of presenting a fuller version of plays which they had been compelled to abridge for their winter season, but why should we take it for granted that they were eager or even willing to do this? The actor-sharers looked upon a play as something that they must buy for use in their business as public entertainers. The conditions of purchase were exactly the same as for buying a cloak, a table, or other ' property ' and, the bargain once completed, the poet had usually neither interest nor right in the play which he had sold. The actors could stage the whole or any part of the play, and, if they thought that alterations were necessary, they might ask the author or another writer to make them. If a dramatist chose to write 500 or 1,000 lines more than they were able to act in winter, they were under no obligation, legal, moral or customary, to restore any of the omitted passages to the play if it happened to

8. *William Shakespeare,* vol. i, p. 215.

remain on the acting list in summer. Other considerations must be taken into account. Any substantial increase in the length of the acting version might, and often did, mean the preparation of new parts for some or all of the cast, and the employment of additional hired men; adding to the length of the play would add to the cost. Actors would probably be reluctant to re-learn their parts, and might believe that the additions would tend to unbalance or spoil an excellent acting version. We learn, too, from the prologues of certain plays that audiences were not very tolerant of over-long plays. The evidence does not support the suggestion that there was a seasonable variation in the length of plays produced on the stage. As the actors did not vary the length of their plays with the season of the year, we may reasonably assume that the afternoon programme was just as long in winter as in summer. The hour of commencement throughout the year was two o'clock. Climatic conditions and the structure of the unroofed theatre combined to limit the duration of the performance in winter to about two hours and a quarter, and no good reason has been advanced why this should have been exceeded in the summer months.

Before proceeding to draw the logical conclusions that follow from these facts, I shall submit for what it is worth another argument in favour of the two-hour acting period. Critics agree that the Elizabethan actors spoke rather more rapidly than ours and that the performance continued from scene to scene without a break; we do not know whether there were act-intervals, or, if there were, how long they lasted. The spectators either sat on wooden benches and stools or stood, exposed to wind, rain, sleet or snow in winter, or to the blazing sun, muggy heat, and malodorous company in summer. Would this audience, composed largely of illiterate Londoners, be able, without excess of mental and physical fatigue, to concentrate its undivided attention for three hours without a break upon such an enthralling melodrama as *Richard III* or such a soul-stirring tragedy as *Othello*? Could such primitive beings pay out the nervous energy needed to endure three hours of imaginative exaltation? The very rapidity of the actors' utterance must have imposed a tiresome strain upon untrained minds, toiling in vain to keep pace with speeches not half understood. In the absence of scenery upon which they might have feasted their eyes, the story, acting, dresses and jig must excite and sustain their interest; if they lost interest, trouble might follow. Spectators irritated by a tiresome play would grow restive, and might hiss, ' cat-call ' and throw missiles at the actors. I doubt whether the more sophisticated modern audience, comfortably seated on padded chairs, would successfully pass such a test of endurance as would be involved in listening to a play for three hours without a break, especially if the stage was bare of scenery. The audience may remain in a modern theatre for three hours, but shrewd managers never require their patrons to listen to the play or opera for more than an hour without providing an interval of five or ten minutes. After deducting the time spent on an overture, music, act-intervals, etc., we shall find that the play itself rarely occupies more than two hours and a quarter. In our theatres, also, the combined ' creations ' of the painter, carpenter, dressmaker, upholsterer, electrician and their colleagues have gradually usurped the places of playwright and player; the theatrical manager of to-day deliberately uses elaborate and costly scenic effects to distract attention from the play, and to relieve any strain imposed on the minds and emotions of the spectators. The strain upon the emotions of the Elizabethan audience was more intense, prolonged, and continuous; there was little or nothing for the eye to see, so the poet could work his will upon the mind and imagination of his audience. Under such conditions a play that lasted two hours would be long enough.

118

PLAY ABRIDGMENT—PART III

ACTING VERSIONS OF ELIZABETHAN PLAYS

THE following facts have been established during the present investigation:

1. Jonson and Shakespeare wrote three-fourths of all the extant plays containing more than 3,000 lines a-piece; plays of this length are about one-eighth of the total number, and therefore are the exception and not the rule.

2. The average length of all extant plays (exclusive of Jonson's) with sound texts, written between 1587 and 1616, does not much exceed 2,400 lines.

3. Dramatists and actors concur in stating that in all the important London theatres two hours were allotted for the representation of a play.

4. Not more than 2,400 lines—this number is, in my opinion, overstated by about 100 lines—could possibly be acted in two hours.

5. The plays presented in the summer months seem to have been no longer than those acted during the winter.

6. The time spent on the whole entertainment, either in winter or in summer at the unroofed theatres, inclusive of play, jig, dances, songs, etc., rarely exceeded the two hours and a half between two o'clock, the hour of commencement, and half-past four o'clock when daylight was failing in winter.

7. There are those who may object that I interpret too literally the almost unanimous statement of the dramatists concerning 'the two howres traffique of our Stage'; I am content to reply that Shakespeare, Jonson, Fletcher and the rest state in plain words a fact well known to them all, and I prefer to accept their explicit statements than put my trust in critics who try to explain some three hundred years later that 'two' means 'three.'

I

The first and by far the most important consequence that must be deduced from the above facts is, that, if the actors adhered rigidly to the limit of two hours for the representation, all plays exceeding 2,300 to 2,400 lines in length would be liable to abridgment and usually would be abridged. If they extended the time to two hours and a quarter the length of the play might reach to about 2,600 to 2,700 lines. A play of 3,000 lines would last more than two hours and a half; we have evidence of the abridgment of at least two such plays. We have no definite contemporary statement that it was the custom of the actors to make an acting version from the author's manuscript of a play if it exceeded 2,400 lines; we are not informed that even such unusually long plays as *Richard III* (3,600 lines) and *Cynthia's Revels* (4,268 lines) were abridged. Our conclusions on this, as on all other questions involving Elizabethan stage practice and the conditions under which plays were written and produced, must, at the best, continue to be reasonable inferences from scanty and casual allusions; too often for a pennyworth of fact modern critics give us a pound's worth of conjecture. I have shown that the average length of the plays written for the Elizabethan and Jacobean stage was very little more than the number of lines that could be played in the two hours which dramatists and actors say were allotted for representation. This closely-linked chain of facts compels us to deduce the definite and logical conclusion that the acting versions of plays presented on the Globe or Blackfriars stage would not usually exceed 2,400 lines; accordingly, longer plays would be more or less drastically curtailed. I estimate that about 40 per cent. of all our extant plays were staged in the form of abridgments; it may be doubted whether a play of 3,000 lines was ever acted on the public stage. I now offer some evidence in support of my assertion that abridgment of plays was customary, not occasional.

Versions of Elizabethan Plays

Plays preserved in contemporary manuscripts are perhaps the most important source of our information on the subject of acting versions. About thirty such manuscripts of plays undoubtedly written for the public theatre have survived; some of them have appeared in facsimile reprints during the past thirty years. Those

TABLE I

NUMBER OF LINES OMITTED IN MANUSCRIPT PLAYS

Name of play.	Number of lines.	Number of lines omitted.	Number of lines spoken.
Orlando Furioso (c. 1590) (Orlando's part, Dulwich MS.)	532	212	320(Q)
John a Kent and John a Cumber	1,672	34	1,638
Sir Thomas More	2,689	467	2,222
1 *Richard II*	2,934	104	2,830
Edmond Ironside	2,061	196	1,865
The Cuck-Queanes	2,139	—	2,139
The Faery Pastoral	2,417	—	2,417
The Second Maiden's Tragedy ..	2,213	164	2,049
The Honest Man's Fortune ..	2,742	40	2,702
The Faithful Friends	2,442	101	2,341
Sir John Van Olden Barnevelt ..	2,530	92	2,438
Charlemagne	2,656	5	2,651
The Welsh Ambassador	2,284	29	2,255
The Captives	2,816	163	2,653
Dick of Devonshire	2,541	—	2,541
The Parliament of Love	2,476	34	2,442
Believe as You List	2,525	—	2,525
Average Length ..	2,446	—	2,358

which have been used as playhouse or prompt copies usually indicate the 'cuts' made by the actors either in compliance with the orders given by the Master of the Revels or for the purpose of adapting or shortening the play for representation. Some passages are crossed out by being struck through with the pen or by cross-hatching; passages marked by the actors for omission are

121

usually distinguished by their being enclosed in brackets or by the presence of a line at the left-hand side of the script. In the table above I give the total number of lines in each of certain plays in manuscript, most of which contain lines marked for omission; in a second column is given the total number of lines to be excised; in a third the number of lines that may have been spoken on the stage. I have arranged the plays in what I take to be the chronological order of composition, and have included four plays which contain no marks of abridgment. My list consists of seventeen plays only; four of Percy's plays are as yet unprinted, and some manuscript plays are not playhouse copies, and were printed soon after they had been played.

Upon the figures contained in Table I certain comments may be worth making.

1. No extant play in manuscript, written to be acted on the public stage, is 3,000 lines in length.

2. The average length of sixteen unabridged plays in manuscript is 2,446 lines a play. This result is in exact agreement with the average of 2,447 lines a play, which was obtained for 204 extant printed plays with sound texts written by all authors other than Jonson during the years 1590 to 1616.

3. The average length of the acting versions of these sixteen plays is 2,358 lines a play; this average agrees quite well with the total of 2,300 to 2,400 lines which was calculated to be the greatest number of lines that could be acted on the Elizabethan stage in the customary playing time of two hours.

4. Though each of these plays, except I *Richard II, The Honest Man's Fortune,* and *The Captives,* could be acted without any abridgment in less than two hours and a quarter, substantial reductions in length were made.

5. Almost all plays in manuscript contain passages marked for omission, most of which do not appear to have been made in compliance with the orders of the censor.

6. The number of lines cut out by the actors does not appear to have borne much relation to the length of the play. Thus 196 lines, mostly in short passages of two or three lines, were cut out of the short play *Edmond Ironside,* whilst only 104 lines disappear from the long chronicle play I *Richard II.*

7. William Percy, the author of *The Cuck-Queanes* and *The Faery Pastoral,* writes, ' I suppose these plaies be somewhat too long ' for a two-hour performance, and suggests the omission of ' some of the songs.' If these two plays were acted, they certainly would be abridged. Thus we have evidence that fourteen out of sixteen plays left in MS. were shortened for representation.

The evidence obtained from plays in manuscript, though not as much or as convincing as could be wished, helps to support and is supported by the facts and conclusions obtained from a study of plays in print. The conclusions, numbered (2) and (3) above, cannot be coincidences; and the fact that most of the plays in manuscript were more or less abridged helps to establish the conclusion that abridgment was a custom, the rule rather than the exception. Our knowledge of stage history is too scanty for us to say definitely that all these plays were staged; perhaps, too, some of these manuscripts were not used as ' prompt ' or playhouse copies.

It is a remarkable fact that the three best preserved of the ' bad ' or surreptitious quartos of Shakespeare's plays are not very much below 2,300 to 2,400 lines, which I take to be the maximum length of an acting version prepared for a performance intended to last not more than two hours. Each of the authentic plays was too long to be acted in its entirety, and the stage adapter— perhaps Shakespeare himself—would find it necessary to prepare an acting version. The original plays contain:

3 Henry VI (folio)	..	..	..	.. 2,904 lines.
Romeo and Juliet (Q 2)		..	..	.. 2,989 „
Hamlet (Q 2)	..	..	..	.. 3,674 „

The pirated versions contain:

True Tragedy of Richard Duke of York	..	2,124 lines.
Romeo and Juliet (Q 1)	..	..	..	2,228 „
Hamlet (Q 1)	..	..	..	..	2,154 „

The equivalent of about one line in every four has been excised from 3 *Henry VI* and *Romeo and Juliet*; *Hamlet* has suffered more severely. The corrupt and garbled texts of the surreptitious quartos were probably derived from ' copy ' furnished to the printers by some dishonest actors, who compiled them from their tattered ' parts ' and from recollections of the genuine acting versions; the latter, in their turn, represent a systematic cutting down of the authentic plays to a definite length, and were probably from 200 to 300 lines longer than the corrupt quartos. The fact that the first quarto of *Hamlet* is about the same length as *The True Tragedy,* though the genuine *Hamlet* is 760 lines longer than 3 *Henry VI,* suggests that the authentic acting versions of the two plays did not differ much in length. I shall discuss other problems concerning the relation of the ' bad ' quartos to the authentic texts later.

Sir E. K. Chambers doubts whether we can separate with any certainty the loss due to abridgments made by the play-adapter prior to or during representation from the loss due to the garbling or forgetfulness of the dishonest persons who supplied the printers with the copy for the ' bad ' quartos. Discussing the relationship of the two quartos of *Romeo and Juliet,* he says:

> A report does not account for everything. Very possibly the report is of a text shortened for performance. Q 1 has 2,232 lines and Q 2 has 3,007. It is hardly possible to distinguish the reporter's omissions from others, but several lacunæ in long speeches or dialogues may be ' cuts.'[1]

Of such a text as the first quarto of the *Merry Wives* this statement is true; in the better preserved scenes of such a text as the first quarto of *Romeo and Juliet* we

1. William Shakespeare, Vol. 1, p. 342.

can, in my opinion, distinguish with some confidence and an approach to certainty original 'cuts' from the reporter's omissions or mutilations.

The most important difference between the 'bad' quartos and the authentic versions is the difference in length. If we accept the principle that the acting versions of plays were of such a length as permitted them to be acted in about two hours, we can explain how the 3,674 lines of *Hamlet* (Q 2) and the 2,904 lines of 3 *Henry VI* came to be reduced to 2,154 lines and 2,124 lines respectively, in the surreptitious quartos; these latter totals represent hap-hazard abridgments of abridgments cut to a standard size. Two hours was the usual amount of time allotted for the representation of a play, and thus curtailment of over-long plays must have been an established stage practice. Consequently we must examine the authentic texts of such plays as 2 *Henry VI, 3 Henry VI, Romeo and Juliet, Henry V* and *Hamlet,* not as lovers of poetry or students of the drama, but with the eyes of an Elizabethan play-adapter, whose business it was to prepare an acting version of about 2,300 to 2,400 lines for the stage.

Romeo and Juliet (Q 1) is 761 lines shorter than Q 2; we may reasonably assume that 500 to 600 lines represent original 'cuts' made by the play-adapter, and may debit the remaining 250 to 150 lines to the account of the reporter. Let us examine the better preserved portion of the first scene I. i. ll. 79-236. Of 158 lines of verse after the entry of Prince Escalus, Q 1 omits 69 lines, 68 are identical in the two versions, 11 have one word altered or omitted, and 10 exhibit more change but are obviously derived from the original lines; not a line has been added. Parts of the speech of Prince Escalus (ll. 80-83, and ll. 90-93), some of Benvolio's first speech (ll. 108-111), most of Montague's first long speech (ll. 129-138), all his second long speech (ll. 144-153), and the conclusion of the dialogue between Benvolio and

Romeo (ll. 215-236) are not in Q 1 and are, in my opinion, original 'cuts;' I do not think these 54 lines were spoken on the Elizabethan stage.

The passages omitted are precisely those which an abridger would cut out, if he must shorten the play without doing harm to its acting value; he would omit the concluding twenty-two lines of the first scene because the same two characters discuss almost the same topic more briefly at the end of the next scene. Some later 'cuts' remove poetical padding of little dramatic worth; thus the fantastic piece of Elizabethan preciosity put into the mouth of a commonplace mediæval mother with its grotesque and over-elaborate comparison of Paris's face to a book (I. iii. ll. 81-95) would certainly have been struck out by any play-adapter fit for his job. Other passages not found in Q1, such as I. iii. ll. 51-58; I. iv. ll. 17-28; II. iii. ll. 9-14; III. iii. ll. 118-134, and many others were probably not parts of the Elizabethan acting version.

Some remarks on the points just raised may be worth making. In the first place all the omissions cited above are of passages that both the plot and the actors could very well spare; they occur in scenes otherwise very well preserved, and are preceded and followed by groups of lines reported almost verbatim. If we assume that the whole of Q 2 was spoken on the stage, nature must have endowed the reporter responsible for Q 1 with a most unusual type of memory, one that was apt to fail him most inexplicably when it was at its best. Thus he gives us eight lines of Friar Laurence's first speech almost literatim, forgets six lines, and then continues without the loss of a line and with one interpolation and a few small verbal changes to the end of the scene, only the final couplet being omitted. The six forgotten lines are the least interesting portion of a long soliloquy. Idolatry will easily convince itself that this didactic passage subserves some subtly conceived dramatic end, but the most ingenious and lynx-eyed hunter of missing lines will find it difficult to deduce from the first quarto version of the friar's speech, even with the help given by the fuller version of the second quarto, any reason for suspecting that a 'cut' had been made at the end of the eighth line. Here, as elsewhere, the reporter's gift of forgetfulness is used most judiciously, and his lapses of memory come upon him only when he comes upon clumps of lines of such little dramatic value that any play-producer would excise them. Q 1, in its better reported scenes, is, in my opinion, a better acting play than Q 2; and the good judgment shown throughout the better preserved scenes in the choice of the passages to be omitted is strong proof that some competent person made the choice; the vagaries of the reporter's recollections had nothing to do with the majority of the important omissions.

In the second place, if we assume that Q 2 was acted without abridgment and Q 1 is the result of some haphazard process of partial disintegration, we have another remarkable feature of Q 1 to explain.

Q 1 has lost 41 per cent. of 385 lines contained in eight long speeches, each more than thirty lines in length, present in Q 2—of three such speeches written for Juliet no less than 70 per cent. have disappeared; the remainder of Q 2 is reduced by only 24 per cent. This differential treatment of long speeches is not peculiar to *Romeo and Juliet*; the speeches over thirty lines in the other four 'bad' quartos—I omit *The Merry Wives*—have suffered much more seriously. The four received texts contain fifty-one such speeches (1,940 lines) in all; the four corresponding 'bad' quartos have lost 53 per cent. of the total number of lines in these speeches as against a loss of 37 per cent. for the remainders of the original plays. Moreover, speeches under thirty lines were much more drastically abridged than the dialogue and the shorter speeches. The following figures refer to all the five plays that have parallel texts. The number of speeches

127

of not less than ten lines each was reduced from 336 for the received texts to 162 for the first quartos. The five received texts consist of 6,473 lines of speeches, each of not less than ten lines each, and 9,407 lines of dialogue and short speeches; the five first quartos show losses of 2,907 lines of long speeches and 2,903 lines of dialogue, *i.e.*, the long speeches have lost 45 per cent., the dialogue, etc., 30 per cent. If we assume that reporting is responsible for all the differences in the reported texts, these results are exactly the reverse of what ought to have been anticipated. Dialogue and the numerous short speeches in which several characters have a share are not so readily remembered as long speeches, and are much harder to report correctly or completely. A 50 per cent. greater loss of dialogue than of speeches would not have been an unexpected result; actually we have nearly 50 per cent. heavier loss of speeches than of dialogue. The simplest and most probable explanation of this remarkable variation from the result expected is to be found in the history of the texts of the 'bad' quartos; they are garbled and mutilated abridgments of the acting versions. In preparing these from the author's manuscripts the play-adapter cut down long speeches more severely than the rest of the play, partly because he found it comparatively easy to remove groups of lines from speeches without doing much injury to the plot, and partly because audiences were beginning to dislike the long speeches so common in moralities and interludes. An indication of this dislike is given in *Hamlet*. After the first player has declaimed the first thirty lines of his speech, Polonius interjects, ' This is too long,' and Hamlet mockingly retorts, ' It shall to th' Barbars, with your beard.' The reporter and his unscrupulous comrades made up the ' copy ' for each of the ' bad ' quartos from the acting version in which long speeches had been more heavily cut than the rest of the play. The following suggestive table illustrates the application to *Romeo and Juliet,* Q 1 and Q 2, of what has been written above.

TABLE II

Title of version.	Total No. of lines in version.	No. of lines in speeches of 10 lines or more.	No. of lines in rest of version.	
Q 2	2,989	1,054	1,935	
(Acting Version) ..	2,400	(a) 847	1,553	Calculated on Q 2.
		(b) 759	1,641	Calculated on Q 1.
Q 1	2,228	705	1,523	

How were the 2,989 lines of Q 2 reduced to the 2,228 lines of Q 1? Rejecting the possibility that the reporter and his associates were responsible for the entire loss, I suggest that intermediate between Q 2 and Q 1 there existed an acting version, which, I assume, ran to no more than 2,400 lines, the greatest number that could be acted in the two hours specifically named in the prologue. My figures show that the play-adapter must have removed 589 lines of Q 2, more or less, and the reporter must have failed to remember 172 lines of this acting version. Let us suppose that in preparing it from the author's manuscript the company's play-adapter cut down both the long speeches and the dialogue proportionately to the totals given for each in Q 2 in the table. This abridgment, containing 847 lines of long speeches and 1,553 lines of dialogue, would be spoken on the stage by the actors and would be subsequently reduced by the reporter and his fellow-pirates to the 2,228 lines present in Q 1. Reference to the table will show that the above supposition implies the omission in Q 1 of 142 lines of long speeches and only 30 lines of dialogue. This result is so exceedingly improbable that we must reject the original hypothesis that the adapter reduced both long speeches and dialogue by about a fifth. The figures appearing to the right of (b) in the table represent what is probably a fair approximation to the true distribution of long speeches and dialogue in the unknown acting version from which Q 1 is derived; they are calculated on the assumption that in this lost acting version the number of lines of long speeches bore to the number of lines of dialogue the same ratio as we find in the table for Q 1. This assumption cannot involve an error of any magnitude. The difference between 847 in (*a*) and 759 in (*b*), or eighty-eight lines, represents the extra toll taken by the play-adapter of speeches not less than ten lines in length. In other words, I assume that the play-adapter struck out about 20 per cent. of the 2,989 lines present in Q 2, omitting 28 per cent. of the speeches of 10 lines or more, and slightly over 15 per cent. of the dialogue and short speeches. The reporter responsible for the 'copy' of Q 1 forgot 172 lines of this acting version, the only *Romeo and Juliet* that he knew.

Some other pieces of evidence, tending to support the conclusions enunciated above, may be offered. Upon the relation between the length of plays and the time available for acting them we may call in authors such as Marston, Jonson, Barnes, and Webster, and corroborate their evidence by citing the words of Moseley, the publisher of the first folio of Beaumont and Fletcher. The interesting induction to *The Malcontent* explains how a play of 1,908 lines grew to 2,531 lines; the actors speak:

SLY. I would know how you came by this play?

CUN. Faith, sir, the booke was lost, and because twas pittie so good a play should be lost, we found it, and play it.

SLY. I wonder you would play it, another company hauing interest in it?

CUN. Why not Maleuole in folio with vs, as Ieronimo in Decimo sexto with them? They taught vs a name for our play: wee call it *One for another*.

SLY. What are your additions?

BUR. Sooth, not greatly needefull, only as your sallet to your greate feast—to entertaine a little more time, and to abridge the not receiued custome of musicke in our Theater. I must leaue you, sir.

In 1604 a play of 1,908 lines was long enough for Blackfriars but rather short for the Globe. The 'additions' of about 600 lines were 'not greatly needefull' and were inserted 'to entertaine a little more time'— about half an hour. The boys at Blackfriars played and sang, and their music was part of the performance; with the King's men 'the custome of musicke' was 'not receiued.' The play, thus augmented, might last about two hours and ten minutes; as the additions were written to order, we may be certain that the augmented *Malcontent* was long enough for all the needs of the company. Probably most dramatists restored to their plays prior to publication all passages excised by the actors. Thus Jonson professes that the text of *Every Man Out of His Humour* represents the play

> as it was first composed by the author B. I., containing more than hath been Publickely Spoken or Acted,

a supererogatory confession—it runs to over 4,400 lines. Later he says of *Epicoene* (3,541 lines)

> there is not a line, or syllable in it changed from the simplicity of the first copy.

All of his plays, except perhaps *The Case is Altered,* must have been very heavily 'cut;' Barnes's play, *The Devil's Charter,* was acted before King James in 1607, but before it was printed it was,

> more exactly reuiewed, corrected and augmented since by the author for the more pleasure and profit of the Reader.

Evidently 3,015 lines were too many for a performance at Court. Webster's *Duchess of Malfi* (3,037 lines) was first produced not later than 1614; the author informs us that

> it was Presented priuately, at the Black-Friers; and publiquely at the Globe, By the Kings Maiesties Seruants. The perfect and exact Coppy, with diuerse things Printed, that the length of the Play would not beare in the Presentment.

We do not know how much the actors cut out, but the author gives us some first-hand evidence that in

1614 a play of 3,000 lines could not be acted without abridgment either at Blackfriars in winter or at the Globe in summer. About this time Jonson, Shakespeare, Beaumont and Fletcher tell us in the prologues or epilogues of three plays, each acted at these theatres, that 'two short hours' were allotted by the actors for the representation of a play; Webster's remark makes it quite certain that at neither of these theatres, neither in winter nor in summer—were the two hours stretched to the two hours and a half required for acting the play without abridgment. Some later references do not concern my present inquiry; Humphrey Moseley, however, in his address, 'The Stationer to the Reader,' prefixed to the first folio of Beaumont and Fletcher's *Works,* says:

> When these Comedies and Tragedies were presented on the Stage the Actours omitted some Scenes and Passages (with the Author's consent) as occasion led them; and when private friends desir'd a Copy, they then (and justly too) transcribed what they acted. But now you have both all that was then Acted, and all that was not; even the perfect full originals without the least mutilation.

Probably the stationer was puffing his own wares; he forgets to tell us the names of the plays to which those 'scenes and passages' were restored, and we are without any means of testing the accuracy of his statements. We learn, however, that, prior to 1616, the actors were in the habit of making abridgments for the stage with the consent of the authors—perhaps this was a concession to their rank. Probably this statement rests on the authority of Lowin, Robinson and Benfield, three of the signatories to the dedication, actors whose connection with the King's men went back to the days of Beaumont and Shakespeare. Moseley must refer to plays written before 1616, because, being the longest, they were most likely to have been abridged. Only seven of the thirty-four plays in the first folio exceed 2,700 lines in length, the remainder average barely 2,400 lines apiece. Abridgment of long plays continued, but the average length of new plays fell steadily after 1616. If we may accept the testimony of the writer of the undated prologue to *The Coxcomb,* long plays were disliked by certain audiences as early as 1610. We read:

> The work it self too, when it first came forth,
> In the opinion of men of worth,
> Was well receiv'd and favour'd, though some rude
> And harsh among th' ignorant multitude
>
> . . . .
>   condemn'd it for its length
> That fault's reform'd.

The extant play runs to 2,411 lines, and is probably the abridgment. Heywood, however, deprecates the 'teadious sceanes' and 'lengthening out' of *The Iron Age, Part II* (c. 1614-1615), which does not much exceed 2,300 lines. The prologue to *The Humorous Lieutenant* promises,

> All new things you shall see
> And these disposed to all the mirth you may;
> And short enough we hope.

This play was not produced before 1619 if the actor's list is that of the first performance; it is 2,690 lines in length. A manuscript of this play dated 1625 omits thirty-eight lines found in the first folio and adds seventy-five new lines; evidently we cannot rely on Moseley's claim that he restored all the excised passages. Abridgment was more prevalent than he thought.

II

The second conclusion that follows from the acceptance of two hours as the normal period of time allotted by the actors for the representation of a play and of 2,300 to 2,400 lines as the normal length of the acting version is, in reality, contained in what has been written above; its importance deserves an explicit and separate statement.

I must insist strongly on the deduction that Shakespeare's longer plays were not exempt from this customary abridgment; consequently I hold that only

133

seven of his plays, viz., *Comedy of Errors, Two Gentlemen of Verona, Midsummer Night's Dream, Macbeth, Timon, The Tempest* and *Pericles* could be represented without any abridgment. The remaining thirty plays would, in my opinion, be shortened by amounts varying from 50 to 1,350 lines. Even if the time allotment was occasionally increased by a quarter of an hour, no less than eighteen plays, including almost all the histories and all the great tragedies except *Macbeth,* would be severely cut down. We have not a scrap of evidence to support the suggestion, which is implicit in much of past and present criticism, that Shakespeare was so highly esteemed in his own day that all his plays were acted as written. When he began his work as a dramatist the custom of the stage permitted the actor-partners to use as much of a play which they had bought as would serve the two hours' traffic of their stage. We do not know whether later in his career he desired to break a custom that the actors believed was essential to the successful conduct of the theatrical business on which rested their own and Shakespeare's prosperity; but in that era the most brilliant dramatist could not pretend to dictate his own terms. For the wares that he had for sale there was, at any rate until 1600, but one other buyer—Phillip Henslowe; that way lay beggary and the Marshalsea. So the actor and man of business philosophically submitted to the mutilation of the plays written by the poet and artist.

Of thirty plays too long to be acted in their entirety, accident and dishonesty have fortunately preserved no less than six in parallel texts, one sound, the other corrupt. Now that critics are abandoning the extraordinary theory that the 'bad' quartos were the poet's first sketches of plays which, after revision and considerable expansion, took the form in which they appeared in later quartos and the first folio, their great importance is being recognised.

I shall have something to say on this theory a little later; I have already termed these 'bad' quartos corrupt abridgments of acting versions made by the actors from the authentic texts. I have also given a small sample of the abundant internal evidence available in these quartos to prove that abridgment of long plays was a stage custom during the years 1592-1602. Acceptance of play abridgment as a practice of Elizabethan actors does not entitle us, however, to assume that a play has been cut down because it is much shorter than is usual with an author.

Recently Professor J. Dover Wilson[2] has put forward a theory that the normal length of a play for the London stage in Elizabethan days was about 3,000 lines, and thus we understand why he looks for and finds evidence of 'cuts' and 'drastic abridgment' in certain of Shakespeare's shorter plays. The results givin in my previous essay, *The Length of Elizabethan and Jacobean Plays,* prove that 'plays for the London stage' averaged about 2,500 lines; an average implies as many below as above it.

Wide variation in the length of an author's plays was characteristic of the golden age of our drama; monotonous uniformity in length is one of the marks of the silver age and decadence. Practically all the important dramatists wrote plays that differ in length by anything from 800 to 2,000 lines. Thus Marlowe's *Dido* (1,735 lines) is 935 lines shorter than *Edward II* (2,670 lines); Middleton's *No Wit, No Help Like a Woman's* (3,018 lines) exceeds his early comedy *Blurt, Master Constable* (2,054 lines) by nearly 1,000 lines; whilst almost the same difference exists between Beaumont and Fletcher's *A King and No King* (3,089 lines) and *Wit Without Money* (2,135 lines). Dekker's bright comedy *A Shoemaker's Holiday* (2,136 lines) is nearly 900 lines shorter than *The Honest Whore, Part II* (3,022 lines). The excessive difference between Jonson's two plays, *The*

2. New Shakespeare, *Two Gentlemen of Verona*, p. 81.

Case is Altered (2,525 lines) and *Every Man Out of His Humour* (4,452 lines), is partly explained by his habit of rewriting and expanding the original manuscript of the acted play prior to publication, but the extant texts of *Sophonisba* (1,611 lines) and *The Fawn* (2,841 lines), though differing by 1,230 lines, probably represent the author's original manuscripts. We may expect that the writer of thirty-seven plays would exhibit even greater variation in length than any of his contemporaries, because more of his plays have survived; actually the difference in length between short plays, such as *The Tempest* (2,015 lines), *Midsummer Night's Dream* (2,102 lines) and *Two Gentlemen of Verona* (2,193 lines), and such long plays as *Othello* (3,229 lines), *Coriolanus* (3,279 lines) and *Cymbeline* (3,264 lines), is about the same as that between the two plays of Marston's mentioned above.

Seeing that such literary dramatists as Marston, Chapman and Middleton edited for publication plays of such widely varying length, we may ask Professor Wilson to explain why he assumes that a short play of Shakespeare's is an impossibility. If the 1,611 lines of *Sophonisba* are all that Marston wrote, why must we suspect that 300 or 400 lines have been excised by the actors from the *Comedy of Errors* (1,753 lines)? Chapman edited *Cæsar and Pompey* (2,086 lines), which was probably written about the same time as *The Tempest* (2,015 lines); consequently I do not accept Professor Wilson's dictum that the received text has been clearly abridged, and abridged in the main by 'Shakespeare himself,' especially when his enumeration of the 'signs of this abridgment' begins with the statement, '*The Tempest* is the shortest text but two in the canon.'[3] The other 'signs' include 'broken lines,' unmetrical lines, 'unsystematic mingling of verse and prose,' 'the immense second scene,' obscurity of sense, etc. Were these

3. New Shakespeare, *The Tempest*, p. 79.

'signs' characteristic of Shakespeare's short plays only, such conclusions might deserve consideration and perhaps some measure of acceptance; but short lines and unmetrical verses abound in the poet's longest plays where they must be otherwise explained than as a consequence of abridgment. The size of the second scene is no proof of cutting; much longer scenes are found in *Richard III, Love's Labour's Lost, Henry IV, Hamlet, Measure for Measure, Timon* and *Winter's Tale*. Nor am I able to accept as 'signs' or proof of abridgment the dropped threads and loose ends of the story so characteristic of Shakespeare's plot-weaving. He wrote for his audience at the Globe and had no thought of making his plots critic-proof. *The Tempest* is not, in my opinion, the acting version of a longer play; it is short, but with the help of the songs, the mask, the dances and the drunken pranks of Caliban and company it would last out the two hours which Jonson, Fletcher and Shakespeare unite in telling us was the time allotted for a play during 1610-1613.

Probably some of the plays in the first folio are acting versions of longer lost originals; but literary sportsmen, on the look out for the spoor of an acting version, would do well to rid themselves of the notion that it is 3,000 lines long. No less than thirty plays contain each more than the maximum number of lines playable in two hours; is not their presence in the folio or the quartos the very best evidence that they are unabridged and contain all that the poet wrote?

III

The third important inference that may be deduced from the existence of a time-allotment not much exceeding two hours for the representation of a play, and its logical corollary, an acting version somewhere about 2,300 to 2,400 lines, is that Shakespeare neither revised his own plays nor rewrote the plays of others in the manner ascribed to him by recent critics.

Henslowe's diary gives us some information on the prevalence and character of revision as practised by the dramatists writing for two London companies. During the five and a half years, 1598-1603, he makes reference to about 180 plays, and records payments, some very small, for the making of 'additions' to seven plays and alterations in eight others. Due allowance being made for duplication, changes appear to have been made in about one play in ten; neither revision nor rewriting played much part in plays belonging to the Admiral's men. The practice of making additions to plays prior to revival, after they had been off the acting list for two or three years, added considerably to their length, but did not affect in any way the custom of abridgment. The term seems to have meant either entirely new scenes or new passages, each of some length, added to the old scenes, which were unaltered. The total number of lines added bore no proportion to the length of the play. Thus 174 lines (prologue, three new scenes and an enlarged epilogue) were added to the 1,505 lines of *Mucedorus* prior to its performance before James I; whilst 318 lines in five long passages were inserted in suitable scenes of *The Spanish Tragedy*, which was originally 2,825 lines in length. Dekker received £2 10s. for additions, probably not less than 200 to 300 lines, to the extant *Sir John Oldcastle* (2,898 lines). Marston collaborated with Webster in writing the 'not greatly needefull' additions to *The Malcontent* (originally 1,918 lines). The 613 new lines consist of the induction, two new scenes and nine passages of varying length. Farcical sketches, 242 lines in all, were added as an additional scene to the first edition of *A Fair Quarrel* (2,272 lines).

Additions usually affected very few of the characters in the original play, and, except for the cost of writing them, added nothing to the cost of producing the play. Thus the additions written for *The Malcontent* and *Mucedorus* require no additional actors, those for *The Spanish*

Tragedy one new actor (the painter's part), etc. The new matter was written to order and seems to have been of a special character, *e.g.* a new prologue or epilogue or both for the Court. The additions to *The Malcontent* are comic or satiric, those for *The Spanish Tragedy* pander to the morbid interest of the audience in stage displays of madness, real or assumed. Usually they did not affect the story; the actor-managers gave the public what it wanted. The inclusion of these additions in such a long play as *The Spanish Tragedy* would result in some 'cuts' of the older scenes of the play, and Jonson probably alludes to this when he speaks of 'the old Hieronimo (as it was first acted).' If the manager of the company could strike out some passages or scenes that had failed or ceased to interest the audience, the cost of making additions to the parts of popular actor-sharers may have been more than offset by a reduction in the number of hired actors previously needed for the discontinued scenes.

The practice of making additions to old plays does not seem to have been common. Shakespeare may have made some 'additions' to his own plays on English history and to *Titus Andronicus*; their loose structure would permit the insertion of scenes or long passages subsequent to the composition of the original plays. We have no evidence that he did this, but he has left us two examples of his way with old plays in *King John* and *King Lear,* and their importance in any study of his methods of revision has not hitherto been estimated at its true value. *King John* is an early play, whilst *King Lear* belongs to his best period.

A comparative study of these plays and their sources shows how drastic and thorough his revision was. Except for an odd fact or two, he seems to have used no other raw material for *King John* than what he found in the *Troublesome Raigne*, yet though identity of theme usually leads to some identity in language, he has performed the miracle of changing entirely the thought and its expression, metaphor, simile, and all the distinctive part of the vocabulary of the old play. One line alone remains and a few phrases. The result is that the vocabulary of the *Troublesome Raigne* is as close to that of *Lucrece* and of the plays on Henry VI as to that of its daughter play, *King John.*

The following table gives the number of the rarer words present in the *Troublesome Raigne,* and also found in the plays named.

TABLE III

RARE WORDS COMMON TO *Troublesome Raigne* AND *Play* NAMED

Name of play or poem.	A	B	C	Total.
1 *Henry VI*	2	7	18	27
2 *Henry VI*	6˙	9	12	27
3 *Henry VI*	6	6	11	23
Lucrece	7	9	14	30
King John	6	8	14	28

A gives the number of words peculiar to the play.
B gives the number of words found in play named and in one other play of Shakespeare's.
C gives the number of words found in play named and in two other plays of Shakespeare's.

Of the twenty-eight 'rare' words, common to the *Troublesome Raigne* and *King John,* no less than twelve are words necessary to the plot for which no exact synonyms exist, e.g., *excommunicate, priory, tithed, abbey, abbot, legate, see, toll, ungodly,* etc.; of the rarer words in which Shakespeare had a choice, sixteen only are common to *King John* and its source play.

Most readers of our drama written before 1594 are struck with the sameness of the language, and any one who has studied the plays of Marlowe, Greene, Peele, Kyd and the young Shakespeare realises that they seem to share a common vocabulary. The *Troublesome Raigne* belongs to this period, and any attempt to use its vocabulary for the purpose of discovering its author is baulked by the fact that the so-called vocabulary clues lead indifferently to each and every one of the authors named. Thus of the rarer words found in this play Marlowe has 62, Greene 50, and Peele 45. The vocabulary of *King John* is very interesting because Shakespeare has deliberately weeded out the stale and overworked words and phrases which he had taken over from his predecessors as part of the poetical outfit of a dramatic poet. Nearly 10 per cent. of the vocabulary of *King John* consist of previously unused words, and no less than 109 words are either of his own coinage or first used by him in our literature. If he enlarged the vocabulary, he reduced the length of his play by 400 lines compared with that of his original, and did not increase either the number or the length of the speeches; as usual, he introduced plenty of vigorous dialogue and used the language of men, not that of poetical puppets.

The poet has made such great changes in and additions to the subject-matter of *King Lear* that what he has left of the old *King Leir* is scarcely recognisable. The vocabulary of the latter is much inferior to that of the *Troublesome Raigne,* and only twelve of its scarce words find a place in *King Lear,* which has a richer vocabulary than any other play except *Hamlet*.

This brief account of the transformation of the *Troublesome Raigne* into *King John* tells us how the young Shakespeare rewrote a contemporary play; in *King Lear* we have an example of his methods when he was at the zenith of his powers. I profoundly distrust the exceedingly ingenious theories which ultra-modern critics have elaborated from little or nothing to explain how Shakespeare partially rewrote or half-revised a play drafted by another man. They entirely ignore the abundant evidence which *King John* and *King Lear* afford us of the way in which he rewrote old plays, and pin their faith to partial recasts which we have no evidence ever existed.

Literary revision of plays written for the public stage seems to have begun with Jonson, and was restricted in the main to the group of dramatists that came under his influence. Jonson made a thorough revision of *Every Man in His Humour* between 1598 and 1616. He added the prologue, varied the length of the acts, increased the number of scenes from twenty to thirty-three, changed the place of action from Italy to England, renamed most of the characters, and made hundreds of verbal and phrasal changes in the text. The length of the play is slightly increased; excluding the prologue he added seventy-four lines. Only a few additions exceed two or three lines, and he struck out many lines and some short passages of the earlier copy. He increased one speech from thirty to sixty-six lines, and added ten lines to another, but he struck ont one speech of thirty-one lines and reduced another of the same length to eight lines. Chapman prepared a revised edition of *Bussy D'Ambois* for the press which was issued seven years after his death. He made over 200 changes, great and small, in the text of 1607; they are well distributed throughout the play, and most of them affect a word or two in a line. Exclusive of the prologue and epilogue (36 lines), which may not be Chapman's, the second edition (2,586 lines) is longer than the first by 145 lines. Chapman made 49 alterations which run to a line or more; he added 127 entirely new lines to Q 2, struck out 69 lines of Q 1, and replaced 48 other lines of Q 1 with 135 lines. One of the passages struck out of Q 1 is fifty lines in length; to balance this he substitutes seventy lines of Q 2 for eight lines of the original. The new matter is mostly dialogue, and except in five passages nothing is added to the speeches. Fletcher probably revised the second edition of *The Maid's Tragedy* which is said on the title-page to be ' newly perused, augmented, and inlarged.' The augmentation amounts to seventy-seven lines, including three passages over ten lines a-piece.

142

Versions of Elizabethan Plays

We get a little information on the subject of revision and abridgment, most of it of a somewhat negative character, from plays of which more than one edition was printed. If an author saw a play through the press he might be trusted to take care that nothing was left out; if passages were omitted or suppressed in the first impression they could be easily inserted in the second, as plays were usually re-set. Under such conditions we may assume that the absence of any change in the second edition means that nothing had been omitted in the first. Comparison of the various editions of plays compels us to realise that many dramatists said with Heywood, ' It neuer was any great ambition in me to bee in this kind Volumniously read,' and they did not often trouble themselves either to correct the blunders of the press or the corruptions of the text, or to remove gags introduced by the actors, or to insert anything omitted in the first edition. At least a hundred plays, including twenty-four of unknown or uncertain authorship, reached a second edition; but in spite of puffing statements on the title-pages of second and later issues that the play had been ' revised,' ' amended,' ' refined ' or ' newly corrected and augmented,' we rarely find anything new except some additional errors of the press. Thus, in the second edition of *Mother Bombie,* twenty of the seventy errors found in the first edition are corrected, but no less than sixty-seven new corruptions are introduced.[4] The third quarto of *Richard III* is declared to be ' newly augmented ' —nothing was added. Except for the very doubtful instance of *Richard III* we have no evidence that Shakespeare made a literary revision of any of his plays or saw those which were printed in his lifetime through the press. Not one made its bow to the public to the accompaniment of a dedication or preface or address to the reader or set of congratulatory verses; each seems to have been silently hurried to the printers with all its many imperfections untouched.

4. R. W. Bond, *Works of John Lyly,* Vol. 3, p. 166.

I must now grapple with the theorists who insist that the first quartos of *Romeo and Juliet, Henry V, Merry Wives* and *Hamlet* were the poet's 'first sketches' of the plays printed in the 'good' quartos or the folio.

Any study of a 'bad' quarto must begin with the acceptance of the fundamental fact that the text is not derived directly from the manuscript of any competent author, but is a corrupt, garbled, ungrammatical and probably mutilated version of some such original. The first quarto of *Romeo and Juliet* may be a corrupt abridgment of Shakespeare's 'first sketch,' but it cannot be, and is not, his 'first sketch.' Professors Pollard and Wilson suggest that Shakespeare rewrote an old play on Romeo and Juliet, and subsequently revised his own play, particularly Acts III-V. Q1

> represents an abridged version of Shakespeare's first revision of an older play eked out by what the pirate could remember of the later version.[5]

The extant Q 1 is almost long enough for 'the two howres traffique of our Stage' mentioned in the prologue; if we assume that Q 1 omits about 150 lines of Shakespeare's early version, his 'first sketch' would be long enough to last two hours and could be played without abridgment. Q 2 exceeds Q 1 by 761 lines, an amount that would add forty minutes to the two hours required for acting the 'first sketch.'

Let us suppose that Q 2 is an enlarged revision of Q 1. The added matter has a high poetic but low dramatic value, and in no way resembles 'additions' such as we find in the *Malcontent, Mucedorus* or *The Spanish Tragedy*. It has no special theme or characteristic, gives very little scope for action, and lacks interest for an audience. The original text does not remain unaltered, but has been revised line by line. Very little of Q 1 has been omitted; many words, phrases and half-lines have been inserted, and new passages, short and long, have been

5. Times Literary Supplement, August 14, 1919.

introduced in almost every scene of the play. Nearly all the fresh matter is amplificatory of what is already in Q 1. Yet Shakespeare has not rewritten Q 1 as he did the *Troublesome Raigne*; the text of his original, wherever it is of good quality, though corrected, is preserved. The new matter is in no way superior to the old; thought, poetry, style, versification and vocabulary are at the same level. No new scene, episode, or incident has been added to the story, though Q 1 has been increased by more than a third. Shakespeare has not made a literary revision such as was made by Jonson or Chapman; in their revisions omissions are almost as numerous as additions, and the original ratio between the total length of the longer speeches and that of the remainder of the play is maintained. The increase of the total length in *Every Man in His Humour* equals 3 per cent., in *Bussy D'Ambois* 6 per cent.; in Q 2 of *Romeo and Juliet* 34 per cent.

The most remarkable change that Shakespeare made in this so-called second revision was to lengthen almost all the long speeches in Q 1, the increase amounting to nearly half the total lines added to it. Here follow some details.

TABLE IV

	Q 1	Q 2
Speeches not less than 30 lines each	3	10
Speeches not less than 20 but under 30 lines ..	8	8
Speeches not less than 10 but under 20 lines ..	20	39
Total of speeches not less than 10 lines ..	31	57

The theory suggests that Shakespeare increased the number of long speeches by 84 per cent. and their length by 50 per cent.; he added only 27 per cent. to the rest of Q 1. He follows no definite plan in doing this. He may be supposed to have had an actor's eye for what pleased the audience, yet he made practically no addition to the

145

K

speeches given to such popular characters as Mercutio and the Nurse, and more than doubled those spoken by Juliet and her mother, which rise from 105 to 243 lines. Most of the additional lines given to them have little or no dramatic value, and would certainly have been cut out by the adapter. Precisely the same change occurs in the *Contention*; the 64 lines of speeches given to Queen Margaret are increased to 171 in *2 Henry VI;* in the *True Tragedy* she speaks 94 lines, which become 176 in *3 Henry VI*. This lop-sided method of lengthening a play was not adopted by any authors in making additions or a literary revision; the provision of more poetry and rhetoric for the ladies may be well enough as a flourish of Elizabethan gallantry, but few of the lines would get past the adapter.

Shakespeare did not use this unusual method of speech expansion in rewriting old plays written by others; why should he reserve it for the revision of his own ' first sketches '? The speeches in *King John* and *King Lear* are neither longer nor more numerous proportionately to the length of the respective plays than the speeches in the corresponding source-plays. The *Troublesome Raigne* has seventy-one speeches of not less than ten lines (eleven of thirty lines or more), amounting in all to 1,306 lines; *King John* has seventy-three speeches of not less than ten lines (eight are thirty lines or more), totalling 1,266 lines. We know, too, that the adapter usually cut down long speeches unless they gave scope to the actors or were necessary to the understanding of the plot; why would a dramatist, especially one who was also an actor, increase the length of almost all the long speeches in the ' bad ' quarto of *Romeo and Juliet* by 50 per cent., and of those in *Hamlet*, Q 1, by over 100 per cent.?

Romeo and Juliet, Q 1, if freed from corruption, is a good acting play; if Shakespeare did revise it a second time the second revision was literary and not for dramatic purposes. ' Additions ' made to a play seem to have

146

added very little to the cost of representation except for
the fee paid to the author; any needed excisions from or
additions to the actors' parts could be made by the book-
holder. Jonson would probably not be paid for his literary
revision of *Every Man in His Humour,* but, if it were
staged, some new parts must be prepared, the actors
would have trouble in half-forgetting the old lines and
in memorising the new, the number of rehearsals would
be increased, and the scanty leisure of the company corre-
spondingly decreased. A dramatic revision such as the
'first-sketch' theory postulates would be a greater
nuisance to the actors than a literary revision, and would
have the additional disadvantage of entailing extra cost.
The author must be paid almost as much as for a new play,
though perhaps no more than 300 or 400 lines of the new
matter would be used; a new set of parts must be made
ready, additional actors must be hired, and perhaps some
costumes bought.

I cannot accept the double revision theory as an adequate
solution of the problems raised by the co-existence of
such parallel texts as the first and the second quartos of
Romeo and Juliet. Professors Pollard and Wilson ignore
the existence of two extant examples of the method
adopted by Shakespeare in rewriting old plays; I do not
believe that he rewrote another man's *Romeo and Juliet*
in stages, two acts perhaps early in 1593, and the remaining
three acts a couple of years later. The theorists forget
that the poet's first revision of the old play, extending
mainly to the first and second acts, would be cut down,
if necessary, to standard size. What sane man would
waste his time in adding more than 200 lines of non-dra-
matic poetry to these acts, if he knew that the actors would
decline to risk any alteration in a play that was such an
excellent 'get-penny'? The whole theory rests on
Professor Wilson's untenable dogma that 'the normal
length of a play for the London stage in Elizabethan days
was about 3,000 lines '; his ' abridged transcript ' was the

official acting version. I think that Shakespeare may have made glorious booty of an old play on *Romeo and Juliet* very much as he did of the *Troublesome Raigne,* and the result was subsequently Q 2. This would be reduced by the adapter in the usual way to an acting version of about 2,400 lines; the corruption and mutilation of the latter produced Q 1. If some members of the recently reconstructed Chamberlain's men had acted in the source-play, the presence in this ' stolne and surreptitious ' text of non-Shakespearean matter may be explained.

IV

My fourth conclusion is that neither the folio versions nor the quarto versions of the seven plays, each of which exists in parallel ' good ' texts differing substantially in length, are the acting versions. Below is a table giving for each play:

1. The total number of lines in the received text (Cambridge edition, 1863-1866).

2. The total number of lines in the earliest good quarto text.

3. The number of lines of the received text not found in 2.

4. The total number of lines in the first folio text.

5. The number of lines of the received text not found in 4.

TABLE V

GIVING NUMBER OF LINES IN PARALLEL TEXTS

Name of play.	1	2	3	4	5
Richard III	3,600	3,389	211	3,570	30
Richard II	2,755	2,590 Q 1 2,751 Q 4	165 4	2,705	50
2 *Henry IV*	3,180	3,006 Q 1 2,898 Q 2	174 282	3,140	40
Hamlet	3,762	3,668 Q 2	94	3,537	225
Othello	3,229	3,055	174	3,222	7
King Lear	3,205	3,092	113	2,899	306
Troilus and Cressida	3,329	3,291	38	3,323	6

N.B.—I have treated the two issues of *2 Henry IV* as two separate editions.

Versions of Elizabethan Plays

Critics are in substantial agreement that the differences in length between the quarto and the folio versions of these plays are due to 'cuts' made with a view of shortening them for the stage. This explanation is very probably correct, but their silence suggests or implies that the 'cuts' recorded in the table were the only ones made, and that the shorter abridged texts were the acting versions. Two of these are in the folio, and five in the quartos. If we must accept them as the acting versions, the length varies in a most remarkable way from 2,590 lines (*Richard II*) to 3,537 lines (*Hamlet*). The time saved by making these omissions varies from less than two minutes for *Troilus and Cressida* to over a quarter of an hour (*King Lear*). The time required for acting the abridged version would range from about two hours and ten minutes for *Richard II* to a full three hours and ten minutes for *Hamlet*; to this time must be added perhaps ten minutes for the inevitable jig. Much more striking differences might occur in a week's programme consisting entirely of Shakespeare's plays, such as:

Monday	..	2 to 5.15 p.m.,	*Hamlet* (3,537 lines).
Tuesday	..	2 „ 3.50 p.m.,	*Comedy of Errors* (1,753 lines).
Wednesday	..	2 „ 5.10 p.m.,	*Richard III* (3,389 lines).
Thursday	..	2 „ 4 p.m.,	*The Tempest* (2,015 lines).
Friday	..	2 „ 5.5 p.m.,	*Troilus and Cressida* (3,291 lines).
Saturday	..	2 „ 4.5 p.m.,	*Midsummer Night's Dream* (2,102 lines).

In each instance I have added ten minutes for the jig, but the duration of the performances has not been over-estimated. Variations such as these in the duration of consecutive performances would scarcely be endured in our day, but they would be intolerable and impossible in an Elizabethan theatre open only in the afternoon. The custom of a daily change of programme began with the building of our first theatre and continued down to less than a century ago; it would make some uniformity in the duration of performances given in the daytime not merely desirable but necessary. If the duration depended solely

on the original length of a new play the audience patron-
ising it would not know whether they would be able to
leave the theatre at four or five o'clock; and as the title of
the play to be acted was not announced till the end of the
previous day's performance, country visitors and residents
of the more distant parts of London would scarcely dare
to risk a visit to the theatre, especially in the short days of
winter, if they were likely to be detained till after half-
past four. We must take into account, also, the influence
of the plague upon the theatre. Thus, for the years
1606-1608 and 1610 the London theatres were closed each
year from about the second week of July to the middle of
November or the beginning of December; in 1609 they
were shut all the year, except for two or three weeks in
December. Thus the majority of the performances given
during these five years would take place on the short days
of winter and early spring. Every aspect of business,
common sense, the convenience of actors and audience, and
public policy would combine to tie the companies to a
strict observance of the undertaking given by Lord
Hunsdon on behalf of his men to begin ' at two and haue
don betwene fower and fiue.' The maintenance of this
agreement meant the making of acting versions. I have
shown that the playing-time of two hours, the number of
lines (2,300 to 2,400) that could be acted in that time,
and the average length of the plays written for the public
stage (2,505 lines) dovetail very well into one another.
Consequently the length of the acting version must have
been based on the two hours allotted for representation
and would tend, within reasonable limits, to become fixed.
Chaos would have resulted if it bore any definite relation to
the extremely variable length of the plays bought by the
actors. Though I cannot give any but a simple explanation
of the difference between the parallel texts, I think the
real acting version of each of these plays was much
nearer to 2,300 than to 3,000 lines.

My last conclusion is that our Shakespeare, in his own day the most popular and thriving dramatist, was first, and, above all, a poet and creative artist. No other deduction seems possible, if we contrast the great length of his plays with the moderate requirements of the acting versions. Thirty of his thirty-seven plays exceed 2,400 lines, and the excess varies from 30 to 1,360 lines. With him began, and with him went out, the practice of writing plays far too long to be acted without abridgment; the year of his death witnessed the performance of Jonson's *The Devil is an Ass,* the last play but one of more than 3,000 lines in length. The early York and Lancaster tetralogy averages 3,062 lines a play, the three later Lancastrian plays 3,105 lines each; the four great tragedies (*Macbeth* is almost certainly abridged) run to an average of 3,071 lines a-piece, whilst the two later Roman plays and *Cymbeline* average 3,186 lines each. Thus he steadily maintained throughout his twenty years of dramatic work his early habit of writing as much as the poet-artist thought fit, apparently indifferent to the deformed abridgments of his masterpieces which the actors put upon the stage. Alone of all the important dramatists, he kept on his course, and did not, as did the others, gradually measure the length of his plays by 'the actors' yardstick. He seems to have accepted philosophically and without complaint the custom of making abridgments; whether he was called upon to play the Roman father and mutilate the child of his brain we do not know. Stage custom and the abject dependence of the playwrights upon their paymasters, the actors, left him and others Hobson's choice in this matter. Jonson who shouted from the housetops his grievances against other dramatists, the audience, and the actors is silent on this business of abridgment. That the actors did cut his plays we know by his postulating ' two short howers ' for the 3,066 lines of *The Alchemist,* and his covenanting ' for the

space of two houres and an halfe, and somewhat more ' for
the 4,344 lines of *Bartholomew Fair*; had they abridged
them badly or overmuch the gentleman would certainly
have given tongue.   *A priori* it might seem unlikely that
such an experienced dramatist as Shakespeare, of whose
previous plays no less than eighteen or nineteen had been
heavily cut, would have written the 3,229 lines of *Othello*
or the 3,279 lines of *Coriolanus*; he knew that at least a
quarter of each play, including much of his finest poetry,
would not be spoken on the stage, and that neither these
plays nor others would be published in his lifetime.   Yet
Shakespeare could not have been entirely free from some
touch of 'that last infirmity of noble mind'; how otherwise are we to explain the never-ceasing prodigality of his
genius under conditions that seemed to cut off any hope of
more than temporary fame?

Shakespeare must have been an even more invincible
idealist than his friend Jonson, and when he began to write
a play the poet-artist took charge and pushed the actor-
sharer into the background.   With the gradual disappearance from the stage of the men who had grown to
manhood in the days of the great queen, a more calculating
generation of playwrights succeeded, who prudently econo-
mised their efforts and wrote little more than was likely
to be used.   After 1616 the average length of plays
steadily fell, and even the survivors of the great
age went with the tide.   Jonson wrote no more
three-thousand-line plays, and his five Carolean comedies
average 2,750 lines each, or 830 lines less a play than
his early work.   The thirty-one plays attributed to
Fletcher fell from 2,580 lines a play to 2,368; Middleton's seven plays average 2,323 lines each, a fall of
162 lines a play; Heywood's ten plays are reduced to 2,342
lines each, as against an average of 2,511 lines for his
earlier plays.   Massinger's eighteen average 2,373 lines
each; Ford's eight, 2,404 lines each; Shirley's thirty-three,
2,252 lines each.   The average for an incomplete total of

127 plays is 2,386 lines a play as compared with the earlier average of 2,626 lines for 144 plays written by the best-known dramatists. It is interesting to note that the average length of 122 plays (Jonson's omitted) written during the period 1616-1642 is 2,370 lines, which is almost identical with the average of 2,379 lines for each of 167 plays (Jonson's and Shakespeare's are omitted) during the previous twenty-six years, 1590-1616. Here we have a striking proof that the conditions under which plays were written and produced during the fifty-two years (1590-1642) did not vary very much.

My conclusion is that Pope's epigram is almost the reverse of the truth. It is untrue that Shakespeare

> For gain, not glory, wing'd his roving flight,
> And grew immortal in his own despite.

That he wrote for money and got a competency is true, yet he gave his fellows God's plenty for their pieces of silver and remained an artist to the end.

WAS THE SECOND PART OF *KING HENRY THE FOURTH* CENSORED ?

PREFATORY NOTE

In an article on the Quarto of *2 Henry IV* which appeared in the *Times Literary Supplement* for Thursday, September 25, 1930, Professor L. L. Schücking suggested that the censor may have been responsible for the omission of certain passages of this play found in the first folio version. By a remarkable coincidence I had read a paper entitled 'Was *Henry IV* Censored?' at a meeting of the Melbourne Shakespeare Society on Friday, October 3, 1930, and had independently reached conclusions in general agreement with Professor Schücking's suggestions. Professor G. H. Cowling, Professor of English Literature in the Melbourne University, and then President of the Society, urged me to publish my paper, and I prepared it for the press. When my article was almost ready, I discovered that I had been anticipated and put it aside; but, as my work elaborates and supports the thesis somewhat tentatively advanced by Professor Schücking, it seems worth printing.

M Y title takes the form of a question, because the answer cannot be much better than a conjecture with a background of facts, a guess on the right side, I hope, of probability. We know that a play written for the public stage in the time of Elizabeth ran the gauntlet of a double censorship. Before it could be acted, the company must submit the complete manuscript to the Master of the Revels for his written 'allowance;' before it could be printed, a licensing chaplain or other 'corrector' of the press appointed by the Archbishop of Canterbury or the Bishop of London must give the printer his imprimatur.

The Master of the Revels or his deputy kept a sharp look out for direct or indirect allusions to the queen and her court, to the Council, noblemen and other people of importance, and to religion, politics and foreign affairs; after 1605 he hunted such small game as oaths or asseverations. The extant specimens of his comments

are not numerous, but they suggest that the Elizabethan
and Jacobean play-censors were as curt and peremptory
in their commands to the actors as his Georgian successors
are to modern playwrights. He might and occasionally
did ban a play, and would strike out passages regardless
of the injury done to the plot or the action, but he did
not rub salt into the wound by giving reasons for what
he did, and did not cant about morality. Almost all his
income came from the fees charged for the performance
of duties, many self-imposed, as censor of plays. Zeal
meant more money and he was very zealous. He took
all public amusements for his province, and displayed a
more than modern ingenuity in devising new taxes to be
extorted from unresisting victims. He charged the companies a substantial and gradually increasing fee for
giving his 'allowance' to a play, and levied toll on
itinerant showmen who turned a penny by exhibiting
baboons, lions, puppets, or performing dogs, apes, horses
or bears. He charged each theatre-owner 10s.—afterwards raised to 15s.—a week for each week during
which the theatre was open, and sold the companies
dubiously legal dispensations, entitling them to break the
law and to act during Lent, Christmas and other forbidden seasons. When he became press censor of plays,
he took bribes for refusing a licence to print plays owned
by the actors. He got quite a lot of dirty money in every
possible disreputable way. His master-stroke of rapacious
extortion was his 'acceptance' of two 'benefit' after-
noons, one in summer, one in winter. He thus records this
'gift' in his notes:—

> The Kinges Company with a general consent and alacritye
> have given mee the benefitt of too dayes in the year, the one
> in summer, thother in winter, to bee taken out of the second
> daye of a revived playe, att my owne choyse. The house-
> keepers have likewyse given their shares, their dayly charge
> only deducted.[1]

What a long tale of tyrannical exactions must be behind

1. Sir E. K. Chambers, *Elizabethan Stage*, vol. I, p. 370, n.

the apparently sincere belief of this humorless brigand-in-office that his victims paid him blackmail with 'alacritye'! Much of the above relates to a period subsequent to Elizabeth's reign; her Master of the Revels in 1600, Sir Edmund Tilney, seems to have been autocrat rather than blackmailer.

No such golden spur pricked on the censors of books to a rigorous execution of their far more difficult task. Money makes the mare to go, even when a licensing chaplain is in the saddle, and the censorship of books other than religious seems to have been more than a little perfunctory. A period of slackness would follow a year or two of inquisitorial vigilance; such small fry as ballads and plays might at any time slip through the wide meshes of the censor's net and reach the press whilst authority dozed. Authority was very wide awake, however, in June, 1599. Satirists and epigrammatists had been raging furiously for more than a year, and the censors-in-chief resolved to make an end of the turmoil. Archbishop Whitgift and Bishop Sancroft wrote to the Wardens of the Stationers' Company and ordered them to burn certain books written by Hall, Marston, Gilpin, Davies and others and to call in all the unsold copies of the pamphlets written by Harvey and Nashe, whose seven years' brawling had ceased to amuse literary London. On the 4th June 'theis bookes presently thereuppon were burnte' states the record in the *Stationers' Register*. The existing evils thus removed, the prelates took thought for the future, and issued their orders to the Wardens of the Company:—

'That no Satyres or Epigrams be printed hereafter: That noe Englishe historyes be printed, excepte they bee allowed by suche as haue aucthorytie; That noe playes be printed excepte they bee allowed by such as haue aucthorytie.'[2]

The Archbishop seems to have enjoyed himself as chief censor and did not stint himself of such pleasures. More than ten years previously he had personally undertaken

2. Arber, *Transcript of the Registers of the Stationers' Company, 1554-1640,* vol. III, p. 677.

the castration of the third volume of Holinshed's
Chronicle (second edition) removing 132 pages of rather
free criticism of Elizabeth's statesmen and officials. He
had banned *The Metamorphosis of Ajax,* written by the
queen's godson, John Harington, after three editions had
been sold. A glance through the list of twelve plays
printed from 1597 to 1599 does not disclose any play
except *Richard II* which had given displeasure to the
Government. Though the Archbishop was no friend to
the Puritans, he certainly intended to warn printers and
censors to keep an eye on plays.

Whitgift had forced John Hayward in March, 1599, to
withdraw the effusive dedication to the Earl of Essex
from his short history entitled *The First Part of the Life
and raigne of King Henrie the IIII.* This book was
really an account of the deposition and death of Richard
II, and would recall Shakespeare's play, acted for the first
time probably in the early part of 1595 and printed towards
the end of 1597. This and the next two editions lack the
' Parliament ' or ' deposition ' episode which appears first
in the fourth edition (1608); this omission must be the
result of the censor's activity, because, as Professor
Schücking says, it ' almost spoilt the play.' I do not agree
with his opinion that the abdication scene was acted; my
reason is that unusual alterations were made in the last
speech of Bolingbroke's as it appears in the early quartos.

The quarto and the folio texts of this scene are substantially the same up to the end of Carlisle's protest against
the dethronement of Richard. The scene in the folio is as
follows :—

NORTH. Well haue you argu'd Sir: and for your paines,
Of Capitall Treason we arrest you here.
My Lord of Westminster, be it your charge,
To keepe him safely, till his day of Tryall.
May it please you, Lords, to grant the Commons Suit?

BULL. Fetch hither Richard, that in common view
He may surrender: so we shall proceede
Without suspition.

YORKE. I will be his Conduct.

BULL. Lords, you that here, etc.

157

Then, after the entrance of Richard, follows the abdication scene. After the departure of Richard, Bolingbroke speaks these two lines:—

BULL.   On Wednesday next, we solemnly set downe
        Our Coronation: Lords, prepare your selues.   Exeunt

All leave the stage except the Abbot, Carlisle and Aumerle, and the dialogue proceeds:—

ABBOT.   A wofull Pageant haue we here beheld.
CARL.   The Woes to come, the Children yet vnborne,
         Shall feele this day as sharpe to them as Thorne.

The version in the first quarto reads:—

NORTH.   Well haue you argued sir, and for your paines
         Of capitall Treason, we arrest you here:
         My Lord of Westminster, be it your charge,
         To keepe him safely till his day of triall.
BULL.   Let it be so, and loe on Wednesday next,
         We solemnly proclaime our Coronation,
         Lords be ready all.   Exeunt.
         Manent West. Caleil, Aumerle.
ABBOT.   A wofull Pageant haue we heere beheld.
CAR.   The woe's to come, the children yet vnborne,
         Shall feele this day as sharp to them as thorne.

An almost complete version of this scene appeared for the first time in the quarto of 1608, and undoubtedly represents what the poet originally wrote. The omission of the 165 lines beginning with the last line of Northumberland's speech and concluding with the departure of Richard makes meaningless both the line

A wofull Pageant haue we heere beheld

and Carlisle's two lines spoken in reply. Possibly these three lines may not have been marked for omission in the author's manuscript, and yet may have been omitted in the representation; it may be that the actors presented the abdication in dumb-show, and thus the three intruding lines would be relevant. Two deductions emerge from a comparison of the two versions. First, the presence in the first quarto of the three meaningless lines quoted above is almost sufficient to prove that Shakespeare did not edit it.

Second, the connective words spoken by Bolingbroke, ' Let
it be so, and loe ' found only in the first three quartos,
must be an interpolation inserted after the poet had written
the play, because they cannot be fitted into the complete
version first printed in the fourth quarto. They seem to
have been added to smooth over the exceedingly abrupt
change from the arrest of Carlisle to Bolingbroke's
announcement of his intended coronation. Who wrote
these words? I think it most improbable that they are
Shakespeare's; he would not have altered for the worse
the two lines with which, in the folio, Bolingbroke ends
this part of the scene, and would not have written such an
unmetrical half line as ' Lords, be ready all.' He would
almost certainly have inserted two or more complete lines
of blank verse to bridge over the clumsy transition from
Carlisle's arrest to Bolingbroke's coronation, and would
have struck out the three lines which the omission of the
abdication scene had made superfluous. The first quarto
speech smacks of the play-adapter. The changes made are
of especial interest because we have here one of the very
few instances of an alteration in the text of one of Shakespeare's plays made for the purpose of healing a wound
due to a ' cut '; usually the broken ends of a mutilated
passage were drawn together, and any resulting hiatus in
syntax or sense remained unbridged. Shakespeare, I have
suggested, did not see the first quarto through the press;
and I do not ascribe this or any other change in the ' copy '
from which the play was printed to the desire of providing
readers of the play with a good text. The addition of
the words, ' Let it be so, and loe,' was made, in my opinion,
for the representation, and the abdication scene was not
presented on the stage.] We shall find in the history of the
time the reasons why authority banned this scene.

Why did the Master of Revels forbid the public representation of the deposition of Richard II? Two or three
years previously he had permitted the staging of similar
scenes in *3 Henry VI* and *Edward II*. What mysterious

spell did the two-century-old story of Richard's fall and murder cast over Elizabeth that not merely plays but even dull chronicles relating to that episode aroused the royal vigilance and wrath? For an answer to these questions we must look into the history of her reign. Simpson says

> By some means Richard II had early become a political nick-name of Elizabeth.[3]

It seems to go back at least as far as 1578. Sir Francis Knollys, whose wife was the queen's first cousin, wrote a letter[4] to Secretary Wilson declining to give unwelcome advice to the queen.

> For who woll persiste in gyuing of safe counsayle, if her Maiestie woull persiste in myslyking of safe counsayle? Nay who woll not rather shrynkingly (that I may say no more) play the partes of King Richard the Second's men, then to enter into the odious office of crossing of her Maiesties wylle?

The result, he says, is the cold shoulder to those that give honest counsel,

> and then King Richard the Second's men woll flock into courte apace, and woll show themselues in theyr colors. From which cumpanye the Lord blesse her Maiestie.

At the end is a postcript that commands respect for his courage :—

> I pray you hyde nothing of my letter from her Maiestie?

If Secretary Wilson did as Knollys asked, the Queen would learn what plain blunt men thought of her and her flatterers. Mrs. Strickland relates a somewhat similar story about the rough-mannered, hard-swearing but honest Lord Hunsdon, the queen's first cousin. In a letter written before 1588 he sarcastically observes, in allusion to his own want of interest at court, ' I never was one of Richard II's men.'[5] Apparently this phrase had become a term of contempt applied to the flattering

---

3. *The Politics of Shakespeare's Historical Plays,* Transactions of the New Shakespeare Society, 1874, p. 410.
4. Wright, *Queen Elizabeth and Her Times* (1838), vol. II, p. 74-5.
5. Strickland, *Lives of the Queens of England,* vol. IV, p. 727.

courtiers that surrounded Elizabeth, who, in her turn, soon got the nick-name Richard II. A reference to it occurs in a letter of Raleigh's, dated July 6, 1597, to Sir R. Cecil:

> I acquaynted the Lord Generall (Essex) with your letter to me and your kynd acceptance of your entertaynemente; hee was also wonderfull merry att your consait of Richard the Second.[6]

The queen knew her nick-name. In August, 1601, after the execution of Essex, she had a conversation with William Lambarde which he committed to paper. He was showing her 'his Pandecta of all her rolls, bundells, membranes, and parcells that be reposed in her Majestie's Tower at London,' and when he came to those concerning the reign of Richard II, the queen exclaimed, ' I am Richard II. Know ye not that?'

w.L.   Such a wicked imagination was determined and attempted by a most unkind Gent. the most adorned creature that ever your Majestie made.

HER MAJESTIE. He that will forget God, will also forget his benefactors; this tragedy was played 40tie times in open streets and houses.[7]

The Queen seems to have received this nick-name originally because, like Richard, she was overfond of flattery and gave flatterers and favourites undue influence in public affairs. Acute observers soon divined, however, an extraordinarily close resemblance between the two monarchs in ideals, system of government, and political position and difficulties. Her steady depression and harsh treatment of the old nobility merely continued the Tudor policy, but in excluding them from public office and her Council she resembled Richard in his last years of absolute rule. She filled her court and the great offices of State with her relatives on her mother's side, Leicester, Essex, Buckhurst, Knollys and Hunsdon, just as Richard aggrandised his step-brothers, the Hollands, whom he created

6. Edwards, *Sir Walter Raleigh,* vol. II, p. 169.
7. Nichols, *The Progresses and Public Processions of Queen Elizabeth,* 3 vol. iii, p. 552. Quoted from Chambers.

dukes. Most of her many serious troubles arose primarily from religious discord which had no small share in Richard's ruin; his support of the Lollards and quarrel with Archbishop Arundel alienated the Church. Like Richard she had no heir of her body, and was encompassed throughout her reign with all the dangers to her life and throne arising from a disputed succession. For two centuries after the accession of King John in 1199, the crown of England had passed without question from father to his eldest son except in the instance of Richard, the last of six kings. He was the only son of the preceding king's eldest son, and was a minor when he ascended the throne. He had neither son nor daughter, neither brother nor sister to succeed him; his successor must come from one of the numerous descendants of his grandfather, Edward III. Parliament had chosen the next of blood, Roger Mortimer, Earl of March, as heir presumptive, and had subsequently rejected the proposal made by John of Gaunt that his eldest son, Henry Bolingbroke, should be chosen as heir. The unmarried Elizabeth was, like Richard, the last of her dynasty in the direct line; she was, in 1600, without any relative of the blood royal nearer than some third cousins.

Her subjects expected her successor to come from the descendants of her grandfather Henry VII. The prudent queen steadfastly refused to give herself a rival by naming her heir, and haughtily commanded her parliaments not to meddle in matters of state. At her death her successor was still unnamed. Parliament had been compelled to leave unchanged the settlement of the succession made in the reign of Henry VIII which excluded the Stuarts, and as late as 1593 a prominent member, Peter Wentworth, was sent to the Tower for asking leave to introduce a bill regulating the succession, and died there three years later. So spineless were the members that a motion for the release of imprisoned members was rejected without a division![8]

8. *Political History of England,* vol. IV, p. 463.

Four books had been written and printed abroad on the question of the succession; prudent men wrote what they thought and hid the manuscript for future ages to read. The last book appeared late in 1594. It was entitled *A Conference about the next Succession to the Throne of England,* and its author was called R. Doleman. The real authors were Cardinal Allen and Robert Parsons who, in a spirit of impish malevolence, dedicated it to the Earl of Essex, the great favourite of the queen, and the head of the party in favour of continuing the war with Spain. They mischievously attempted to inspire in the queen suspicion of her great subject by declaring in the dedication that 'no man is like to have a greater part or sway in deciding of this great affair than your Honor,' at the same time they endeavoured to stir up his vaulting ambition, ever too ready to overleap itself, by reminding him that he came from 'the most famous and noble house of Bouchers' and was himself descended from Edward III. But their malice missed its mark; the queen herself showed Essex the book, and readily accepted his excuse that he knew nothing of book or authors. Camden says

> They traduced most of the Kings of England as meer usurpers and all of the Blood-Royal in England as illegitimate and uncapable of succession.

They canvassed the claims of more than a dozen claimants, and decided in favour of the title of The Infanta of Spain. The book was full of frank criticism of the past and present, and created a mighty stir. Even as late as February, 1601, when Essex was on trial for rebellion, the prisoner charged Sir Robert Cecil with saying to Sir William Knollys, 'The Infanta's title comparatively is as good in succession as any other.' Cecil passionately defended himself, and proved that the charge arose from a misunderstanding of a conversation held on the subject of Doleman's book. The dedication to Essex was a master-stroke of jeering irony; the authors had previously accused Elizabeth of being led astray by

163

unworthy favourites and had compared Cecil, Leicester and Hatton to such 'caterpillars of the Commonwealth' as Gaveston, Spencer, Bushy, Bagot and Green. They declared that by squandering on such minions much of the money wrung from the gentry and merchants she had lost the hearts of nobles and commons as Richard had. The numerous counts in the indictment framed against Richard related in the main to specific Acts of misgovernment; if we compare the principles underlying Richard's system of government with those of Elizabeth's, we shall find that she held, as did Richard, that the royal prerogative towered above and over-rode statute and common law, that she made the same arbitrary and illegal use of proclamations and of her so-called dispensing power, and had, for nearly forty years, ruled England very much as, in the opinion of his parliament, Richard had misruled it two hundred years before. He was declared to have been deservedly deposed for abuse of his regal powers; consequently Elizabeth who called herself Richard the Second, was equally deserving of deposition. Like the Richard of Shakespeare she claimed to rule by right divine; unlike him she had her claim almost universally allowed by her subjects. The liberty of the subject was as much or as little as she chose to grant him. When she addressed her last Parliament in 1601, all the members knelt in her presence. That an ephemeral body which met for a few weeks about once in three years should dare to criticise the acts of its semi-divine creator seemed to her ridiculous topsy-turvydom. Had any member ventured to hint at deposition, he would have tasted the axe on Tower Hill. The 'Parliament' scene of *Richard II* was censored partly for the reason that the queen refused to permit her subjects to look upon such a degrading spectacle as the deposition of an anointed King by order of a parliament that a king could make or unmake.

The fatal word deposition had been thundering in Elizabeth's ears for more than forty years. She never sat securely on her throne, and was forced to trim her sails to every cross breeze that blew. In 1567 the Scots had made war on Queen Mary, imprisoned, exiled and deposed her, set up her infant son in her place, and stubbornly refused to obey Elizabeth's commands to restore her. In 1570 all England was amazed to hear that a papal bull deposing Elizabeth and absolving her subjects from their allegiance had been nailed to the gates of the Bishop of London's palace. The rebellion of the northern earls, Ridolfi's, Parry's and Babington's plots, and the Spanish Armada, had each as its avowed end her deposition or death. But though the nation was loyal to the queen, new ideas, entirely subversive of absolutism and the doctrine of divine right on which Tudor absolutism was based, were in the air. When Elizabeth asked the Scottish envoys why they had deposed their lawful queen, they horrified her by stoutly maintaining that the nation was the source of all power and was free to elect or depose its ruler, and that laws were enacted to restrain the arbitrary rule of kings. They declared that resistance to the tyranny, mis-government or persecution of the monarch was the right and even the duty of the subject. The Jesuits easily outdid the Calvinists in whole-souled advocacy of the right of the nation to protect itself against the tyranny or misrule of the sovereign. Thus Cardinal Allen and Parsons declared in 1594 :—

> Yea not only hath the Commonwealth authority to put back the next inheritors upon lawful considerations, but also to dispossess them that have been lawfully put in possession, if they fulfil not the laws and condicions, by which and for which, their dignity was given them.[9]

Proceeding from this general proposition to a particular case, they discussed at great length 'the lawfulness or unlawfulness of King Richard's deposition,' and decided that if a king becomes

> a Tyrant, a Tiger, a fearse Lion, a ravening wolfe, a publique enimy, and a bloody murtherer, it were against al reason both natural and moral, that a Commonwealth could not deliver itself from so eminent a distruction.[10]

9. Quoted from Doleman's *Conference on the Succession* (1594).
10. *Ibid.*

They adroitly stressed such of Richard's misdemeanours and crimes of misrule as were chargeable against Elizabeth and her Council, and so insinuated that the queen who said 'I am Richard the Second' must also be looked upon as a 'Tyrant,' 'ravening wolfe' and 'publique enimy.' If the Lord Chamberlain's men produced Richard II early in 1595 when the calumnious truths of this mischief-making book were fresh in the memories of the queen and her court, Sir Edmund Tilney would certainly strike out the suggestive 'deposition' scene from the manuscript of the play submitted for his allowance. In vain had the poet coated the pill of deposition with the sugar of a sermon on divine right. Without any other omission than this scene, the play was printed late in 1597, when official vigilance dozed.

Both parts of *Henry IV* had probably been written and played before February 25, 1598, when the first part was entered on the *Stationers' Register*. Professor Schücking puts the origination of the second part a year later, 'early in 1599,' but I prefer to accept the evidence summarised by Sir E. K. Chambers[11] in favour of the earlier date. The press censor seems to have left untouched the references made to *Richard II,* which are few in number and found only in two scenes. But the ghost of Richard continued to walk in print. Early in 1599 Dr. John Hayward, whom Camden calls a man of sense and learning, gave to the world his short history, to which I have already made reference. The book contains nothing new, covers almost exactly the same period of history as Shakespeare's play, and does little more than relate the known facts of Richard's misrule, fall, deposition and murder. He proved his learning by inventing after the fashion of Thucydides and Livy suitable speeches for Richard, Archbishop Arundel, Bolingbroke, Carlisle and others. Carlisle's speech, spoken after and not before the coronation of Bolingbroke, discusses 'what should be

11. *William Shakespeare,* vol. I, p. 383.

done with King Richard' and extends to more than ten
pages of a closely printed small quarto. He surveys
Kingship and Kings from David to Elizabeth, drags in
references to Lycurgus, Ambiorix, Nero, Domitian,
Nebuchadnezzar and the prophets, tags his arguments
with numerous texts from the Bible, borrows some
epigrams from Tacitus, and concludes his speech with
a peroration not unlike the prophetic utterance in
Richard II. The author does not take sides or express
his own judgments, and does not stress, as did Cardinal
Allen and Parsons, the justice and necessity of the
deposition, but he takes pains to heap up the evidence
against Richard, and condemns perfunctorily and without
severity the ambition, crooked policy and usurpation of
Bolingbroke. He thus leaves on the mind of a reader
the impression of a partisan history. The speech composed for Archbishop Arundel when he was in exile
obliquely and by implication glanced at Elizabeth, her
courtiers, favourites and Ministers. Arundel says that
Englishmen are not subjects but

> abiectes and flat slaues: not to one intractable Prince onely,
> but to many proud and disdainfull fauourites, not always the
> same, but euer new. And no sooner haue we satisfied one,
> but hungrie masters are streightwayes set vpon us, who haue
> more endamaged vs by extortions and bribes, then the enemie
> hath done by the sword. What vnusual kindes of exactions
> are dayly put in practise? Without either mesure or end,
> and often-times without need.[12]

For Bagot, Bushy and Greene the reader would substitute
Leicester, Hatton, Raleigh and Essex. We hear, too, the
same complaint as had been made less than five years
before by Cardinal Allen and Parsons:—

> The King hath cut away the chiefe of the nobilitie, and the
> commons hee hath pared to the quicke, and still hee harrieth
> us as a conquered countrie.[13]

Hayward's dedication to the Earl of Essex is, for the
times, not excessively fulsome; he gives Essex all his

12. Hayward, *The First Part of the Life and raigne of King Henrie the IIII*,
1599, p. 63.
13. *Ibid.*, p. 64.

numerous titles of honour, adding 'Magnus siquidem es, et presenti iudicio et futuri temporis expectatione.' Discerning readers asked themselves why the author had chosen to write on this particular episode of the national history at that particular time, and why he had dedicated the story, then two centuries old, of the deposition of an unpopular king by a popular nobleman to the queen's favourite, by far the most popular noble of his time, the man who had asked for and obtained the command of the powerful army then being collected for the subjugation of the rebels in Ireland. At the request of Essex, the Archbishop of Canterbury ordered the printer to remove the dedication, and thus helped the sale of the book; 'no book,' said the printer, 'ever sold better.' A second edition was called for and the town continued to talk. Was Essex the author and was he attacking his enemies in the Privy Council? Was the dedication to him a covert and sinister suggestion that he should play the part of Bolingbroke, and use his popularity and army to remove from the Council members with whom he was at variance? Did he intend, if successful in Ireland, to make himself master of England? Modern writers express their wonder that such a stir should have been caused by a rather dull recital of facts already better told in the chronicles of Halle, Holinshed and Stowe. We must not forget that such bulky and expensive volumes could not be bought by any but the well-to-do. Hayward's book was little better than a pamphlet, not much longer than such a play as Jonson's *Every Man Out of His Humour,* and would cost, perhaps, a shilling. It would be sold at London bookstalls and in the larger country towns, and would be read by five times as many people as read Holinshed. Hayward may have been, probably was, in complete ignorance of the queen's nick-name and of the current court gossip concerning the quarrels between Essex and his mistress, but his choice of subject and of dedicatee was very

unfortunate, especially at that juncture. The earl took
his army to Ireland, mismanaged the campaign, lost half
his troops by disease, concluded what was little better
than a treasonous truce with the leader of the rebels,
perhaps toyed with rebellion, and finally returned to England in defiance of the queen's explicit orders. He was
placed in confinement, and suspicions of his conduct and
motives being aroused, was refused access to the queen
and the court. His royal mistress was determined to
humble him to the dust, and she put the pettiest slights
upon him. She caused the title-page of the first volume
of the second edition of *Hakluyts' Voyages* to be cancelled, because it contained a reference to 'The famous
Victorie atchieved at the citie of Cadiz, 1596,' in which
Essex had been a leader; and she ordered the censor to
cut out the text 'of the briefe and true report' of the
expedition. She would not permit any one to see him
without her permission, and she sent no answers to his
numerous letters asking for pardon. After suffering
virtual imprisonment for nine months he was put on
trial in June, 1600, for the culpable mismanagement of
the Irish expedition. One of the minor counts in the
indictment framed against him was the acceptance of
Hayward's dedication, and, in July, Hayward, the printer
Wolfe, and the licenser Harsnett were repeatedly questioned concerning the authorship and publication of the
book. Hayward was arrested, rigorously cross-examined
by Bacon, and threatened by the queen with the rack
unless he disclosed the name of the real author; the
attempt to implicate Essex failed, and after an imprisonment for six months in the Tower, Hayward was re-
leased. He did not write a second part of 'that most
treasonous booke,' as an official called *The First Part of
the Life and raigne of King Henrie the IIII*. The suspicions of the queen and her advisers were not removed
by this failure. When Essex was tried in February,
1601, for his mad rebellion, the lawyers renewed this

charge, and declared that the book 'was penned on purpose as a Copy and encouragement for deposing the Queene.'

Fate or accident played Shakespeare and his fellows a scurvy trick when they became involuntarily involved in the rebellion of Essex by giving a 'request' performance of *Richard II* on the afternoon of the day immediately preceding the outbreak. Professor Schücking suggests that the players 'were known as supporters of Essex (vide *Henry V*)',[14] but they were loyal servants of the Lord Chamberlain, Henry Lord Hunsdon, the nearest blood relation of the queen, a man from relationship and inclination averse from taking any part in court factions. Two of the actors gave evidence at the trial which makes it clear that *Richard II* was staged on February 7th, not from any sympathy with Essex or his plots, but because certain men of rank were willing to pay for the special performance. I cannot accept Professor Schücking's suggestion that the actors jettisoned certain passages of *2 Henry IV*, when it was printed, because 'it was necessary to give proofs of loyalty or at any rate to avoid giving further offence.' The testimony of Phillipps[15] is decisive on this point.

> The Examination of Augustyne Phillypps seruant vnto the L. Chamberlyne and one of hys players taken the xviiith of Februarii 1600 vpon hys oth
> He sayeth that on Fryday last was sennyght or Thursday Sr. Charles Percy Sr Josclyne Percy and the L. Montegle with some thre more spak to some of the players in the presans of thys examinate to haue the play of the deposyng and kyllyng of Kyng Rychard the second to be played the Saterday next promysyng to gete them xls. more then their ordynary to play yt. When thys Examinate and hys fellowes were determyned to haue played some other play, holdyng that play of Kyng Richard to be so old & so long out of vse as that they shold haue small or no Company at yt. But at their request this Examinate and his fellowes were Content to play yt the Saterday and had their xls. more then their ordynary for yt and so played yt accordyngly.
>
> Augustine Phillipps.

14. *Times Literary Supplement*, September 25, 1930.
15. Quoted from Sir E. K. Chambers, *William Shakespeare*, vol. II, p. 325.

Sir Gilly Meyrick, one of the accused men, Mr. Attorney Coke and Francis Bacon accept and corroborate this statement. Essex was not present at the performance, but absence did not exculpate him. The lawyers charged him with the crime of having seen the play frequently, perhaps five or six years previously,

> the Erle himself being so often present at the playing thereof, and with great applause giving countenance and lyking to the same.[15a]

The action of the conspirators in bespeaking on Friday and attending on Saturday a 'play of the deposyng and kyllyng of Kyng Rychard the second' became a count in the indictment against Sir Gilly Meyrick, the steward of Essex. Bacon drew from these facts this inference:—

> So earnest hee was to satisfie his eyes with the sight of that tragedie which hee thought soone after his lord should bring from the stage to the state, but that God turned it vpon their owne heads.[16]

Cheyney justly terms the rebellion, 'a planless, hopeless, meaningless rising;'[17] it certainly fizzled out like a damp squib, but did not even a temporary success mean the overthrow of the government and civil war? Essex himself had grown reckless and desperate since the beginning of December, 1600, and was surrounded by dangerous men capable of such mad ventures as Thomas Lea's plot to seize the queen and force her to set Essex free. Sir John Harington has given us a glimpse of Essex shortly before the end.

> It resteth wyth me in opynion, that ambition thwarted in its career, dothe speedilie leade on to madnesse; herein I am strengthened by what I learne in my lord of Essex, who shyftethe from sorrowe and repentance to rage and rebellion so suddenlie, as well prouethe him deuoide of good reason or righte minde. In my laste discourse, he vttered strange wordes borderinge on suche strange desygns that made me hasten forthe and leaue his presence. Thank heauen! I am

15a. Ibid., Vol. II, p. 323.
16. *Ibid.*, vol. II, p. 326.
17. Cheyney, *A History of England* (1926), vol. II, p. 534.

safe at home, and if I go in suche troubles againe, I deserue
the gallowes for a meddlynge foole. His speeches of the
Queene becomethe no man who hath mens sana in corpore
sano. He hathe ill aduysers, and muche euyll hathe sprunge
from thys source. The Queene well knowethe how to humble
the haughtie spirit; the haughtie spirit knoweth not how to
yield, and the mans soule seemeth tossede to and fro, like the
waues of a tróbled sea.[18]

Deposition scenes in prose, poem or play were not
likely to escape the censor's vigilance for a year or two
after the events of 8th February, 1601. Authors might
carouse an extra quart of wine when they heard that
the mad bull authority had tossed and gored the press
' corrector ' Harsnett, but their pleasure would be dashed
with the thought that such tossing and goring would
encourage the others to do more than their duty.
Drayton apologised in advance for errors that he uncon-
sciously could not help committing. All copies of his first
book, *The Harmonie of the Church,* had been destroyed
by the censor except those which Archbishop Whitgift
kept in his library. Consequently when he transformed
his *Mortimeriados* into *The Barons' Wars* (published
1603) he knew that he was sliding on the thinnest ice
in making any reference to the deposition of Edward II.
He blunderingly deprecates official censure in this
anacolouthic stanza:

> Pardon me, Art, that striving to be short,
> To this intent a speech delivering,
> And that at full I doe not here report
> Matters that tuch deposing of the King,
> My faithful Muse, O doe not thou exhort
> The after times to so abhor'd a thing,
> To show the reasons forcibly were laide
> Out of thy feelings what he might have said.

Drayton got his epic unmutilated into print; a less known
man, afterwards Sir Francis Hubert, was not so fortunate. We do not know when he wrote his long epic
poem entitled *The Historie of Edward the Second,
surnamed Carnaruan, one of our English Kings: together*

18. *Nugae Antiquae,* ed. by H. Harington (1804), vol. I, pp. 179-180.

with the fatall Downfall of his two vnfortunate Fauorites Gaueston and Spencer. It finally appeared in 1629, though a spurious edition had been printed the previous year. The author tells us:—

> This innocent child not of my body, but of my brain is surely of full age; for it was conceived and born in Queen Elizabeth's time but grew to more maturitie in King James.

According to the publisher it was by 'supreamest authoritie forbidden to be printed.' We may fairly assume that the refusal of a licence to print this poem may be dated sometime between 1599 and 1603; after the accession of James, the Court was far less touchy on the deposition of Kings dead two or three hundreds of years.

The publication of Hayward's book, the compulsory withdrawal of the effusive dedication to Essex, the departure of the latter and his army to subdue the Irish rebels, his failure and return to London in defiance of the queen's orders, his disgrace and nine month's confinement, his semi-public trial at York House, and the subsequent cross-examination of the printer Wolfe, the press licenser Harsnett and Hayward, followed by the arrest the imprisonment of the latter, kept London in a simmer of excitement from early in 1599 to July, 1600. On the 23rd August, 1600, Andrew Wise and William Aspley

> Entred for their copies under the handes of the wardens— the second parte of the history of Kinge Henry iiijth with the humours of Sir John Falstaff: Wrytten by master Shakespeare.[19]

The title-page bears the date 1600; this means that the first and only extant quarto would be printed at some time between the 23rd August and the end of 1600. Professor Schücking says that

> the date 1600—allows of a space for the appearance of the book from the end of August to the end of March, 1600-1601.[20]

19. Arber, *Transcript of Stationers' Register*, vol. III, 170.
20. *Times Literary Supplement*, September 25, 1930.

Did the printers date their books according to the then official year beginning on March 25th? Dr. Greg gives good reasons for his opinion that plays were dated according to the calendar year; and if we compare the dates of entry on the *Stationers' Register* with the dates of publication of all plays printed during the last five months of the calendar year for each year of the period 1590-1616, we obtain results which strongly support Dr. Greg's conclusion, though they are not quite decisive of the question.

The Cambridge editors make the following remarks on this edition :—

> In some copies of the Quarto the first scene of Act III is left out altogether. The omission seems to have been discovered after part of the edition had been struck off and rectified by the insertion of two new leaves. In order to make this insertion, the type was taken to pieces in part of the preceding and subsequent leaves, so that there are two different impressions for the latter part of Act II and the beginning of Act III, Scene 2.[21]

They give a little more detail later :—

> In the earlier impression which we call Q1, the whole of Act III, Sc. 1, was omitted, but inserted in the latter (Q2), and in order to make room for this insertion two new leaves were added to sheet E, but as the new matter did not exactly fill up the two leaves required, the pagination was altered. Hence in Q2, Sig. E3, Recto is made to terminate at 'how now, what's the matter?' (II. 4. 342) which is seven lines from the bottom in Q1. The two become again identical at 'strong and of good friends' (III. 2. 99), the first line of Sig. F.[22]

Professor A. W. Pollard says of *2 Henry IV* :—

> Moreover, in the play, when the omission of the first scene of Act III was discovered, copy for it was forthcoming, and Quire E was reprinted in six leaves instead of four to contain the additional matter.[23]

A few years later he explains the make-up of Q2 more fully :—

21. Clark and Wright, *Works of Shakespeare* (1863-66), vol. IV, pp. xi-xii.
22. *Ibid.*, vol. IV, note VIII, p. 485.
23. *Shakespeare's Quartos and Folios* (1909), p. 68.

When the first issue was finished the printer discovered that he had omitted something in Act III, he therefore cancelled E3 and E4 and reprinted them adding E5 and E6 to contain the omitted matter.[24]

Describing one of the copies of Q2 in the British Museum, the authors say:—

'British Museum. $6\frac{3}{4}$" × $4\frac{5}{8}$". With two stubs left from the cancelled leaves in Sheet E. "George Steevens" on title. —Pressmark C. 12.9.20.'[25]

Professor Schücking remarks:—

The whole beginning of the third act appears to have been originally left out by the printers, so that they afterwards felt compelled to reset one sheet, adding two new leaves—a most unusual procedure. It evidently was not caused by mere accident—the inadvertency would be almost too gross.[26]

I agree with this opinion, and think that the omission of this scene was due to the activities of the censor.

The fortunate preservation in the 'Steevens' Copy of the leaves E1 and E2 with the two stubs remaining after the cancelled leaves E3 and E4 had been cut away from the original sheet E in Q1 explains the make-up of Signature E in Q2. It contains six leaves. Two of these, E1 and E2, are part of Signature E as it is found in the original impression (Q1); the other four leaves, Signatures E3-E6, are a new sheet of four leaves found only in Q2. As the two leaves, Signatures E1 and E2, are identical in Q1 and Q2, it is certain that as many copies of the original sheet containing these two Signatures were printed as of each of the other Signatures, A, B, etc.

Almost all editors and commentators state or tacitly assume that the omitted scene was inserted in Q2 either while Q1 was being printed or almost immediately after the discovery of the omission. This statement or assumption is neither necessarily nor even probably correct. Both parts of *Henry the Fourth* had been theatrical successes, and two, if not three, editions of *1 Henry IV*

24. Bartlett and Pollard, *A Census of Shakespeare's Plays in Quarto*, p. 26.
25. *Ibid.*, p. 26.
26. *Times Literary Supplement*, September 25, 1930.

had been published in the two previous years. We are entitled to assume that Wise and Aspley printed the customary 1200 copies of *2 Henry IV*. Perhaps 600 copies were ready for sale by November, 1600, the remainder being left in sheets till ordered. As Shakespeare apparently did not see any of his plays through the press, the absence of this scene, if it was accidental, would probably not be discovered till the play was put on the market. When the printers were informed of the defect, they would agree to rectify it; but in fairness to the booksellers who had bought copies of Q1, Wise and Apsley would probably not insert the omitted scene in the unbound remainder until all the copies of the first issue had been sold. I agree with Professor Schücking that *2 Henry IV* ought to have been an Elizabethan ' best-seller '; we have contemporary evidence of the popularity not only of Falstaff but of Pistol and the two justices. Yet for some mysterious reason no second edition was required; it is absurd to suggest that no copy of the second edition of a book exists (assuming a second edition was published) when seventeen copies of the first edition are known. A prosaic yet perhaps true explanation is that there was in 1600-1601 a temporary glut of new plays. Sixteen new plays (including five of Shakespeare's) had been printed during 1600, and seven more in 1601. In addition fourteen new plays had been published during 1598 and 1599; eighteen second editions of popular plays had also appeared, among which were five of Shakespeare's. During 1601 no less than thirteen of his plays would be simultaneously on sale. The conditions of the book market would tell against the rapid sale of even such a fine play as *2 Henry IV,* and the printers would probably not set up the type for the new sheet E3-E6 containing the omitted scene until fresh orders came in for the book. It may be that the second issue did not make its appearance for some months or even years after November, 1600; if the sale was very slow, they might

176

endeavour to quicken it by adding the missing scene. If we accept the opinion of bibliographers that the contemporary popularity of an Elizabethan play may be held to vary directly with the number of editions printed and inversely with the number of copies of the first and second editions now extant, we must admit that *2 Henry IV* failed to sell. No less than seventeen copies, including eight of Q1 and nine of Q2 survive of the one edition printed; it would seem that about the name number of copies of each issue was sold. Later I shall discuss the possibility that the omission of the scene in Qi was not accidental; it may be, too, that the sale of the play was temporarily prohibited.

Modern criticism, in the main, accepts the opinion of the Cambridge editors upon the relation existing between the text of the quarto and that of the folio. They say:—

> The version in the First Folio was probably printed from a transcript of the original MS. It contains passages of considerable length which are not found in the Quarto. Some of these are amongst the finest in the play, and are too closely connected with the context to allow of the supposition that they were later additions inserted by the author after the publication of the Quartos. In the manuscript from which that edition was printed, these passages had been most likely omitted, or erased, in order to shorten the play for the stage.[27]

Writing of these omissions from the Quarto, Mr. H. A. Evans says:—

> There is no need to suppose any other cause for their absence, nor is any other motive apparent than that of reducing the length of the play.[28]

Sir E. K. Chambers says (I omit details):—

> There are several passages, aggregating 168 lines, not in Q. . . . and as the absence of some of these leaves *lacunae* in the sense, they may all be taken as 'cuts' in Q. On the other hand, F omits about forty lines found in Q. These are mostly short passages not likely to be cuts. They are probably not all to be explained in the same way. Some may

27. Clark and Wright, *The Works of William Shakespeare* (1863-66), vol. IV, p. xii.
28. Griggs, *Facsimile of Quarto of '2 Henry IV,'* Introduction.

M

be due to slips of F printer, and others—to emendation. But a few suggest that the censorship of profanity has been extended to passages of indelicacy—and in one case anti-patriotic criticism.[29]

Professor L. L. Schücking is the first critic to suggest that the reason for the ' cuts ' in the Quarto is not abridg-ment for representation on the stage. He says:—

The most remarkable and puzzling characteristic of the Quarto is its cuts.

Later he declares:—

The aim of these lines is to show that the character of the cuts seems rather to point to some sort of hasty intervention perhaps during the very printing, which may have had political reasons.[30]

Professor Schücking declines to accept the explanation that the omission of 171 lines in a play extending to 3180 lines was made for the purpose of shortening the play for the stage. He thinks that acting versions did not usually exceed 2600 lines; in my opinion all plays exceeding 2400 lines in length were liable to abridgment and were usually abridged. He believes—and I share his belief—that some at least of the ' cuts ' in the Quarto of *2 Henry IV* were made for political reasons.

The number of lines in the received text, the two issues of the quarto, and the folio text, together with the distribution of the verse and the prose in each, is set out below.

Text	No. of Lines of Verse	No. of Lines of Prose	Total No. of Lines
Quarto (First Issue) = Q1 ..	1281	1617	2898
Quarto (Second Issue) = Q2	1389	1623	3012
First Folio	1552	1588	3140
Received Text (Cambridge) ..	1560	1620	3180

The difference of 108 lines between the number of lines of verse in Q1 and Q2 respectively represents the length

29. *William Shakespeare*, vol. I, pp. 380-1.
30.. *Times Literary Supplement*, September 25, 1930.

178

of the scene omitted in Q1 and inserted in Q2; the extra six lines of prose found in Q2 are not due to any change or increase in the actual text but to the various yet unnecessary devices used by the printer in filling up the new sheet E3-E6 for which he had been supplied with an insufficient amount of 'copy.' Had he spaced all the ten entries and exits which he printed in Q2 in the same generous way as he did eight of them there would have been no need for him to reduce slightly the width of the eight new printed pages, to increase the number of the letters in spelling certain words or to tinker with all the prose text of the four leaves belonging to Signature E in Q1, and a better balanced page would have been the result. The change in the appearance and make-up of the new pages in Signature E could not escape the reader's notice because the paper-saving printer had elsewhere grudged space for necessary stage directions. The prose passages omitted in the folio belong to the comic underplot and are relatively unimportant; why they were omitted must remain a matter of conjecture. Q1 omits 279 and Q2 171 lines of poetry, nearly all in eight passages, each of considerable length. These omissions are in themselves of the highest importance poetically and dramatically; they come entirely from the main and serious part of the play, and in Q1 reduce the verse by more than a sixth of the total. The excision of these passages injures the coherence and intelligibility of the main story, and causes four bad breaks in the sense. The ratio of the number of lines of verse to the number of lines of prose for the folio version of *2 Henry IV* is much lower than for any of the tragedies or other histories, English or Roman. The loss of 279 lines of verse makes this ratio lower for Q1 than for any play of Shakespeare except the four comedies written shortly afterwards. The result is to thrust the comic underplot into such prominence, especially up to the end of the first scene of the fourth act, that the play becomes a comedy in a historical setting rather than a true chronicle or history play with some comic relief.

The first group of 'cuts' consists of passages which may be removed from their context and the play without seriously affecting the sense or the continuity of thought or the plot. The strictest and most meticulous scrutiny cannot detect or suggest any allusion to Elizabethan politics; the passages are of poetical or amplificatory rather than dramatic value. Had these been the only portions of the play to be omitted, editors would be almost certainly correct in asserting that these groups of lines were struck out 'in order to shorten the play for the stage.' The list of passages includes the following:—

    (i)   I. i. ll. 166-179
    (ii)   I. iii. ll. 21-4
    (iii) I. iii. ll. 36-55
    (iv) II. iii. ll. 23-45.

In all 61 lines have been omitted in order to abridge the play.

The second group of omitted passages have as a common characteristic some reference to Richard II, his reign or his deposition and death. They are essentially dramatic in quality and are necessary either to the immediate context or to the main story of the play or to both context and plot. Apart from these allusions to Richard II, a suspicious censor, in touch with the gossip and intrigues of the court and with a good knowledge of domestic and foreign affairs of the last four months of the year 1600, would find in this play plenty of what he or others might reasonably take to be covert references to the events, politics and persons of the day. These passages are

    (i)   I. i. ll. 189-209
    (ii)   I. iii. ll. 85-108
    (iii) III. i. ll. 1-108
    (iv) IV. i. ll. 55-79
    (v) IV. i. ll. 103-139

These passages amount in all to 215 lines, or 107 lines

if the omission of III. i. ll. 1-108 is to be considered an accident.

Not much comment is necessary on the first group of omissions. In preparing an acting version, such passages as these were usually struck out, even if they came from the pen of a Shakespeare, for the excellent reason that they had little interest for the majority of the audience and could not be efficiently declaimed.

(i) The first passage omitted (I. i. ll. 166-179) is a string of platitudes on the fortune of war. Morton has fled from the ' bloodie field by Shrewsburie ' to the

> Worme-eaten-Hole of ragged stone,
> Where Hotspurres Father, old Northumberland,
> Lyes crafty sicke.

He tells the earl that the conspiracy is broken and his son slain. The bereaved father for once forgets himself, and, throwing away his ' nice crutch,' would bind his ' Browes with Iron ' to meet

> The ragged'st houre, that Time and Spight dare bring
> To frowne vpon th' enrag'd Northumberland.

His retainers and fellow-conspirators, alarmed for his reason and health, exclaim,

> TRA. This strained Passion doth you wrong, my Lord.
> L. BAR. Sweet Earle, diuorce not wisdom from your Honor.
> MOR. The liues of all your louing Complices
> Leane on your health, the which if you giue-o're
> To stormy Passion, must perforce decay.

Here ends all that the quarto retains of Morton's speech; the folio omits the line spoken by Travers and continues :—

> You cast th' euent of Warre (my Noble Lord)
> And summ'd the accompt of Chance, before you said
> Let vs make head: It was your presurmize
> That in the dole of blowes, your Son might drop,
> You knew he walk'd o're perils, on an edge
> More likely to fall in, then to get o're:
> You were aduis'd his flesh was capeable
> Of Wounds, and Scarres; and that his forward Spirit
> Would lift him, where most trade of danger rang'd,

Yet did you say go forth: and none of this
(Though strongly apprehended) could restraine
The stiffe-borne Action: What hath then befalne?
Or what hath this bold enterprize bring forth,
More than that Being, which was like to be?

With such cold comfort and platitudes does Morton try
to calm the 'stormy passion' so· unusual in that shifty,
calculating political Janus. The actors were not fond of
moralising in bulk and preferred speeches which
gave more scope for appropriate action. Morton is a
minor character, little better than a messenger; he tells
his tale and appears no more. Any need for his presence
on the stage ends with the news that he has to give, yet
the poet makes him speak right on and hold the stage
from his entrance. By the omission of this speech, which
the acting version is better without, and of all but two
lines of his next speech Morton ceases to usurp, even
temporarily, the place of Northumberland in the play.

(ii) The next passage omitted (I. iii. ll. 21-4) consists
of four lines which partly explain and partly amplify the
thought contained in the two lines that precede them.
Lord Bardolph's next speech (ll. 27-33) supplies all
that is needed in the way of interpretation, and neither
the sense nor the context is much affected by the
omission. The actors very drastically curtailed the same
speaker's **very**

(iii) long speech (I. iii. ll. 36-62), retaining only the
final seven lines. They first struck out the opening six
and a half lines in which he likens the prospects of the
conspiracy to the hopes of getting fruit from forward
buds which frosts may destroy; they then removed the
much longer and rather tediously elaborate comparison
between drawing the complete plan of a house before
commencing to build it and perfecting all the details
necessary for a successful campaign before beginning
war. Similes from nature and over-worked comparisons
rarely escaped the erasing pen of the play-adapter. The

actors left Lord Bardolph the last seven lines, which are
a sufficient answer to the optimism of Hastings.

(iv) We may regret that Kate Percy's beautiful
tribute to her dead husband (II. iii. ll. 23-45) went the
way of much fine dramatic poetry, and was not spoken on
the Elizabethan stage. Hotspur was a poet and inspired
poetry in all that knew him, even in his arrogant, brutal,
selfish, scheming father, who could never make up his
mind whether it was more profitable for him to fight
than to stay at home. Yet this beautiful eulogy, so admirably becoming and natural in the mouth of the widow,
has the fault of being dramatically superfluous in this
play; the actors preferred a well-told tale to the finest
poetry, and as Hotspur was not a chracter in *2 Henry
IV,* they probably cut out most of the speech as a digression. Professor Schücking thinks 'the curtailment of
the fine speech of Hotspur's widow is remarkable';
I am astonished that so much of it was left. The actors,
in making an acting version, invariably reduced long
speeches more severely than dialogue, and just as invariably cut out a much higher proportion of the lines spoken
by the boys taking female parts than of the lines spoken
by adult actors. I am convinced that no boy ever spoke
the 37 lines of Kate Percy's speech in a public theatre
during the period 1598-1642.

Professor Schücking suggests that Shakespeare had
Essex in mind when he drew this brilliant portrait of the
dead Hotspur, and that the players expunged these lines
for fear of giving offence to the court. It is true that
Essex had much of Hotspur in him and, like him, became
a rebel. The salient facts, however, do not square with
these suggestions. When these lines were written,
whether they are to be dated 1597, 1598, or even in the
early months of 1599, Essex was basking in the sun of
royal favour and was on the pinnacle of popular reputa-
tion; even when the play was entered on the *Stationers'
Register,* most people thought that his star was but

momentarily eclipsed. If either the players or the press censor struck out these lines because they believed that this praise written for the dead Hotspur would be taken by the queen and her Council to be praise of Essex, then in disgrace, why did they not make a clean sweep of the entire eulogy? Why did they permit the finest part of this magnificent panegyric to remain?

> For His, (honor) it stucke vpon him, as the Sunne
> In the gray vault of Heauen: and by his Light
> Did all the Cheualrie of England moue
> To do brave Acts. He was (indeed) the .Glasse
> Wherein the Noble-Youth did dresse themselues.

I submit that the presence of these five lines in the abridged quarto proves that the press-corrector was not responsible for striking out the 22 lines immediately following this passage. Five lines were enough for the needs of the actors; the censor would strike out all or none.

We have ample evidence that the original stage name of Falstaff was Oldcastle. The important family of Brooke had taken the good name of the Lollard martyr, Sir John Oldcastle, under its protection, and had enough influence to compel the Chamberlain's men to make the change. This must have occurred before the date of the entry of Part One on the *Stationers' Register,* February 25, 1598, because the only traces of the name Oldcastle left in *1 Henry IV* are a joke on his name that in consequence of the alteration lacks point, and an unmetrical line (II. ii. 1. 101) of blank verse.

> Away, good Ned, Falstaffe sweates to death.

The substitution of the original word *Oldcastle* would restore this verse to normality. Evidently Shakespeare did not revise *1 Henry IV* for the press. I think the change was made before much of part two was written. The prefixing of *Old.* instead of *Fal.* to the speech commencing I. ii. 1. 113 may be as fairly ascribed to the sub-conscious memory and momentary forgetfulness of the poet not long after he had written Part One as to a failure to strike out an original *Old.* prefixed here. The name Falstaff occurs in six blank verse lines, viz., in II. iv. ll. 338, 344; IV. iii. ll. 25, 81; V. ii. l. 33; and V. v. l. 92; in each the substitution of Oldcastle for Falstaff would render the blank verse irregular. The verses are probably as the poet wrote them. The epilogue as it appears in the quarto tells its own story. It originally ended with the prayer for the queen which in the quarto follows the words 'promise you infinitely,' and in the folio are the last words spoken. Henry Brooke, Lord Cobham from March, 1597, was a good deal of a fool, and may have insisted on a public apology as well as the omission of Oldcastle's name. Sir E. K. Chambers is probably correct in suggesting that the company may have thought it politic to make a formal but not too slavish acknowledgment of their fault in libelling Oldcastle; in consequence Shakespeare scribbled two additional paragraphs, one announcing a dance, the other promising a re-appearance of Falstaff in *Henry V*. The actual apology, viz., ' For Old-Castle dyed a Martyr, and this is not the man ' would be meaningless to us if we did not have the key to the puzzle; for the audience it would be ample and self-explanatory. I think *2 Henry IV* must have been staged a few months after the first part was produced, if the apology was spoken on the stage; it would have been quite stale, had it been made, as Professor Schücking suggests, eighteen months or more after the offence. The confusion which the misplacement of the prayer for the queen creates for readers of the quarto is, in my opinion, an additional proof, if more proof was needed, that Shakespeare was indifferent to the manner in which his plays were printed.

Professor Schücking does not distinguish, as I do, between the two different kinds of ' cuts ' made, and seems to be in doubt whether they were the work of the actors or the printer. He says:—

The anxiety of the players would have been all the better founded as they were known as supporters of Essex (*vide* H. V. 5) and had become practically involved in the insurrection by their performance of *Richard II* on the eve of it. It was necessary to give proofs of loyalty or at any rate to avoid giving further offence. But even if the printer felt solely responsible, it would be intelligible that he preferred not to scandalize the authorities.[31]

Professor Schücking assumes that the printer had not set up a line of *2 Henry IV* by February 8, 1601, though it is dated 1600 and had been entered five and a half months previously. This assumption seems to me untenable. Obviously the easiest and simplest way of avoiding trouble with the authorities would have been to stop the printing of a book on which no work had been done by buying back the manuscript, refunding the money paid for it. Had the play been already printed as completely as in the received text, and been left in sheets, the printer could not have made the excisions in the quarto without re-setting the whole of every page of the play. If no portion of the play, however, had been printed by February 8, how came the printer to make the mistake of omitting to print the first scene of the third act?

I assume that *2 Henry IV* was written late in 1597 or very early in 1598, and received Tilney's 'allowance' probably without the loss of a line. There was not a cloud in the political sky. *Richard II* minus the deposition scene had been licensed for the press and printed, and in due course *1 Henry IV* also received an imprimatur. There was nothing topical in the account of an apparently purposeless rebellion that had occurred two centuries before to alarm the most cautious or suspicious licenser of plays. The actors would prepare their acting version, cutting out perhaps 600 or 700 lines, the majority of which would be likely to come from the verse. The play would be very frequently acted for about six or nine months, and thereafter at less frequent

31. *Times Literary Supplement*, September 25, 1930.

intervals; in a couple of years it would be off the acting list except for occasional revivals. When the company sent the 'copy' for the play to Wise and Aspley in August, 1600, what reason was there for the actors to think that a play, allowed by the Master of the Revels and acted before crowded audiences of admirers, was likely to give offence to the authorities? The printer or publishers would submit the manuscript to the press licenser, and would probably be astonished to discover that certain passages had been marked for omission. He would print what the licenser had left. Did printers arrogate to themselves the right of censoring plays? Perhaps some did when they had evaded the law. This play had, however, been entered 'under the handes of the wardens,' and the publishers had almost certainly obeyed the ruling laid down by the prelates in 1599 'that noe playes be printed excepte they bee allowed by suche as haue aucthorytye.'

Professor Schücking says:—

> Of the eight cut passages (including III. i.) no fewer than five mention King Richard II and his tragic fate.[32]

Though he recognizes that *2 Henry IV* was almost certainly abridged for representation, he assumes that all the passages omitted in the quarto were removed by the actors or printers 'perhaps during the very printing.' My own studies in the abridgment of Elizabethan plays have taught me to consider the subject-matter of each passage excised in relation to its context, the plot of the play and current history. I came to the conclusion that the passages which, in my judgment, the censor would strike out and the actors retain, in part at least, had in common the peculiarity that each contained a reference to King Richard II or the events of his reign. I was confirmed in my opinion on discovering that every allusion to Richard, his reign, actions, deposition and death had disappeared from the first issue of the quarto. This

32. *Times Literary Supplement*, September 25, 1930.

remarkable fact seems to have escaped the notice of commentators, and cannot be explained satisfactorily except on the assumption that some one purposely struck out these passages. Altogether there are eleven references to Richard II in the folio; they are to be found in one or other of the following passages: I. i. 1. 205; I. iii. ll. 98, 101; III. i. ll. 53, 63, 67, 88; IV. i. ll. 58, 115, 125, 139. All have disappeared from Q1, and this disappearance is not the result of coincidence or accident.

A study of these omitted passages makes it certain that the actors did not strike them out in order to shorten the play for the stage; if so, they cut out either too little or too much and left some ugly gaping wounds in the text that an audience would notice. The person responsible for this group of excisions had some political purpose in mind. This is also Professor Schücking's opinion, but I cannot accept his suggestion that out of sheer fright the actors or the printer did the press censor's work for him. I entirely dissent from his opinion

> that the insurrection of the dissatisfied grandees against the crown described in *2 Henry IV* contained certain topical allusions.[33]

Shakespeare did not, and could not, insert in a play written not later than March, 1599, and probably much earlier, topical allusions to events some of which occurred nearly two years later. History had merely repeated itself. The sketch of current history already given explains why the press censor, who must have read the play early in August, 1600, before it was entered on the Stationers' Registers would eliminate every reference to Richard II and his reign. Two or three weeks previously licenser Samuel Harsnett, a prebendary of St. Paul's, had been put through the Elizabethan 'third degree' by Francis Bacon, and had been asked by that super-subtle gentleman to explain many things which no licenser could hope to explain. He was accounted fortunate, I suspect, in that he escaped imprisonment for not being able to guess in March, 1599, what the Govern-

33. *Times Literary Supplement*, September 25, 1930.

ment would object to in August, 1600. But Archbishop
Whitgift had apparently instructed his satellites to keep
a sharp eye on plays for expression of opinion on religion,
affairs of state and the Council; accordingly the licenser
belittled the importance of Archbishop Scroop as leader
of the rebels against King Henry, and removed
from the play certain passages which malice or discontent
might twist into criticism of current politics or the
administration.

I. The first omitted passage (I. i. ll. 189-209) belonging
to the second group of 'cuts' comes from Morton's
speech; it explains the importance and share of Archbishop Scroop in the new conspiracy formed against the
King. The quotation below gives the folio version of the
passage omitted in both issues of the quarto with as much
of the context as is necessary. The passage omitted is
marked at the left-hand side.

L. BAR. And yet we ventur'd for the gaine propos'd,
    Choak'd the respect of likely perill fear'd,
    And since we are o're-set, venture againe.
    Come, we will all put forth; Body, and Goods,

MOR. 'Tis more then time: And (my most Noble Lord)
    I heare for certaine, and do speake the truth:
    The gentle Arch-bishop of Yorke is vp
    With well appointed Powres: he is a man
    Who with a double Surety bindes his Followers.
    My Lord (your Sonne) had onely but the Corpes,
    But shadowes, and the shewes of men to fight.
    For that same word (Rebellion) did diuide
    The action of their bodies, from their soules,
    And they did fight with queasinesse, constrain'd
    As men drinke Potions; that their Weapons only
    Seem'd on our side: but for their Spirits and Soules,
    This word (Rebellion) it had froze them vp
    As Fish are in a Pond. But now the Bishop
    Turnes Insurrection to Religion,
    Suppos'd sincere, and holy in his Thoughts:
    He's follow'd both with Body, and with Minde:
    And doth enlarge his Rising, with the blood
    Of faire King Richard, scrap'd from Pomfret stones,
    Deriues from heauen, his Quarrell, and his Cause:
    Tels them, he doth bestride a bleeding Land,
    Gasping for life, vnder great Bullingbrooke,
    And more, and lesse, do flocke to follow him.

NORTH. I knew of this before. But to speake truth,
This present greefe had wip'd it from my minde.
Go in with me, etc.

In the quartos, these thirty lines are reduced to the
nine that are unmarked. The obvious comment on the
abridged version of the quartos is that Morton and
Northumberland are talking nonsense. What is this news
that Morton hears for certain and that Northumberland
knew before, but had permitted his grief to wipe from
his mind? Too much or too little has been removed from
the folio version. If we add to Morton's two quarto
lines the first and last lines of the passage excised,

The gentle Arch-bishop of Yorke is vp,
And more, and lesse, do flocke to follow him,

we can cut out nineteen lines, keep the sense satisfactory,
and give Northumberland's two lines a meaning. Some
such abridgment as this would have been made by the
actors if they aimed at reducing the length of the play;
they were careless in their ' cuts,' but did not leave the
loose ends so frayed that the audience would notice
them. Another possible mode of abridging the folio
version would be to omit the whole of Morton's speech
and the first two lines of Northumberland's; sense and
continuity would have been preserved but at the expense
of the main plot. The Archbishop is the real leader of
the rebellion, and this speech was written to prepare an
audience that had not seen *1 Henry IV* for his appearance
in the council of rebel leaders at the beginning of the
third scene of the play. The result of this omission in
the quartos is that the third scene presents to us an
Archbishop of whose existence we have had a casual
mention in the previous comic scene. We know neither
his name nor his see, nor the reason why he is actively
plotting against the King. Had the actors cut down
Morton's speech, they would have retained enough to
make the subsequent events intelligible to their audience.
This clumsy ' cut ' suggests the ruthless hand of a censor;

his presence becomes highly probable when we read what
has been omitted in close relation to the history of Elizabeth's reign and the events of the year 1600.

For more than forty years most of England's domestic
and foreign troubles had sprung from the intrigues of
the type of rebel that

> Deriues from heauen, his Quarrell, and his Cause.

The internal political history of Elizabeth's reign is, in
the main, the story of real or imaginary Catholic plots,
contrived or suggested by bishops or other ecclesiastics
who turned religion to insurrection.   Mary Queen of
Scots had assumed Elizabeth's arms and title in 1559,
and with her arrival in August, 1561, began the long duel
which ended at Fotheringay in February, 1587.   The
dangerous rebellion of 1569 had been headed by the
Catholic Earls of Northumberland and Westmoreland.
The Pope had excommunicated the Queen in 1570 and
absolved her subjects from allegiance.   Leslie, the Bishop
of Ross, was a leading spirit in Ridolfi's plot that cost the
Catholic Duke of Norfolk his life.   The approach of the
Spanish Armada was heralded by the re-publication of
the Bull of Excommunication and Deposition accompanied with the grant of a plenary indulgence to all
Englishmen that assisted the invader.   In 1600 the chronic
Irish insurrection had reached a highly critical stage.
During the previous year Essex had lost over 10,000 men
and wasted the equivalent of a million pounds of our
money.   All that Elizabeth got for this very large
expenditure was a treaty with Tyrone which gave Ireland
almost complete home rule.   Tyrone broke the treaty
before the end of the year and appealed to Spain for
assistance; Philip decided to strike a blow at the Achilles'
heel of England.   Early in 1600 Oviedo, a Franciscan
monk, had come from Spain to Ireland with the title of
Bishop of Dublin; in April he conferred with the native
chieftains, gave them £6,000 in money and promised
them Spanish military aid.   More than two years before

Shakespeare and the Homilies

Shakespeare had written of Archbishop Scroop and Bolingbroke,

> But now the Bishop
> Turnes Insurrection to Religion,
> Suppos'd sincere, and holy in his Thoughts:
> He's follow'd both with Body, and with Minde
> And doth enlarge his Rising, with the blood
> Of faire King Richard, scrap'd from Pomfret stones,
> Deriues from heauen, his Quarrell, and his Cause:
> Tels them, he doth bestride a bleeding Land,
> Gasping for life, under great Bullingbrooke,
> And more, and lesse, do flocke to follow him.

When this passage was spoken on the stage in 1597-8, it could not be taken in any but its simple dramatic sense; not even the most captious of critics or 'moralisers,' who, as Nashe says, delighted to 'wrest a neuer-meant meaning out of euerything, applying all things to the present time,' could pretend that these lines covered a reference to contemporary politics or events. In August, 1600, the entire passage shouted politics to a critical reader. An Elizabethan 'decipherer' had the easiest of problems to solve. Oviedo was the 'bishop,' Mary Queen of Scots was 'King Richard,' 'Pomfret' was Fotheringay, Elizabeth, 'Bullingbrooke,' the 'Land' was Ireland. The author, they would say, was voicing the Catholic view of the Irish Rebellion. When the Spanish troops landed in 1601, their captain-general proclaimed 'God's war for maintaining the faith in Ireland,' and declared the queen 'an usurper in Ireland' and that the Irish people owed her no allegiance. I suggest that the Master of the Revels saw no political significance in this passage on his first reading of the play in 1597-8, and that the book censor struck it out, when he read it two years afterwards, for the reasons stated.

II. The third scene of the quarto contains only 62 of the 110 lines written by the poet. Three passages were omitted, two of which have been briefly discussed; the omission of the last passage (I. iii. ll. 85-108) does not affect the context or sense, but does serious injury to the plot and disturbs the balance in the characterisation intended by Shakespeare. The Archbishop loses his one important speech in this scene with the result that he seems the subordinate, a feeble echo of the weak and irresolute nobles instead of being their accepted leader. Lord Bardolph is for delay, gives reasons that are unanswerable, and after the conference takes no further part in the rebellion; the Archbishop agrees with him. Hastings gives reasons for action and the Archbishop assents. In the folio version the Archbishop takes the lead and outlines his plan of campaign; he has one virtue of a leader in that he comes to a decision and declares for war. He resolves to appeal to the people.

> Let vs on:
> And publish the occasion of our Armes.

Then, bishop-like, he preaches a sermon on the text

> An habitation giddy, and vnsure
> Hath he that buildeth on the vulgar heart.

This rebel-prelate had been one of the proctors nominated by Richard to present his resignation of the Crown to Parliament, and had sat on Henry's left hand at his Coronation feast! The sum of his grace's wisdom is reliance for the success of a half-baked plot upon the steady support and firm resolution of the people whom he despises as fickle, changeable and irresolute. The quarto version omits his entire speech, and, as a contemptuous make-weight, transfers to him the line given in the folio to Mowbray,

> Shall we go draw our numbers, and set on?

Thus the futile conference ends, and he leaves the stage, asking his fellow-rebels, ' What shall we do? ' Let any one read the quarto version of this scene, and try to pick out the leader of the revolt. The opening speech of the Archbishop suggests leadership, but he says nothing and comes to no decision; he speaks in all ten and a half lines, appears on the stage for a little more than three minutes, and is then lost sight of for more than two acts. We do not know his name or his see, or his reason for joining the conspiracy. Then at the beginning of the fourth act he reappears as the acknowledged leader of the insurgent army. The censor seems to have attempted to reduce the part played by the Archbishop to that of a minor character. Prior to the fourth act the leaders of the rebellion have appeared in three scenes, which in the folio amount to 392 lines, and in the quarto are reduced to 286 lines. The quarto thus omits 106 lines of these three scenes of which no less than 68 are lines that either refer to the Archbishop or are spoken by him. The leader, the Archbishop, speaks 10½ lines in all.

At first sight it is difficult to understand the censoring of the Archbishop's denunciation of

> our slippery people,
> Whose Love is neuer link'd to the deseruer,
> Till his deserts are past.

In this and many another such speech the characters of Shakespeare echo the contempt felt and expressed by the queen, her nobles, the gentry, the church and scholars for the people; such expressions are commonplaces in the dramatists. Mingled with this contempt was more than a little fear. The queen and her Council looked askance at any noble who affected popularity, and Bacon's advice to Essex on this subject was a timely warning unheeded. Shakespeare has admirably described Bolingbroke's ' Courtship to the common people.'

> How he did seeme to diue into their hearts,
> With humble, and familiar courtesie,
> What reuerence he did throw away on slaues;
> Wooing poore Craftes-men, with the craft of smiles,
> And patient vnder-bearing of his Fortune,
> As 'twere to banish their affects with him.
> Off goes his bonnet to an Oyster-wench,
> A brace of Dray-men bid God speed him well,
> And had the tribute of his supple knee,
> With thankes my Countrimen, my louing friends,
> As were our England in reuersion his,
> And he our subiects next degree in hope.

194

Hayward, too, in his *History,* comments somewhat severely on his desire of being popular. Essex notoriously delighted in the cheers of the London populace, and relied on the support of the citizens for success in his hare-brained rising on Sunday, February 8, 1601. On the following Sunday Cecil issued *Directions to the Preachers,* commanding them to declare from their pulpits that the Council knew that Essex had been scheming to become King, and had connived at the printing of Hayward's book in order that he might be looked upon as another and more popular Bolingbroke. The Government had neither police nor a permanent military force to maintain order, and this weakness made it very suspicious of popularity in such impulsive men as Essex. One thousand resolute men in possession of the Tower and of the Queen's person could have made themselves masters temporarily of London and England.

Archbishop Whitgift, who appointed the press 'correctors' and instructed them in their duties, was a member of the Privy Council and a regular attendant at its meetings. He knew all that was going on at home and abroad. Hayward's book gave much prominence to the part played by Archbishop Arundel in organizing the revolt that cost Richard II his throne and his life. Whitgift would know that in Ireland Bishop Oviedo was publishing 'the occasion of his Armes,' just as Scroop does in *2 Henry IV,* and was calling upon the Irish Catholics to rebel against the usurping queen. In the opinion of the Government heresy and disloyalty grew like two cherries on one stalk; Essex had been coquetting with the Puritans and the Catholics, and at his trial his adherents were denounced as 'a damnable crew of heretics and atheists.'[33a] The chief censor would resolve to minimize the dramatic importance of an archbishop in open revolt against civil authority, and would instruct his deputies to cut down or excise all speeches made by

33a. *Political History of England,* vol. VI, p. 368.

ecclesiastics calling upon the commons to rise in arms against the Government in power. He supported Cecil by compelling the clergy to read *The Directions to the Preachers* issued as a State document, and, being familiar with court gossip, would know the nick-name given to the queen. He would probably object to the frequent allusions made in *2 Henry IV* to Richard II and Bolingbroke at a time when the events of the Essex trial at York House and Hayward's imprisonment had made talk of Richard II and his deposition assume almost the appearance of treason.

III. I have already suggested towards the end of my reference to the two issues of the quarto that, even if the omission of Act III. Scene i. in Q1 was an accident due either to the inadvertence of the printer or to the failure of the Company to supply him with the ' copy,' it is not probable that he would at once set about the cancellation of E3 and E4 of Q1, and the printing of the new Sheet E3-E6 of Q2; he would almost certainly wait till fresh supplies of the play were needed by the booksellers. The great merit of the play and the circumstances amidst which it was published should have advertised *2 Henry IV* if published in November, 1600, and have quickened the sale. It is remarkable that no editions of *Richard II, 1 Henry IV* or *2 Henry IV* were published between 1600 and 1604, whilst the third edition of *Richard III,* and the second edition of the surreptitious *Henry V* (first printed in 1600) both appeared in 1602. Is it possible that shortly after February 8, 1601, the Privy Council prohibited the further sale of *Richard II* and the two plays on *Henry IV*? If the sale of these plays was stopped, Wise and Aspley would be left with a large portion of the edition of *2 Henry IV* unsold. The prohibition would be in force till the death of Elizabeth in March, 1603; for the remainder of that year and the early part of 1604, plague put an end to business. The proprietors might try at some time in

1604 to help the sale of the unsold copies by the inclusion of the omitted scene.

The omission of this scene may not be the fault of either company or printer. Of all the scenes belonging to the main or serious plot this has the least importance and could be omitted without much injury to plot or play. It is movable and could be placed almost anywhere between Act I, Scene iii, and Act IV, Scene i; it might also be an ' addition ' to the play except for certain reasons to be stated later. Though full of exquisite poetry, dramatically this scene of inaction and retrospection is naught and almost superfluous; nothing happens and we learn nothing except that a sick king is still sick and cannot sleep. We hear, too, that Glendower, in whose fate the reader or auditor of *2 Henry IV* has no interest because he is not a character of this drama, is dead. We know that Northumberland has once more left his friends in the lurch, but neither Warwick nor the King has heard this piece of news. The famous invocation to sleep, the sage reflections on ' the reuolution of the Times,' and reminiscences of Richard and Northumberland are natural in the speaker but not much to the purpose of the play. Only about a dozen lines have to do with the action. The title-page of *2 Henry IV* informs us that the King will die before the end of the play in order that we may see the coronation procession of Prince Hal. The most idolatrous admirer of Shakespeare must admit that King Henry is an unconscionably long time in making his first appearance on the stage in the play which bears his name as title. The scene is hardly necessary to create for the audience the illusion that enough time has passed to permit Falstaff to travel from London to Gloucestershire. The conversation between the justices in the opening of the next scene is long enough to satisfy the elastic conventions of the romantic Elizabethan drama on change of locality and passage of time.

197

Shakespeare and the Homilies

Justice Shallow speaks of ' Iack Falstaffe (now Sir Iohn)' and so Justice Silence has the chance of asking the question, ' This Sir Iohn (cousin) that comes hither anon about Souldiers.' We are thus prepared for the entrance of Bardolph, and soon afterwards his master appears. The real difficulty that the omission of the scene would create is that, without it, the King would not present himself to the audience till more than two-thirds of the play were over; he would appear but to die. I am of opinion, therefore, that the actors would not omit this scene in its entirety.

How would the play-adapter treat this scene in preparing the acting version some time in 1597-98? The successful conduct of his company's business as public entertainers required that he should make the most attractive version possible out of the 3180 lines of prose and verse written by the poet. The story must remain coherent and full of interest, and he must retain enough to give the audience pleasure for two hours. Even if the ' two howres traffique ' was extended to two hours and a quarter, the actors would be unable to play all the 2898 lines of Q1, much less the 3007 lines of Q2, or the 3140 lines of the folio. Heavy abridgment was certain. The comic scenes would be slightly pruned; the long excisions would come from the verse. The result might be that in the acting version the prose would be half as long again as the poetry; and the earlier scenes in verse would seem little more than breathing-spaces provided by a kindly-natured author for the actor that played Falstaff. The popular name of these plays seems to have been *Sir John Falstaff* or *Sir John Oldcastle,* and sometimes court officials so named them in their records. Probably almost one-half of this scene would be marked by the play-adapter for omission without making any breaks in continuity that an audience would notice. If we omit the following passages, viz., ll. 9-17, 21-5, 42-3, 47-56, 72-5, 80-7,

94, 102-3, 107-8, we shall find that 66 lines of the original 108 remain and that everything essential to the scene is retained. Anyone who heard it read or declaimed for the first time would not perceive any defect in the sense and would not be aware that any lines had been excised. The King would make his first appearance, would be on the stage for about four minutes and prove by his presence that the title of the play was not a mistake. The audience would be reminded that the rebellion against the King was slowly coming to a head; Falstaff, too, would be completing the first stage of that extraordinary march from his tavern in Eastcheap to the battlefields of Yorkshire by way of Gloucestershire.

When the press censor in August, 1600, took up his blue pencil or the Elizabethan equivalent, he would not be interested in Henry's insomnia or the ceremonious greetings that passed between the King and his nobles; but I think he would pause and perpend when he came upon this passage:—

> KING. Then you perceiue the Body of our Kingdome,
> How foule it is: what ranke Diseases grow,
> And with what danger, neere the Heart of it?
> WAR. It is but as a Body, yet distemper'd,
> Which to his former strength may be restor'd,
> With good aduice, and little Medicine:
> My Lord Northumberland will soone be cool'd.

Even a press censor in 1600 might be excused for believing that in this passage an almost direct allusion was made to court politics. Change ' King ' to ' Queen,' ' Warwick ' to ' Robert Cecil,' and ' Northumberland ' to 'Essex,' and we might be listening to the conversation of Elizabeth with Cecil on the worst of her domestic troubles. For nearly a year the relations between the queen and her former favourite had been growing more and more strained. After virtual imprisonment for eight months he had been put on trial for his mismanagement of the Irish expedition. The result was his suspension from almost all his many public offices and his confinement to his own house; he was refused access to the queen and court, was deprived of his most valuable monopoly, the patent for sweet wines, was heavily in debt and was becoming a desperate man. The censor would undoubtedly strike out such an ambiguous passage; if, as I think, he had decided to remove from the play all references to Richard II and Bolingbroke, he would also mark for omission ll. 57-89 and 88-94. The omission of ll. 38-44 would cause the consequential omission of ll. 1-3 and 36-7. The 52 lines thus struck out by the censor would leave the remainder of the scene barren of anything likely to be of interest to readers or the audience at the Globe. There would remain a poetical rhapsody on sleep, some ceremonious greetings, two short but entirely disconnected discourses on fate and the principles of prophecy, nine lines on the war and rumours of war, and some talk on the King's sickness. What the censor had left could not be presented on the public stage at a time when the 'ayrie of Children' acting at Blackfriars were so high in public favour; even Shakespeare's best seems for a time not to have been good enough. He did not, as far as is known, take any active part in the publication of his plays, but Master Ben Jonson, who was writing for the children in 1600, had recently jeered at two lines of *Julius Caesar*. Shakespeare may have decided not to expose his plays and himself to such ill-natured sneers, and may have suggested to the company to withdraw from publication the inconsequential and disjointed mingle-mangle that remained after the press censor had torn out the vitals of this scene.

Before discussing the cuts in the fourth act, it is worth while considering the effects of the preceding omissions upon the play and especially upon the two concluding scenes of the rebellion. So far comedy and prose have been in the ascendant. The folio version of Acts I-III contains 1765 lines, divided into 500 lines of blank verse

and 1265 lines of prose. The scenes in verse, containing
the serious or main plot, would require about 25 minutes
to act, the comic scenes, almost all in prose, about 65
minutes. Q1 retains all the prose but omits 214 lines of
verse; thus the quarto version requires less than 15
minutes for the 286 lines of verse and 65 minutes for the
prose. Even in the folio version the length and excellence
of the comic element tend to thrust the somewhat lifeless
and disconnected story of the rebellion into the background.
Each verse scene presents to us a different set of persons,
who come upon the stage, speak a few lines, do nothing,
and then disappear from the play. We have no Hotspur
to flash like a meteor through the second part. The conspirators lack a leader to give their futile plots even the
appearance of the unity which the presence of Falstaff
gives to the comic episodes. Up to the end of the third
act, the verse of Q1 bears to the prose much the same
proportion as the half-pennyworth of bread to the sack
in Falstaff's tavern-bill. The comic muse is in her
merriest mood and reigns supreme, and after the end of
the first scene of the play, the two short scenes in verse
seem brief intervals designed to give the actor who played
the part of Falstaff time to ' drink ' his tobacco.

IV. The opening lines of the fourth act present to us
the Archbishop of York in full armour at the head of the
rebel forces. He had hitherto played a small part in the
drama, but the poet who wrote the play as it appears in
the folio version was too good a craftsman not to prepare
his audience for the strange transformation of a prelate,

> The very Opener, and Intelligencer,
> Betweene the Grace, the Sanctities of Heauen,
> And our dull workings,

into what Prince John calls

> an Iron man
> Chearing a rowt of Rebels with your Drumme,
> Turning the Word, to Sword; and Life to Death:

Though he appears once only on the stage prior to this
act, we hear of him in nearly every other scene. When

the rump of the insurgents shattered at Shrewsbury is plotting fresh wars at Northumberland's ' Worme-eaten-Hole of ragged Stone,' Morton tells them that

> The gentle Arch-bishop of Yorke is vp
> With well appointed Powres,

and under the cloak of religion is assembling an army. The poet slips in another reference to him in the next scene. The Chief Justice, outpointed in every round of the wordy duel between Falstaff and himself, makes this home-thrust :—

> Well, the King hath seuer'd you and Prince Harry, I heare you are going with Lord Iohn of Lancaster, against the Archbishop, and the Earle of Northumberland.

Falstaff adroitly parries this with a sarcastic reference to ' all you that kisse my Ladie Peace, at home,' and then turns the implied reproof to his own commendation. The poet thus prepares us for the meeting of the rebel-leaders in the next scene at which the Archbishop presides. Hastings, Mowbray and Lord Bardolph being unable to agree upon a course of action, he makes up his mind and decides for war, resolving on an appeal for support to

> fickle Changelings, and poore Discontents,
> Which gape, and rub the Elbow at the newes
> Of hurly burly Innouation.

Then follow two scenes of comedy, but we are not allowed to forget the war; Gower tells the Chief Justice

> Fifteene hundred Foot, five hundred Horse
> Are march'd vp to my Lord of Lancaster,
> Against Northumberland, and the Archbishop.

We next pick up some loose threads of the conspiracy. Northumberland's wife and his widowed daughter-in-law, Kate Percy, plead to him not to tempt fortune any more :—

> Let them alone :
> The Marshall and the Arch-bishop are strong.

She succeeds in persuading him to abandon his confederates to their fate, as he had before deserted his own son, and he drifts out of the play, a model of irresolution and despair :—

> Faine would I goe to meet the Arch-bishop
> But many thousand Reasons hold me backe.
> I will resolue for Scotland.

Even the famous tavern scene closes on a note of war;
Peto enters to disturb the revellers:—

> The King, your Father, is at Westminster,
> And there are twentie weake and wearied Postes,
> Come from the North.

The King makes his first appearance and after his
soliloquy, discusses with Warwick the character and
conduct of Northumberland, concluding with the remark,

> They say, the Bishop and Northumberland
> Are fiftie thousand strong.

Warwick replies, 'Rumor doth double. . . . The
numbers of the feared,' but the mention of this rumour
keeps present to our minds the Archbishop who has been
so long absent from the stage.

The portrait of the Archbishop in the folio version is
sketched in outline rather than drawn at full length.
Shakespeare has permitted Falstaff and the rest of the
'Irregular Humorists' to overshadow all the other
characters, but he has taken care to harmonize the
speeches and actions of the Archbishop when he makes
his appearance with Morton's account of his activities.
Morton's speech is intended to excite in the audience an
interest in this as yet unknown and unseen member of the
church militant. The poet inserts no less than six other
allusions in various scenes to him as joint leader of the
rebellion; and thus after the flight of Northumberland
we are prepared for his entry in full armour.

Far different is the picture of Archbishop Scroop
which we find in the Quarto. All that relates to him in
the first scene, including Morton's long description of
him and his actions, has been cut out, and, though the
reference to him in the second scene has been retained,
every member of the audience would be so convulsed with
the unequal wit-combat between Falstaff and the Chief
Justice that scarcely any notice would be taken of the

casual remark about an unknown and unseen Archbishop. Thus it comes about that when he appears on the stage in the third scene he lacks the artistic background prepared by the poet; he is unlooked for by the audience and neither does anything nor says anything to explain why a prince of the church is entangled with this knot of conspirators. He fares just as badly afterwards; two out of five incidental allusions to him have been struck out, and all that remains is a mere mention of his name. Shakespeare wrote 32 lines of verse for him; in the quarto he speaks 10½ lines, and not a line of any importance; in the folio there are 35 lines in which other characters make some reference to him; of these, eight lines only are retained in the quarto. He neither acts nor speaks as a leader should. The cumulative effect of these omissions is to reduce the part played by him in the conspiracy before the fourth act to complete insignificance. I have shown that they seriously disturb the characterisation and plot, and I suggest that this was the intention of the person responsible for them, and that these passages were struck out for political reasons.

The result of these abridgments in Q1 is a defective plot; we have no explanation of the appearance of an Archbishop clad in armour at the head of

> moody Beggars, staruing for a time
> Of pell-mell hauocke, and confusion.

We do not know his secret motives, his grievances or the ends that he pursues; it would seem to be a sudden resurgence of hitherto suppressed original sin. When the armies meet, Westmoreland, the King's general, demands of him why he

> Whose Sea is by a Ciuill Peace maintain'd,
> Whose Beard, the Siluer hand of Peace hath touch'd,
> Whose Learning, and good Letters, Peace hath tutor'd,
> Whose white Inuestments figure Innocence,
> The Doue, and very blessed Spirit of Peace,

has turned rebel and soldier. Scroop's reply, as it is given in the folio, offers some reason for his conduct.

> Wherefore doe I this? So the Question stands.
> Briefely to this end: Wee are all diseas'd,
> And with our surfetting, and wanton howres,
> Haue brought our selues into a burning Feuer,
> And wee must bleede for it: of which Disease,
> Our late King Richard (being infected) dy'd.
> But (my most Noble Lord of Westmerland)
> I take not on me here as a Physician,
> Nor doe I, as an Enemie to Peace,
> Troope in the Throngs of Militarie men:
> But rather shew a while like fearefull Warre,
> To dyet ranke Mindes, sicke of happinesse,
> And purge th' obstructions, which begin to stop
> Our very Veines of Life: heare me more plainely.
> I haue in equall ballance iustly weigh'd
> What wrongs our Arms may do, what wrongs we suffer,
> And finde our Griefes heauier then our Offences.
> Wee see which way the streame of Time doth runne,
> And are enforc'd from our most quiet there,
> By the rough Torrent of Occasion,
> And haue the summarie of all our Griefes
> (When time shall serue) to shew in Articles;
> Which long ere this, wee offer'd to the King,
> And might, by no Suit, gayne our Audience:
> When we are wrong'd, and would vnfold our Griefes,
> Wee are deny'd accesse vnto his Person,
> Euen by those men, that most haue done vs wrong.
> The dangers of the dayes but newly gone,
> Whose memorie is written on the Earth
> With yet appearing blood; and the examples
> Of every Minutes instance (present now)
> Hath put vs in these ill-beseeming Armes:
> Not to breake Peace, or any Branch of it,
> But to establish here a Peace indeede,
> Concurring both in Name and Qualitie.
>
> WEST. When euer yet was your Appeale deny'd?
> Wherein haue you beene galled by the King?
> What Peere hath beene suborn'd, to grate on you,
> That you should seale this lawlesse bloody Booke
> Of forg'd Rebellion, with a seale diuine?
> (And consecrate Commotions bitter edge)?

The quartos retain the first two and the last eight lines of the Archbishop's speech, or ten lines instead of thirty-five; the lines excised are marked by a vertical line on the left. The folio version presents us with the Archbishop's defence of the rebellion, and Shakespeare takes care that he gets the worse of the argument. He has no effective answer to Westmoreland's searching questions, and takes refuge in specious or vague generalisations or in assertions that his friends and followers are oppressed and cannot gain an audience with the king to make known their grievances. Westmoreland challenges him to state his personal grievances and bluntly tells him that it is not the business of an Archbishop to redress other men's political wrongs. In the quarto version the prelate cuts a very sorry figure, and has not been left the rag of an excuse for taking part in a rebellion against civil authority. Every plea of justification has been ruthlessly cut out, and after making a half-intelligible and somewhat mysterious allusion to the troubles of the last reign, he rests his defence on the time-honoured quibble that he is in arms not to break the peace but to make a peace that will endure. Here as in earlier parts of the play the quarto consistently lowers the character and dramatic importance of an archbishop who takes an active part in open rebellion against the Government. The lines quoted above offer evidence that the censor and not the play-adapter was responsible for this omission. Westmoreland's three questions

> When euer yet was your Appeale deny'd?
> Wherein haue you beene galled by the King?
> What Peere hath been suborn'd, to grate on you?

are present in both quarto and folio; they refer to lines omitted in the quarto but present in the folio. The quarto text exhibits a bad break in continuity and sense which we cannot reasonably attribute to the actors. Any intelligent member of the audience could not but perceive that Westmoreland must be referring to specific complaints made by Scroop which for some reason had been omitted. A censor might be pardoned for thinking in August,

1600, or later in the year that this speech, especially the part omitted, was full of covert and dangerous allusions to important persons, politics, and the state of England. He would find, too, opinions and doctrines, expressed or implied, subversive of the basic principles upon which the entire fabric of the Tudor paternal despotism in Church and State had been erected; a fundamental tenet of the State religion was questioned, if not denied; and there would seem to be more or less veiled criticism of existing conditions in the England of Elizabeth. The people were loyal, patriotic and proud of their queen who had been on the throne before three-fourths of her subjects had been born. Yet much discontent had existed for some years, due mainly to her interference with trade and manufactures. The ever-recurring expense of the long war with Spain and of the chronic revolt in Ireland meant forced loans without interest, additional taxes, heavy subsidies, and a continuous, extensive and illegal use of the press-gang to fill the army and navy. Recruiting was effected much in the way described by Shakespeare; most men, like Bull-calf, ' had as lief be hanged, as goe ' to the wars. Two-thirds died of wounds or disease, and many who returned were maimed or a charge on the parish rates for life. Yet *2 Henry IV* would probably have passed through the censor's hands without notice but for the untoward circumstances of the times. The prominence given to Richard II and his reign during the Essex trial in June, 1600, and Hayward's imprisonment filled the censors with super-official zeal. Out would go the reference to Richard's death and with it the preceding lines,

> And with our surfetting, and wanton howres,
> Haue brought our selues into a burning Feuer,
> And wee must bleede for it.

This was a text on which gloomy Puritan divines preached two-hour sermons lamenting the wickedness of the times; it is the language of morality-mongers in every age. The declaration of the Archbishop that he had taken up arms, not ' as an Enemie to Peace,' but rather

> To dyet ranke Mindes, sicke of happinesse,
> And purge 'th' obstructions, which begin to stop
> Our very Veines of Life.

would be familiar to readers of Halle and Holinshed; reformation had been the cry of those who had taken part in recent London riots on account of high prices and the injury done to trade by resident aliens. Monopolies and patents were amongst the ' obstructions ' of which complaint was wide-spread.

Far more momentous issues were involved in the next lines of the Archbishop's speech:—

> heare me more plainely.
> I haue in equall ballance iustly weigh'd,
> What wrongs our Armes may do, what wronges we suffer,
> And finde our Griefes heauier then our Offences.

This mediaeval archbishop here enunciates the ultra-modern doctrine that the citizen has the right to rebel against the authority of the State, if, in his opinion, rebellion is likely to pay him better than obedience. If acceptance of the queen's rule was to be a matter of private judgment, the whole system of Tudor despotism would crumble into ruins. When Henry VIII broke with Rome and declared himself Pope of the English Church, his ingenious theologians buttressed up the royal infallibility and supremacy in Church and State by inventing the doctrine of the immediate divine right of Kings. They soon logically deduced two fundamental tenets of the State religion, first, that passive obedience was the chief duty and virtue of all subjects, and secondly, that wilful rebellion against the monarch was the one unforgivable mortal sin; the two homilies on *Obedience* and *Wilful Rebellion* express completely official Tudor opinion on the relation between ruler and subjects. How must the clerical licensers of books, accustomed to read a portion of these two homilies on nine Sundays in each year, have stared and gasped at the Archbishop's declaration that rebellion was not a mortal sin, but a mere matter of business or striking a balance of profit and loss! The zeal of the censors would be trebled when Mariana proved from texts of Scripture that what they termed treason and heresy in the mouth of an Archbishop was sound Catholic doctrine. Probably copies of Mariana's book on *The King and the Kingly Institution* had reached England by the middle of 1600. The author makes short work with the doctrine of the divine right of Kings to govern wrong. The people, he states, had delegated a certain measure of their power to their sovereign but retained the right of recalling it if misused. He considered the

> case of a sovereign elected by the nation or who had obtained his throne by hereditary right, but who sacrificed his people to his lusts, infringed the laws, despised true religion, and preyed upon the fortunes of his subjects. If there existed in the nation any authoritative assembly of the people, or if such an assembly could be convoked, it should warn the sovereign of the consequence of his acts, declare war against him if he continued obdurate, and, if no other resource remained, pronounce him a public enemy, and authorize any person to slay him.[34]

Mariana dedicated to Philip III of Spain a book worthy of Locke or Rousseau; in England Francis Bacon would have argued that the possession of such a book was constructive treason, and John Hayward had been imprisoned and threatened with the rack for the offence of re-telling the story of the deposition of an English King two hundred years before.

Politics in an England ruled by such a despot as Elizabeth was a matter of persons rather than principles. The disgrace of Essex overshadowed in the public mind the war with Spain or even the burning question of monopolies. Everyone in London knew that the once all-powerful favourite of the queen had for nearly a year been denied admission to the court and access to her

34. Quoted from Lecky, *Rationalism in Europe* (1866), vol. II, pp. 169-170.

o

Shakespeare and the Homilies

Majesty. Both the earl and his numerous friends were loud in their complaints that they

> might, by no Suit, gayne our Audience:
> When wee are wrong'd, and would vnfold our Griefes,
> Wee are deny'd accesse vnto (her) Person,
> Euen by those men, that most haue done vs wrong.

The avowed purposes of his unlucky rising were to force his way into the presence of the queen, to remove his personal enemies, Cecil, Raleigh, Cobham, Grey and others from power, and to make 'an alteration of the State,' an ambiguous phrase capable of various sinister meanings. Anyone with a small knowledge of current court gossip, especially one who lived by finding faults in the work of his fellows, would read into these lines a direct allusion to the strained relations of Essex and the Queen. Shakespeare wrote this passage when the favourite was basking in the glorious sunshine of the royal favour; the censor, being concerned only with the present, would strike them out as a too intelligent anticipation of what was to come.

Neither the play-adapter nor the printer, but the press censor is, in my opinion, responsible for the unusual obscurity and want of intelligibility which characterize certain parts of the first scene of the fourth act in the quarto version. A reader will appreciate the full effect of the devastating changes made only if he reads this abridgment in conjunction with the more complete folio text. The extract from the quarto text given below begins with the two opening lines of Archbishop Scroop's reply to Westmoreland's first long speech in this scene, and concludes with four lines of Westmoreland's second long speech in reply to Mowbray. From this point the two versions are in agreement.

BISHOP.   Wherefore do I this? so the question stands:
          Briefly, to this end, we are all diseasde:
          The dangers of the daie's but newly gone,
          Whose memorie is written on the earth,

With yet appearing blood, and the examples
Of euery minutes instance (present now),
Hath put vs in these ill-beseeming armes,
Not to breake peace or any braunch of it,
But to establish heere a peace indeede,
Concurring both in name and quallitie.

WEST.　When euer yet was your appeale denied
Wherein haue you beene galled by the King:?
What peere hath beene subornde to grate on you?
That you should seale this lawlesse bloody booke
Of forgde rebellion with a seale diuine,
(And consecrate commotions bitter edge.)

BISHOP.　My brother Generall, the common wealth
(To brother borne an houshold cruelty.)
I make my quarrell in particular.

WEST.　There is no neede of any such redresse,
Or if there were, it not belongs to you.

MOWBRAY. Why not to him in part, and to vs all
That feele the bruises of the daies before?
And suffer the conditions of these times
To lay a heauy and vnequall hand
Vpon our honors.

WEST.　But this is meere digression from my purpose
Here come I from our princely generall,
To know your griefes, to tell you from his Grace,
That he will giue you audience, etc.

The most remarkable characteristic of the above
continuous extract from the quarto text is the
almost complete absence of any logical sequence in
consecutive speeches. Each speaker in his turn takes
little notice of what has been said to him, and,
instead, either asks some new or unexpected question
or makes some inconsequential statement which
does not spring, as it should, from the previous
speech. The distinctive qualities of Shakespeare's work
are lacking; we miss the lightning-like rapidity in picking
up a doubtful point, the easy and natural transition from
one topic to another, the brisk give-and-take and even
flow of the dialogue, and the lively repartee and word-
play. The reply of Archbishop Scroop to the severe and

211

vigorous attack of Westmoreland is feeble and unconvincing, and consists of nothing but a string of well-worn generalities. He makes no specific complaint on behalf of either his friends or himself; yet Westmoreland in his brusque rejoinder asks him three new and pertinent questions on personal grievances. The mystification still goes on; the Archbiship takes no notice of any of these questions, and utters three cryptic lines referring to 'his brother Generall, the common wealth' and his 'brother borne.' Westmoreland in his turn pays no attention to the words of the Archbishop and his retort,

> There is no neede of any such redresse,

makes our confusion worse confounded by referring to something not to be found in his opponent's speech. Here the folio version does not show us a road out of the maze; it cuts the difficulty and makes some sense of the passage by discarding a line that seems right Shakespeare,

> To brother borne an houshold cruelty.

Spedding has given, in my opinion, a sound explanation of this crux, 'I think some lines have been lost.' In these the Archbishop probably spoke of the need for the 'redresse' of grievances; he also may have answered one of Westmoreland's questions,

> Wherein haue you beene galled by the King?

by citing the circumstances of the execution without trial of his brother, the Earl of Wiltshire, by order of Bolingbroke in 1399, an event to which Shakespeare makes an allusion in *1 Henry IV*. I think that the Archbishop's speeches alone are defective here, and that the censor struck out these passages to deprive him of any excuse for taking part in a rebellion against constituted authority.

We return to sanity and Shakespeare for a moment with the first line of Mowbray's speech. He begins his speech quite naturally by challenging the last sentence

spoken by Westmoreland to Scroop, 'it not belongs to
you.' But the first line of Westmoreland's reply,

But this is meere digression from my purpose,

thrusts us back into blunderland once more. Mowbray
speaks for the first time on what is a personal grievance;
he not merely receives no answer but is completely ignored
—a piece of extraordinary rudeness on the part of an
envoy sent by a prince to persuade rebels to put down
their arms. I decline to believe that the actors were
responsible for such a wantonly stupid destruction of the
sense and dramatic situation. Had the play-adapter found
it necessary to strike 60 lines out of this scene, he could
have easily distributed the 'cuts' so that neither the sense
nor the dramatic value would have been impaired.

(V) The last omission of any importance is the longest
and extends to 38 lines (IV. i. ll. 103-140). The passage
appears thus in the folio; the quarto text omits the 38
lines marked with a vertical line at the side.

MOW. Why not to him in part, and to vs all,
That feele the bruises of the dayes before,
And suffer the Condition of these Times
To lay a heauie and vnequall Hand vpon our Honors?

WEST. O my good Lord Mowbray,
Construe the Times to their Necessities,
And you shall say (indeede) it is the Time,
And not the King, that doth you iniuries.
Yet for your part, it not appeares to me,
Either from the King, or in the present Time,
That you should haue an ynch of any ground
To build a Griefe on: were you not restor'd
To all the Duke of Norfolkes Seignories,
Your Noble, and right well-remembred Fathers?

MOW. What thing, in Honor, had my Father lost,
That need to be reuiu'd, and breath'd in me?
The King that lou'd him, as the State stood then,
Was forc'd, perforce compell'd to banish him:
And then, that Henry Bullingbrooke and hee
Being mounted, and both rowsed in their Seates,
Their neighing Coursers daring of the Spurre,
Their armed Staues in charge, their Beauers downe,

Their eyes of fire, sparkling through sights of Steele,
And the lowd Trumpet blowing them together:
Then, then, when there was nothing could haue stay'd
My Father from the Breast of Bullingbrooke;
O, when the King did throw his Warder downe,
(His owne Life hung vpon the Staffe hee threw)
Then threw hee downe himselfe, and all their Liues,
That by Indictment, and by dint of Sword,
Haue since mis-carryed vnder Bullingbrooke.

WEST. You speak (Lord Mowbray) now you know not what.
The Earle of Hereford was reputed then
In England the most valiant Gentleman.
Who knowes, on whom Fortune would then haue smil'd?
But if your Father had beene Victor there,
Hee ne're had borne it out of Couentry.
For all the Countrey, in a generall voyce,
Cry'd hate vpon him: and all their prayers, and loue,
Were set on Herford, whom they doted on,
And bless'd, and grac'd, and did more then the King.
But this is meere digression from my purpose.
Here come I from our Princely Generall,
To know your Griefes; to tell you, from his Grace,
That hee will giue you Audience: etc.

Thomas Mowbray, Earl of Nottingham and hereditary Earl Marshall of England (one of Essex's titles), was the eldest son and heir of that Duke of Norfolk whom Richard II had banished for life and who had died abroad in 1400. His son inherited in due course his father's lands and all his dignities except the dukedom of Norfolk. Mowbray—he was barely twenty years old—explains that he has joined the rebellion because he will not

suffer the conditions of these times
To lay a heauy and vnequall hand
Vpon our honors.

So far the quarto and the folio versions agree, but the folio version partly explains the meaning of this vague statement. Mowbray is complaining that without any reason he has been degraded from the dignity of Duke of Norfolk by Bolingbroke. He had married Bolingbroke's niece, the daughter of another of Richard the Second's degraded dukes. History had most strangely repeated itself after two hundred years. From Mowbray's sister

had descended the Tudor Dukes of Norfolk, the last of
whom had been attained and executed in 1572 for partici-
pation in Ridolfi's plot against the queen. Like Bolingbroke, she had restored his son

> To all the Duke of Norfolkes Seignories,

except his dukedom. This son in his turn had plotted
against her, and had died in 1596 after being imprisoned
in the Tower for thirteen years. Enemies of the queen,
such as Parsons, Cardinal Allen and Campion charged
her with the deliberate and systematic extermination of
the old nobility, and especially of those families which
traced their descent to Edward III. This charge had been
repeated by the Pope when he republished the Bull of
Deposition against Elizabeth. Under the Tudors the
historic houses of Stafford, Percy, Neville, Pole and others
had been ruined. Had Westmoreland's reply remained in
the quarto text, readers would have been reminded of the
downfall and tragedy of the last English duke and his
son; the thought might come that Elizabeth was as merci-
less as Bolingbroke. The long account of the quarrel
between Mowbray's father and Bolingbroke is little better
than the 'meere digression' that Westmoreland calls it,
and not much more to the purpose than Kate Percy's
eulogy of her dead husband. Some one, the play-adapter
or the censor, struck it out of the quarto, and with it
went the last reference to Richard II in the play. We
have at the end of this passage another reference to the
popularity of Bolingbroke,

> and all their prayers, and loue,
> Were set on Herford, whom they doted on,
> And bless'd, and grac'd, and did more then the King.

The queen knew that she was nick-named Richard the
Second; his enemies termed Essex a would-be Bolingbroke. An alert-minded censor might suspect that many
'decipherers' would make such substitutions for themselves.

The results of this inquiry may be briefly summarized.
Throughout Elizabeth's long reign the succession to the

throne had remained unsettled, and deposition hung over her head like the sword of Damocles. Doleman's treatise on the succession (printed in 1594) and subsequent talk of republishing the Papal Bull deposing the queen and absolving her subjects from their allegiance, stimulated the press censors to activity. The ' Parliament scene ' of *Richard II* was omitted in all editions printed in the Queen's life-time, because she objected to the implied right of a Parliament to depose the monarch. Her favourite Essex had by his unwise conduct alienated her affection, and Hayward's rather effusive dedication to him of his pamphlet on Richard II aroused suspicions which the conduct of Essex in Ireland increased. His mismanagement of the Irish expedition, his trial at York House, and Hayward's arrest and imprisonment tended to keep the censors suspicious and active. The second part of *2 Henry IV* was entered on the *Stationers' Register*, August 23, 1600, and was printed before the end of that year. Certain passages, amounting in all to 279 lines, are missing from the first issue of the quarto version. We must remember that what a dramatist wrote may have been abridged by the actors voluntarily or by the actors or printer under compulsion. It has always been assumed first, that the first scene of the third act was accidentally omitted, and was inserted in the second issue as soon as the omission was discovered; secondly, that the other passages omitted were ' cuts ' made for the purpose of shortening the play for the stage. Almost simultaneously, and quite independently, Professor Schücking in the *Times Literary Supplement* (September 25, 1930), and the author in a lecture given before the Melbourne Shakespeare Society (October 3, 1930) gave reasons for an opinion that certain passages had been banned by authority. I agree with Professor Schücking that the omitted scene was not likely to have been omitted through inadvertence. I think, too, that it is neither necessary nor probable that the error was rectified by the printer as

soon as it was discovered. The remainder of these
omitted passages may be divided into two groups, the first
including those which have no political significance and
are almost certainly ' cuts ' made with a view of shortening
the play for representation, the second consisting of
passages containing references to Richard II as well as
other matter which the most unsuspicious of press censors
might, in August, 1600, believe to glance at contemporary
history and politics. Not one of the eight allusions to
Richard II, no mention of his name or of any event in
his reign has been left in the first issue of the quarto. We
find, too, that as a result of these omissions the part of
Archbishop Scroop, the leader of the rebellion, has been
reduced to insignificance. The actors cannot be held
responsible for these ' cuts ' which injure the context,
story and plot. The laws of probability compel us to
discard chance as a factor. If the actors found that it
was necessary to strike out about a quarter of the first
scene of the fourth act, they had other ways of doing this
than by excising ll. 55-79 and 103-139. They could have
omitted ll. 1-5, 43-6, 63-6, 80-7, 93, 95, 134-9, 154-161,
170-7, 193-6, 210-4, 218-20, or 57 lines out of 228 lines
without doing any harm to the sense or dramatic quality.
Behind the omission of these two long passages there was
almost certainly a definite purpose, and that purpose was
political. We may therefore conclude that the censor
insisted on these omissions as a pre-condition of giving
the printer his imprimatur. Possibly after the play had
been in print for a few weeks, the sale was stopped; there
would be nothing surprising if the queen and the council
prohibited it after the events that ended in Essex's insurrection on February 8, 1601. Public interest in these
plays ought to have been stimulated by the Essex
tragedy, in which a ' request ' performance of Shakespeare's *Richard II* played a small part, but we find
that *2 Henry IV* sold very slowly, and that new
editions of *Richard II* and *1 Henry IV* were not printed

Shakespeare and the Homilies

till the next reign. The poet's most popular plays with the reading public were *Richard III* and *1 Henry IV*, six editions of each play being printed before the appearance of the first folio; *Richard II* with five editions ranked a good third in public esteem. The only one of Shakespeare's chronicle plays printed in quarto that did not reach a second edition was *2 Henry IV*; this apparent want of popularity is inexplicable in view of the fact that a second edition of the surreptitious *Henry V* was required two years after the first edition of 1600. The publication of the two parts of *Robert, Earl of Huntingdon,* in 1601, of *Thomas Lord Cromwell,* the second edition of *Henry V* and a third edition of *Richard III* in 1602, suggests that the vogue of the English history plays with the reading public was not past. But the sale of the editions of *Richard II* (1598), *1 Henry IV* (1599), and *2 Henry IV* (1600) hung fire, and the number of extant copies of each of the last editions printed in Elizabeth's reign, viz., nine of *Richard II,* eleven of *1 Henry IV,* and seventeen of *2 Henry IV* is exceedingly high. This fact suggests that some copies of each edition were bought by persons of good social status, who would take more care of them than was usual. Perhaps over-production of plays about 1600 may be sufficient to explain this slow absorption. If the Council prohibited the sale of these plays in 1601, the second issue containing the omitted scene might not appear till 1604 or even later; it would be impossible to insert the other passages without resetting the type for most of the play.

Conjecture has played a large part in this investigation and cannot venture more than a possible solution. The evidence suggests that the play may have been censored, and though I cannot
                                    so proue it
        That the probation beare no Hindge nor Loope,
        To hang a doubt on,

I have, perhaps, made out a *prima facie* case to send before the high court of literary criticism.

THE VOCABULARY OF *EDWARD III*

SINCE Capel first suggested in his *Prolusions* that
Shakespeare may have a hand or at least a finger or
two in *Edward III*, there has been much throwing about
of brains on this still-vexed question. After a century
and a half of discussion we are not much nearer to a definite conclusion than Capel and his contemporaries; subjective criticism seems about as likely to fix the authorship
as to tell us what songs the Sirens sang. In some ultra-
modern critical fantasies on this theme brilliant balloons
of inference have been blown from the merest specks of
fact. Yet in the play there lies a rich heap of raw material
ready to the hands of those who are willing to do some
rather tedious work. The exceedingly interesting vocabulary has attracted little attention, though one or two critics
have arbitrarily chosen a few words from it to assist
them in buttressing some pre-conceived theory concerning
the authorship. No one has attempted a comparative
study of the vocabularies of this and other plays. I
propose to discuss briefly the full vocabulary of the play
and its relation to the vocabularies of other plays known
to have been written by the authors to whom critics have
ascribed it. I submit certain results and hope that they
will help readers to reach an opinion based on something
other than aesthetic impressions.

Using Crawford's *Concordances to Marlowe* and *Kyd*
and Schmidt's *Shakespeare Lexicon*, I give the number
of words in the plays named below and the average for
each play in its group. In addition I have given the
number of lines in each play and the average length in
lines of each play-group.

TABLE I

Title of Play.	Number of Lines.	Average Length of Plays in Each Group.	Number of Words in Play.	Average Number of Words in Each Play-Group.
1 Henry VI	2676 ⎫		2908 ⎫	
2 Henry VI	3069 ⎬ 2883		3062 ⎬	2903
3 Henry VI	2904 ⎭		2740 ⎭	
Richard II	2755 ⎫	2662	2870 ⎫	
King John	2570 ⎭		2934 ⎭	2902
1 Henry IV	2968 ⎫		3061 ⎫	
2 Henry IV	3180. ⎬ 3105		3163 ⎬	3140
Henry V	3166 ⎭		3195 ⎭	
A Midsummer-Night's Dream .	2102 ⎫		2396 ⎫	
Twelfth Night	2429 ⎬ 2182		2557 ⎬	2516
The Tempest	2015 ⎭		2595 ⎭	
Tamburlaine I	2316 ⎫		2532 ⎫	
Tamburlaine II	2330 ⎬ 2439		2418 ⎬	2449
Edward II	2670 ⎭		2398 ⎭	
Spanish Tragedy	2734 ⎫		2526 ⎫	
Soliman and Perseda	2227 ⎬ 2477		2346 ⎬	2384
Arden of Feversham	2469 ⎭		2281 ⎭	
Edward III	2498	2498	2976	2976

Notes on the above Table

1. For all the plays named except E3 and the three comedies of Shakespeare, the results are given both for each play and for a group of three plays of approximately the same date written by or attributed to the one author. Except the comedies, all these plays are histories or tragedies and have in common such themes as the court, politics, crime, war and love. Accordingly we may expect and we get considerable similarity of vocabulary, and thus may consider the difference in the number of words used to be due in the main to difference in

authorship. I have chosen the three plays of Marlowe because they have the purest texts and are least contaminated by interpolations. I have grouped together the three plays often attributed to Kyd and give figures for purpose of comparison.

2. The number of words present in a play depends upon several factors, the most important of which are the author and his theme; of smaller importance are the length of the play, unless it is exceptional, and the period of his career when the author wrote it. Usually a tragedy or history will contain more words than a comedy of the same length and date. A romantic comedy such as *The Tempest* will make larger demands upon the author's stock of words than a comedy nearer to the life of the day such as *The Merry Wives* (2,634 lines and 2,560 words). *Othello* and *King Lear* are of almost the same length and were written within a year or two of each other; *King Lear* contains 260 words more than *Othello*. Generalisations are difficult to make and not very reliable when made, but we are safe in asserting that the author and his theme will in the main determine the ratio between the length of a play and the number of words used.

3. Marlowe does not seem to have extended his vocabulary very much during the four or five years that probably elapsed between the writing of *Tamburlaine I* and *Edward II*; the latter play shows a lower ratio between the number of words and the number of lines than any other history or tragedy of this period which I have examined. He does not seem to have been a word-collector or word-maker as were so many of his contemporaries, and his stock of fresh words grew slowly. Thus of words not in Shakespeare's plays *Tamburlaine I* has 112, *Tamburlaine II* 97, and *Edward II* only 78. *King John* is exactly 100 lines shorter than *Edward II* and contains 536 words more. The two parts of *Tamburlaine* form really one play. Deducting 1482 words common to the two parts, we have a play of 4646 lines containing 3469 words. This means 406 words more than Shakespeare uses in the 3069 lines of *2 Henry VI*, 534 words more than are in the 2570 lines of *King John* and 96 words more than we find in the 3205 lines of *King Lear*.

4. Shakespeare commenced dramatist with a much larger and more varied stock of words than any of his contemporaries. Heminge and Condell edited the folio under what many modern critics would have us believe was the disadvantage of knowing more about what plays their friend wrote than any man living in 1623. If I defer to the judgment of Shakespeare's 'fellows' and accept *1 Henry VI* as substantially his, I shall ask these critics to put this opinion down to a bias in favour of facts. The three plays on *Henry VI* proved his

possession and skilful use of a larger poetic vocabulary than any other known dramatist of the time, and the large vocabularies of these plays definitely separate them from all other plays of the period ending in June, 1592. The earliest of this trilogy is practically of the same length as *Edward II*, but uses 510 more words. A glance at the figures in the Table shows that Shakespeare more than maintained his supremacy in the world of words, and when play-making was resumed after the re-opening of the theatres in 1594, he poured into each new play a copious stream of new words. In *Richard II* and *King John* he began to discard much of the poetical jargon used in common by all the dramatists, weeding out those 'high-astounding terms' that time and use had staled, and replacing them with new words, replete with freshness and the picturesque vigour of a poet's plenty; no less than 14 per cent. of the total vocabulary of *1 Henry IV* consists of words previously unused, and the percentage of new words— 554 in all—introduced into *Hamlet*, after writing 20 plays, equals 14·5 per cent. of the vocabulary that amounts to about 3800 words.

5. *Edward III* has in proportion to its length the largest vocabulary of any play belonging to the last decade of the sixteenth century that I have examined; in this respect *King John* is the only play that may challenge comparison with it. Who was the author? If the figures in the Table mean anything neither Marlowe nor Kyd had a finger in it. The suggestion that Marlowe, who, about 1592, wrote *Edward II* (2670 lines and 2398 words), also wrote in the same year or a little later *Edward III* (2498 lines and 2976 words) cracks the wind of probability. Tests made on Peele's *David and Bethsabe* and Green's *Friar Bacon* indicate that the stock of words used by either of these dramatists was inferior in number to that of Marlowe; this conclusion is confirmed by other tests such as the comparatively small number of uncommon words and compound forms present in their plays. Critics have a habit of cutting plays such as *Edward III* into pieces, and of assigning arbitrarily portions to Marlowe, Greene, Peele, Kyd, Heywood, or others, but the great size of the vocabulary of *Edward III* makes it impossible for us to accept joint authorship as a reasonable explanation of the variations in the quality of various parts. Elizabethan collaboration in play-writing usually meant that each man wrote a few scenes. Accordingly the total number of words used by two, three or more collaborators in writing a play could not possibly exceed the number that would have been used by the author with the largest vocabulary if he had written the whole of the play instead of a part. If we must

pick from known dramatists one literary parent for this nameless waif, Shakespeare is the man. Each of his plays on English history, not alone those written prior to 1596, but those written subsequently, has a vocabulary comparable in size to that of *Edward III*; as far as vocabulary goes, this play fits naturally into his series of historical plays, and is a misfit if placed among Marlowe's, Greene's, Peele's or Kyd's. The author of *Edward III*, however, may be an unknown man. A large vocabulary may co-exist with a small amount of poetic and dramatic power. I do not think, nor do I imply, that *1 Henry VI* is a better play than *Edward II* because it contains several hundreds of words more; but the possession of an unusually large stock of words is a rare and well-marked literary characteristic, unlikely to be common to two dramatic authors of this short period.

I shall next discuss briefly the inter-relation of the vocabularies of certain plays named below. The facts are set out in the following table, which gives in separate columns the number of words common to selected pairs of plays and the percentage of the total vocabulary of one play which is present in another.

TABLE II

Plays Compared.	Number of Words in Common.	Percentage of Vocabularies Common.		
A. *E.III* and *1 H.VI* .	1604	53·7	per cent. of words in	*E.III*
E.III and *2 H.VI* .	1679	56·4	,, ,,	,,
E.III and *3 H.VI* .	1571	52·4	,, ,,	,,
E.III and *R.II* ..	1558	52·3	,, ,,	,,
E.III and *John.* ..	1539	51·7	,, ,,	,,
E.III and *Tam. I* .	1412	47·4	,, ,,	,,
E.III and *E.II* . ..	1352	45·4	,, ,,	,,
B. *1 H.VI* and *2 H.VI*	1603	55·2	per cent. of words in	*1 H.VI*
1 H.VI and *3 H.VI*	1480	50·9	,, ,,	*1 H.VI*
2 H.VI and *3 H.VI*	1614	59·0	,, ,,	*3 H.VI*
R.II and *John.* ..	1544	53·8	,, ,,	*R.II*
Tam. I and *Tam. II*	1482	58·5	,, ,,	*Tam. I*
Tam. I and *E.II* ..	1280	50·0	,, ,,	*Tam. I*
C. *1 H.IV* and *2 H.IV*	1591	52·2	per cent. of words in	*1 H.IV*
1 H.IV and *H.V* ..	1550	50·8	,, ,,	*1 H.IV*
2 H.IV and *H.V* ..	1624	51·3	,, ,,	*2 H.IV*
M.N.D. and *Temp.*	1046	42·6	,, ,,	*M.N.D.*

N.B.—The number of words present in each play is given in Table I.

Shakespeare and the Homilies

Notes on Table II

1. All our early dramatists seem to have drawn upon what amounted to a common dramatic vocabulary; in fact, the extraordinary similarity of the language used in the tragedies and histories written during the period 1587-1594 tends to cover up and make almost useless for critical purposes the small differences in the use of words due to difference of authorship. Consequently attempts made to find an author or authors for any of the numerous anonymous plays printed during these years or shortly afterwards must ultimately rest, not on clues from vocabulary or phrases, but on the most variable and elusive of tests, the subjective impressions of the critic.

2. The number of words common to any two plays will depend on a variety of conditions. Two plays written on the same theme by the same author will have a larger portion of their vocabularies common than if each play had a different author. It is equally obvious that an author possessing a small vocabulary must repeat more of his words than an author having a larger and more original stock of words. Two comedies or two tragedies written by the same man within a few months would exhibit a closer likeness in vocabulary than if some years had separated the composition of the first from that of the second. We do not expect much resemblance between the vocabulary of a tragedy and that of a comedy even if the one author wrote both. Compare the high percentage of words common to *2 Henry VI* and *3 Henry VI* or to *Tamburlaine I* and *Tamberlaine II* with the lower percentage of words common to *1 Henry VI* and *3 Henry VI* or to *Tamburlaine I* and *E.II*. When Shakespeare burst the bonds imposed by his use of the restricted vocabulary customary with his predecessors, and began to range freely in the treasury of our tongue the percentage of words common to two plays written in rapid sequence fell and continued to fall. The process of re-stocking began in *R.II* and *John* which have 53·8 per cent. of their words the same, continued in *1 Henry IV* and *2 Henry IV* which have 52·2 per cent. of their vocabularies common and in *2 Henry IV* and *Henry V,* for which the percentage falls to 51·3 per cent. Some years afterwards we find that *King Lear* has about 46 per cent. of its words in common with *Othello* though not much more than a year separated the composition of these plays. Reference to the table shows that *A Midsummer Night's Dream* has only 42·6 per cent. of its words in the *Tempest*.

3. Crawford remarked in his introduction to his *Concordance to Marlowe* on the close resemblance of the vocabulary of *E.III*

224

to that of *1 Henry VI*; he probably had in mind the considerable number of unusual words common to both plays. Reference to division A of the table shows that each of the plays on *Henry VI, King John* and *Richard II* contains far more words in common with *Edward III* than does any one of the plays of Marlowe. All critics agree that pairs of plays such as *Tamburlaine I* and *Tamburlaine II* or *2 Henry VI* and *3 Henry VI* or *1 Henry IV* and *2 Henry IV* were written by their respective authors in rapid sequence, and will look upon the high percentage of common vocabulary present in each pair as additional confirmation of inferences based on external evidence, language, style, verse, and theme. Now the percentage of words common to *Edward III* and *2 Henry VI* is very slightly lower than the percentage common to *Tamburlaine I* and *Tamburlaine II* and to *2 Henry VI* and *3 Henry VI*, and is considerably in excess of the percentage common to *1 Henry IV* and *2 Henry IV*. May we logically reverse the reasoning process and conclude that *2 Henry VI* and *Edward III* have the same author because these two plays have the very high percentage of 56·4 of their words in common? Such an inference receives strong support from the close inter-relation of *Edward III* and the five plays, *1 Henry VI, 2 Henry VI, 3 Henry VI, Richard II* and *King John*. *Edward III* is more closely linked in the matter of vocabulary to *Richard II* than is *1 Henry VI* to *3 Henry VI* or *Tamburlaine I* to *Edward II* or *1 Henry IV* to *Henry V* or *2 Henry IV* to *Henry V*.

4. Critics who ascribe *Edward III* to Marlowe have much to explain. The percentage of feminine endings present is very much higher than in any of his signed plays; I shall suggest an explanation of the presence of the fourteen per cent. present in his translation of Lucan. We must also have answers to two questions. Why did Marlowe insert in *Edward III* such a large percentage of words found in five plays written by Shakespeare? Why is there so low a percentage of words common to *Edward III* and his three signed plays? If we follow many critics and accept Marlowe as author of the plays on *Henry VI* and of *Edward III* we have a satisfactory explanation of the close interrelation of these plays in respect of vocabulary. But these critics are not out of the wood. They must explain why 56·4 per cent. of the vocabulary of *Edward III* is present in *2 Henry VI* and only 45·4 per cent. in *Edward II*, though both *2 Henry VI* and *Edward II* were written probably about 1592. They must also explain why 51·7 per cent. of the vocabulary of Marlowe's *Edward III* is found in Shakespeare's *King John*, and only 45·4 per cent. of the words of Marlowe's *Edward III* in Marlowe's *Edward II*.

P

My inquiry has resulted in the discovery of several important facts, which I briefly summarize.

(i) *Edward III* has a larger vocabulary than any other contemporary play of equal length examined.

(ii) Only Shakespeare's plays have vocabularies equal or superior in size to that of *Edward III*. The vocabularies of Marlowe's three plays average 520 words per play less than that of *Edward III*.

(iii) The vocabularies of the plays on *Henry VI* match in size those of *Richard II, King John* and *1 Henry IV*.

(iv) Far more words present in *Edward III* are also found in each of the plays on *Henry VI*, in *Richard II* and *King John* than are found in any signed play of Marlowe's.

(v) The percentage of words common to *Edward III* and *2 Henry VI* is comparable in size to that for *2 Henry VI* and *3 Henry VI* or that for *Tambulaine I* and *Tamburlaine II*; also the percentage of words common to *Edward III* and *Richard II* or to *Edward III* and *King John* is equal or superior to the percentage of words common to *1 Henry IV* and *2 Henry IV* or to *2 Henry IV* and *Henry V*.

So far my facts and conclusions have come either from the total numbers of words present in the chosen plays or from about half of these totals. I propose next to collect and examine some large groups of words present in these plays; I shall then discuss the question whether the results for *Edward III* lead us to Shakespeare or Marlowe. I have grouped together all the words in each play which begin with the more important prefixes. The prefixes selected were ad-, be-, con-, de-, dis-, en-, ex-, for-, in-, out-, over-, per-, pre-, pro-, re-, sub-, and un-, with the variants occurring before varying consonants.

Vocabulary of Edward III

I have grouped together and averaged the totals for the plays on *Henry VI*, for *King John* and *Richard II*, and for the three plays of Marlowe's in order that no undue stress may be placed upon occasional or abnormal results.

TABLE III
WORDS BEGINNING WITH THE PREFIXES NAMED

Prefix.	1 H.VI	2 H.VI	3 H.VI	Average.	R.II	John	Average.	Tam. I.	Tam. II	E.II	Average.	E.III
ad-	47	46	35	43	46	36	41	35	29	36	33	45
be-	29	35	31	32	31	29	30	21	16	24	20	28
con-	74	68	48	63	61	65	63	52	44	45	47	67
de-	45	41	42	43	43	41	42	26	25	27	26	42
dis-	42	33	28	34	49	36	43	28	20	18	22	45
en-	31	20	16	22	24	23	23	28	20	18	22	44
ex-	26	26	14	22	19	21	20	23	21	13	19	21
for-	13	15	19	16	14	15	14	6	4	10	7	7
in-	56	46	50	50	43	52	48	45	51	37	46	46
out- ⎱ .. .. over- ⎰	21	14	15	17	11	15	13	12	8	19	13	12
per-	14	11	13	13	11	18	14	14	10	·10	11	16
pre-	19	14	18	17	12	9	10	13	10	10	11	13
pro-	32	25	21	26	23	24	24	18	12	13	14	26
re-	60	63	57	60	62	60	61	48	51	61	53	63
sub-	30	31	27	29	25	14	20	20	19	19	19	26
un-	30	34	31	32	52	38	45	16	14	27	19	34
Totals . ..	569	522	465	519	526	496	511	405	354	389	382	535

Notes on Table III

(i) The first part of *Henry VI* may be considered by itself; in no other of 28 plays examined by me does this group of words constitute so large a portion of the total vocabulary. The number of words in *1 Henry VI* exceeds the average number present in the three plays of Marlowe by 459, or not quite 19 per cent.; the number of words in *1 Henry VI* beginning with the prefixes named above exceeds the average number for the Marlowe plays by 187, or nearly 50 per cent. *Edward III* is slightly more than 2 per cent. longer than the average length of the three Marlowe plays, yet words beginning with the prefixes named are 40 per cent. in excess of the average number found in the three Marlowe plays. Such great difference in the use of this very important group of words—equal to more than a sixth of the entire vocabulary used—seems explainable only on the assumption of a difference in authorship.

(ii) We find that in *Edward III*, the three plays on *Henry VI*, and in two later plays, *Richard II* and *King John*, the percentage of the play-vocabulary consisting of the words under consideration is almost exactly the same, viz., 17·8 per cent., and is two per cent. higher than the average percentage of such words found in the vocabularies of Marlowe's three plays. Moreover, the total number of words tabulated for each of *2 Henry VI* (522) and *Richard II* (526) is practically identical with that for *Edward III* (535); a detailed examination will prove that this almost exact agreement or identity for the full total extends to the majority of the totals for each group of words beginning with one of the above prefixes. On the other hand the totals shown in the table for Marlowe's plays vary very little among themselves, but exhibit such great inferiority to those for *Edward III* and the plays of Shakespeare that we may almost disregard the possibility that Marlowe changed his vocabulary to the degree necessary for the writing of *Edward III*.

(iii) Comparison of the totals set down in the table shows *2 Henry VI*, *Richard II* and *Edward III* have almost identical totals for words beginning with the prefixes ad-, be-, con-, de-, ex-, in-, pro-, re-, and sub-; these words comprise nearly three-quarters of the total for each of these plays. The variations in the totals for words beginning with the other prefixes are not greater than might be expected. The only important difference occurs in the respective totals for words commencing with the prefix en- and its variants. The number present in *Edward III* is unusually large and exceeds that found for this type of word in any other play whose vocabulary has come under my review. Experimenting with a certain type of word in one play is a habit of Shakespeare's, and has led certain critics astray. Thus 57 words or about two per cent. of the total vocabulary of *3 Henry VI* consists of adjectives ending in the suffixes -ful or -less; in *Henry V* I find 96 adverbs formed from adjectives or participles by adding the suffix -ly. We find no less than 44 words ending with the suffix -ment in *Hamlet* or almost double the number present in

228

any other play; and *Lear* uses 42, and *Cymbeline* 47 words concluding with the suffix -ness.

(iv) The totals for Shakespeare's five plays of words beginning with the prefixes be-, con-, de-, and un- exhibit high differences from the corresponding totals present in Marlowe's three plays. The author of *Edward III* in his aggregates of such words agrees far more nearly with the averages for the plays on *Henry VI* or for *Richard II* and *King John* than with the averages for the plays of Marlowe. Shakespeare had a liking for verbs beginning with be-, and coined 26 such words, one of which, *bethump,* is in *King John.* Marlowe uses these formations more sparingly and did not coin one; he has only one more word of this type in his three plays than we find in *Richard II* and *King John.* The difference between Marlowe's and Shakespeare's plays in the totals of words commencing with the prefix de- is very marked, and constitutes a distinctive difference in the vocabularies of the two authors. Shakespeare averages for the history plays and the great tragedies 40 a play, or about the number found in *Edward III.* He has an especial liking for words beginning with the prefix un-; they amount to about 4 per cent. of his total vocabulary, and the large number that he has invented helps us to differentiate his plays from those of his predecessors and contemporaries such as Marlowe, Greene, Peele, Kyd, Chapman, Fletcher and others. Beginning a short survey with *2 Henry VI* we discover that he inserted some such words of his own coinage in almost every play; there are seven in *2 Henry VI,* three in *3 Henry VI,* five in *Lucrece,* eight in *Richard II,* eight in *King John,* seventeen in *Hamlet,* and so forth. I count only four in the seven plays of Marlowe, there being one each in *Tamburlaine I, Tamburlaine II* and *Edward II;* Greene has three in his five plays and his poems, and Peele three in his works. My list shows that *Richard II* has almost as many words commencing with un- as we find in both parts of *Tamburlaine* and *Edward II* taken together— yet we have critics who assign *Richard II* to Marlowe! *Edward III* has 34 words beginning with un-, of which three are new to literature. Thus once again we are led to Shakespeare rather than to Marlowe.

A glimmer of light may be thrown upon this question by a brief study of the use made by Marlowe and by Shakespeare of words ending in certain suffixes. Below is a table containing for each play named under a separate heading the total number of :

I. *Adjectives* ending in the suffixes -able, -ant, -ary, -ate, -ent, -ful, -ible, -ish, -ive, -less, -ous, and -y.
II. *Nouns* ending in the suffixes -ance, -ence, -er, -ment, -or, and -tion.
III. *Adverbs* ending in -ly.

I have grouped plays by Marlowe and Shakespeare in threes, except for *Richard II* and *King John*. I have added a column giving the percentage which the total for each play is of the entire vocabulary.

TABLE IV

WORDS ENDING WITH CERTAIN SUFFIXES

Plays.	No. of Adjectives.	Average for Group.	No. of Nouns.	Average for Group.	No. of Adverbs.	Average for Group.	Total for Play.	Average for Group.	Percentage of Play Vocabulary.
Tam. I ..	163 ⎫		107 ⎫		43 ⎫		313 ⎫		12·36
Tam. II ..	156 ⎬	148	84 ⎬	92	37 ⎬	42	277 ⎬	282	11·45
E.II	124 ⎭		84 ⎭		47 ⎭		255 ⎭		10·63
1 H.VI ..	190 ⎫		137 ⎫		47 ⎫		374 ⎫		12·86
2 H.VI ..	209 ⎬	197	141 ⎬	133	57 ⎬	53	407 ⎬	383	13·58
3 H.VI ..	191 ⎭		121 ⎭		55 ⎭		367 ⎭		13·39
E.III	199	199	128	128	58	58	385	385	12·93
R.II	179 ⎫		142 ⎫		70 ⎫		391 ⎫		12·62
John.	191 ⎭	185	162 ⎭	152	79 ⎭	74	432 ⎭	412	14·73
1 H.IV ..	161 ⎫		189 ⎫		76 ⎫		426 ⎫		13·91
2 H.IV ..	154 ⎬	164	201 ⎬	202	75 ⎬	82	430 ⎬	449	13·60
H.V	176 ⎭		218 ⎭		96 ⎭		492 ⎭		15·34

Vocabulary of Edward III

(i) The figures given in the table show that on the average *Edward III* and the three plays on *Henry VI* contain over a third more words of the type included than the plays of Marlowe, and that *Richard II* and *King John* average not quite half as many again. After making such adjustments as would eliminate the effects due to differences in the size of the vocabularies of the plays the advantage of *Edward III* and Shakespeare's plays over Marlowe's ranges from 12 to 25 per cent.

(ii) The same conclusion as in (i) is expressed less strikingly in the figures of the column giving the percentage of the total vocabulary which words ending in the suffixes named constitute in each play. The plays on *Henry VI* and *Edward III* average 1·7 per cent. more such words than Marlowe's plays and the five later histories of Shakespeare 2·8 per cent. more. If we assume that four years elapsed between the writing of *Tamburlaine I* and *Edward II* we perceive that Marlowe definitely reduced in successive plays not only the total number of words ending in the suffixes named but also the percentage of such words present in the vocabulary of his last play. On the other hand, in the four years that may have separated the composition of *2 Henry VI* and *King John*, Shakespeare definitely increased both the total number of these words and the proportion of them present in the vocabulary. Marlowe decreased adjectives and nouns in about the same ratio, keeping the adverbs about the same; in *Richard II, King John* and subsequent plays we notice a slight fall in the number of adjectives which is more than counterbalanced by the great and continuous increase in the number of nouns and adverbs.

(iii) Unusually large differences between the plays of Marlowe and those of Shakespeare occur in the totals for words ending certain suffixes. Thus the plays of Marlowe average per play 37 adjectives ending in -ble and -y, the plays on *Henry VI* 62 a play; *Edward III* has 62. Marlowe's plays average 47 words a play for agent nouns ending in -er and -or, and abstract nouns ending in -ance and -ence; the corresponding average for such nouns in the plays on *Henry VI* is 77 per play. *Edward III* has 62.

(iv) I have said that Shakespeare gradually abandoned much of the poetical jargon common to the early dramatists and restocked his vocabulary with words rare in poetry or new to literature. In the plays on *Henry IV* and *Henry V*, are

231

continued two processes which he began in *Richard II* and *King John,* the first, a diminution in the number of adjectives ending in the suffixes -ful, -less, -ous and -y, and the second, a much freer use, especially in poetry, of nouns ending in -er, -ment, -or and -tion. Thus *2 Henry VI* has 148 adjectives and 106 nouns ending in one or other of these suffixes, whilst in *Henry V* the poet practically reverses these totals with 102 adjectives and 153 nouns. His gradual increase in poetry of nouns ending in -tion is worth notice, because Puttenham in his *Arte of English Poesie,* first printed in 1589, attacks the use of such words in verse. 'Chiefly in your courtly ditties,' he says, 'Take heede ye vse not these maner of long polisillables and specially that ye finish not your verse with them as retribution restitution remuneration recapitulation and such like; for they smatch more the schoole of common players than of any delicate Poet Lyricke or Elegiacke.'[1] Elsewhere he remarks, 'some wordes of exceeding great length, which have bene fetched from the Latine ink horne or borrowed of strangers, the use of them in ryme is nothing pleasant, saving perchaunce to common people, who reioyse much to be at playes and enterludes—and therefore be as well satisfied with that which is grosse, as with any other finer and more delicate.'[2] Shakespeare did not pay much attention to theorizing on the language of poetry. He has 33 'long polisillables,' ending in -tion in *3 Henry VI,* 51 in *Richard II,* 64 in *King John,* 80 in *2 Henry IV,* 86 in *Othello* and 103 in *Hamlet.* *Edward III* has 46, ten more than the average for the plays of *Henry VI.*

(v) The totals found in *Edward III* for adjectives, nouns and adverbs ending in the above suffixes are in remarkable agreement with those for *2 Henry VI* and *3 Henry VI;* they exceed the highest totals for any of Marlowe's plays by nearly 25 per cent. The aggregate for *Edward III* is only two more than that for *Richard II;* the differences in the group totals are not more than might be expected in two plays written by the one man.

A comparative study of the compound words in *Edward III* and other plays makes possible some interesting inferences. Compounds form about 4·6 per cent. of the total vocabulary of Shakespeare's early plays and

1. *Arber's Reprint,* p. 140.
2. *Ibid.,* pp. 95-6.

about 3·5 per cent. of the words in Marlowe's, Greene's and Peele's plays. I give separate lists for the plays and the poems of each author. The 5 plays of Shakespeare included in (a) are *1 H.VI, 2 H.VI, 3 H.VI, R.III* and *Titus,* the 4 plays in (b) are *Love's Labour's Lost, Romeo and Juliet, King John,* and *Richard II.*

TABLE V

COMPOUND WORDS

A. PLAYS Author.	No. of Plays.	Total No. of Lines in Plays.	No. of Compounds.	No. of Adjectival Compounds.	Percentage of Adjectival Compounds.		
Shakespeare (a) ..	5	14,771	641	292	45·6	per cent.	
„ (b) ..	4	10,965	580	259	44·7	„	„
Marlowe	7	14,955	464	159	34·3	„	„
Greene	5	10,379	326	77	23·6	„	„
Peele	4	7,070	219	66	30·1	„	„
Edward III		2,498	136	58	42·6	„	„
B. POEMS							
Venus and Lucrece		3,049	226	160	70·8	per cent.	
Hero and Leander . } *Ovid and Lucan ..* }		4,178	263	160	60·8	„	„
Greene's Poems ..		3,366	119	57	47·9	„	„
Peele's Poems . ..		2,451	101	49	48·5	„	„

In poems Shakespeare uses a somewhat higher proportion of compound words than Marlowe, who in his turn employs them more freely than Greene or Peele. In drama, Marlowe and Peele have about the same proportion of compounds; reference to the table shows that in the plays grouped in (a) Shakespeare uses 40 per cent. more compounds than Marlowe, in the plays grouped in (b) 70 per cent. more; calculations are made on the basis of equality in the number of lines. The above table suggests two important and well-defined characteristics which serve to differentiate early Shakespearean drama from the signed work of his predecessors and contemporaries. The first is the higher percentage of compound words already mentioned. The second and more significant is the difference in the percentage and use of adjectival compounds. The total number of these in the five plays grouped in (a) is almost equal to the combined total for the 16 plays of Marlowe, Greene and Peele. The disparity is even more marked if we compare the total of 259 such compounds for the 10,965 lines contained in the 4 plays included in (b) with the total of 302 for the 32,404 lines in the 16 dramas of his predecessors. This freer use of adjectival compounds is an essential element of Shakespeare's style in his early undoubted plays, and critics who dispute the authenticity of the plays included in (a) will need all their ingenuity to find a satisfactory explanation. It would seem that in his use of compounds the language of Shakespeare's early plays does not differ very much from the language of his long poems. I suggest that *Venus* and *Lucrece* were written during the plague years 1592-4 after he had done some dramatic work and at a time when the making of plays was suspended. Marlowe, on the other hand, seems to have thought the language of his translations of Ovid and Lucan and of *Hero and Leander* unsuitable for drama, and I suggest that he deliberately cut down the proportion of adjectival compounds. It may be remarked that the ratio of the number of compounds other than adjectival to the number of lines does not vary much for the four dramatists. The following table exhibits the subdivision of compound words found in the plays of Marlowe and Shakespeare into two main groups.

TABLE VI

COMPOUNDS IN PLAYS NAMED

Play.	No. of Compounds.	Average per Play-Group.	No. of Adjectival Compounds.	Average per Play-Group.	Compounds Other than Adjectival.	Average per Play-Group.
Tamburlaine I ..	83 ⎫		40 ⎫		43 ⎫	
Tamburlaine II .	73 ⎬	81	25 ⎬	31	48 ⎬	49
Edward II . ..	86 ⎭		29 ⎭		57 ⎭	
1 Henry VI . ..	127 ⎫		55 ⎫		72 ⎫	
2 Henry VI . ..	137 ⎬	129	57 ⎬	57	80 ⎬	72
3 Henry VI . ..	123 ⎭		59 ⎭		64 ⎭	
Richard II . ..	110 ⎫		62 ⎫		48 ⎫	
John	122 ⎬	116	62 ⎬	62	60 ⎬	54
Edward III . ..	136	136	58	58	78	78

Notes on this Table

(i) I have chosen the three plays of Marlowe in which word-compounds are the most numerous; there are only 65 compound adjectives in his other four plays. This table seems to exhibit the comparative poverty of his plays in compound words; but, if we take into account the difference in average length, the three chosen plays of Marlowe have proportionately almost the same number of compound words other than adjectival as have the five plays of Shakespeare. *Edward III* and the three plays on *Henry VI*, however, average 54 per cent. more adjectival compounds than do the three plays of Marlowe, and *Richard II* and *King John* average between 80 and 90 per cent. more. These calculations make the necessary allowance for variations in the lengths of the plays. Compound adjectives, particularly such as end in participles are, in the main, the invention of the poet in whose works they are found; in the number, percentage, and variety of these formations Marlowe's plays fall far below *Edward III* and the plays on *Henry VI*.

(ii) I need not labour the point that *Edward III* must be grouped with the plays of Shakespeare, if we are to be guided by the results given in the above table.

More than three-fourths of the compound adjectives present in the early dramas of Shakespeare are either compounds of the parasynthetic type or end in a past or present participle. The latter group constitutes more than half of the adjectival compounds and may be sub-divided into two main groups as will appear in the subjoined table. The plays and poems of Shakespeare are those enumerated in Table V.

TABLE VII
COMPOUND PARTICIPIAL ADJECTIVES

A. POEMS

Author.	No. of Lines.	No. of Compound Adjectives.	Total No. of Participial Adjectives.	Noun, Adj. or Adverb + Present Participle.	Noun, Adj. or Adverb + Past Participle.	Total No. of Compounds Noun + Participle.
Shakespeare	3,049	160	98	49	49	31
Marlowe	4,178	160	109	37	72	55
Greene	3,366	57	30	11	19	9
Peele	2,451	49	35	8	27	4
Totals		426	272	105	167	99

B. PLAYS

Author.	No. of Lines.	No. of Compound Adjectives.	Total No. of Participial Adjectives.	Noun, Adj. or Adverb + Present Participle.	Noun, Adj. or Adverb + Past Participle.	Total No. of Compounds Noun + Participle.
Shakespeare (a) ..	14,771	292	165	68	97	46
„ (b) ..	10,965	259	150	57	93	48
Marlowe	14,955	159	77	22	55	13
Greene	10,379	77	46	11	35	5
Peele	7,070	66	25	2	23	1
Totals (omitting (b))		594	313	103	210	65
Edward III	2,498	58	37	23	14	9

A. Poems

The percentage of compound participial adjectives present in Shakespeare's poems, if calculated on the total number of compounds present (see Table V) is slightly in excess of that for the poetry of Marlowe; the figures given in the above table suggest a superiority the other way. Except for the obvious facts that Shakespeare uses compounds with a present participle more freely than Marlowe and that the latter employs considerably more compounds with the past participle, not much difference exists in their use of such compounds in poetry.

B. *Plays*

We may, I think, exclude both Greene and Peele from the list of possible authors of *Edward III* merely on the figures given for their poems and plays in the above table. They do not favour the use of compound epithets either in poems or the drama. Greene's total of 77 for his five plays compares very unfavourably with the 58 found in *Edward III*; Peele's total of 66 in four plays does not read much better. Greene has 46 participial compounds all told, but no less than fifteen occur in *The Looking Glass* in which Lodge had a share; there are then eight a-piece for each of his other four plays. This number is insignificant when contrasted with the 37 participial adjectives present in *Edward III*. Both Greene and Peele belong to the earlier school of poets and in their plays and poems make a very sparing use of compounds ending in a present participle. Greene has 22 altogether in 13,745 lines of poetry and drama, Peele only 10 in 9521 lines; *Edward III* has 23 such compounds in 2498 lines. Finally, the almost entire absence of compound adjectives consisting of a noun followed by a participle in the plays of Peele and in those of Greene (except in *The Looking Glass*) tells almost decisively against any possibility that either of those dramatists wrote *Edward III* in which nine such compounds occur.

Marlowe's early use and subsequent disuse of compound adjectives ending in a participle present an interesting problem for solution. We find a considerable number of such compound epithets in his poetry, but he appears to have restricted deliberately the use of such formations in his plays. Only twenty-two compounds ending in a present participle are present in his seven plays, distributed as follows:—Three each in *Tamburlaine II, Faustus, Dido* and *Jew of Malta,* one each in *Edward II* and *Massacre at*

237

Paris, and eight (all but one semi-compounds beginning with ' ever,' and ' never ') in *Tamburlaine I.* Shakespeare has eight compounds ending in a present participle in *1 Henry VI,* 14 in *2 Henry VI,* 13 in *3 Henry VI,* 23 in *Richard III,* and 10 in *Titus*; the same type appears freely in succeeding plays, e.g., 10 in *Comedy of Errors,* 17 in *Love's Labour's Lost,* 14 in *Richard II,* 16 in *Romeo and Juliet,* and 10 in *King John.* The presence of twenty-three such compounds in *Edward III* tells almost as strongly against the authorship of Marlowe as against that of Greene or Peele; Shakespeare is the only known dramatist of the time who uses these formations with the necessary freedom in plays. Unlike Greene and Peele who use these epithets very seldom even in their poetry, Marlowe seems to show a liking for them in his translations and his long poem; it may be said that he was making an experiment with participial epithets in *Edward III.* I venture to suggest that Marlowe introduced compounds with present participles into his translations for the same reason as caused him to fill the blank verse of Lucan with some fourteen per cent. of feminine endings; he was undertaking translation from a foreign tongue under the stress of a self-imposed restriction. In attempting line-for-line versions of Ovid's *Amores* and of Lucan's *Pharsalia,* Book I, he thrust himself into the tightest of metrical strait-jackets; his task was to compress a fifteen or sixteen-syllable Latin hexameter line into a ten-syllable line of English blank verse. Accordingly ' Amore capta ' becomes *love-snared*—a gain of three syllables, ' nocte volantis ' becomes *night-flying*—a gain of two syllables, and so on. The poet must have shuddered at the cacophonies of the translator. Hence arose from necessity that large percentage of eleven-syllable lines in the translation of Lucan; and to this cause we must attribute the fifteen per cent. of eleven-syllabled rhymed couplets in his translation of Ovid. The blank verse of *Tamburlaine* and *Edward II* shows us the verse that he wrote as a poet freed from metrical shackles; the verse of Lucan is largely a study in the art of compression.

Vocabulary of Edward III

We have seen that in his plays Marlowe drastically reduced both the number and the proportion of compound adjectives ending in a present participle; and he almost completely discarded compounds consisting of a noun followed by a past or present participle. In his poems this type of compound is numerous, there being 55 out of 109 compounds ending in participles or about one-half. I have suggested in the preceding paragraph a reason for the excessive use of such formations. In his plays they number 13, but 8 of these are in *Dido*, and only 5 in the remaining six plays; we may assume, therefore, that Nashe, a famous maker of 'boystrous compound wordes,' may be responsible for their appearance in that play. Peele has not one in his plays and only 4 in his poems; Greene has 5 in his 5 plays (4 in *The Looking Glass*) and 9 in his poems. Kyd has none in *The Spanish Tragedy* and 6 in *Cornelia*, a translation from the French and not intended for the public stage. Shakespeare uses this type of compound indifferently in poetry or drama. In his poems they number 31 out of 98 compound participial adjectives, in his 5 early plays 46 out of a total of 165 such compounds, and in 5 succeeding plays 67 out of a total of 169. There are 7 in *1 Henry VI*, 8 in *2 Henry VI*, 8 in *3 Henry VI*, 15 in *Richard III* and 8 in *Titus*; in plays written two or three years afterwards we find 9 in *Love's Labour's Lost*, 16 in *Richard II*, 14 in *Romeo and Juliet* and 9 in *King John*. *Edward III* has 9 such compounds, and thus fits well in either of the above groups, but would seem misplaced among the plays of Marlowe.

Many modern critics are inclined to accept the second scene of the first act and the whole of the second as Shakespeare's work. These scenes amount to almost exactly one-third of the play; let us call this third A (836 lines), and the other two-thirds B (1,662 lines). It may be of interest to state how the rarer words present in the vocabulary are distributed between A and B. I find that 124 words of *Edward III* are not found in any of Shakespeare's works; 54 of these are in A, 70 in B.

Another 112 words of *Edward III* occur in only one of Shakespeare's plays or poems; of these 49 are in A and 63 in B. Thus of 236 'rare' words 103, instead of the expected 79, occur in the scenes attributed to Shakespeare, and 133, instead of 157, in the rest of the play. I find also that *Edward III* contains 50 words 'new' to our language, of which 24 (instead of the expected 17) are found in A, and 26 (instead of the calculated 33) in B. The types of 'new' main-word present in A, e.g., *encouch, foragement, abide* (n.), *soar* (n.), *snaily, vasture,* and the three new words beginning with un- suggest the way of the young Shakespeare with words. Marlowe has no nouns new to literature ending in the suffixes -ment or -ture and, as was stated above, did not invent many words commencing with un-; tests such as these, however, being based on fragmentary data, can at best, lead to doubtful inferences. We must not neglect, however, some evidence which points to homogeneous authorship of the two parts. I have said *Edward III* contains 37 adjectival compounds with a participle. These are distributed 13 in A, 24 in B, or practically in the ratio of the respective lengths of A and B. The sound inference would be either that the two parts have the same author, or that, if two collaborators worked upon the play, both used such compounds freely and in the same way. The second inference is contrary to the known facts, and implies the existence of an unknown dramatist who played the excessively sedulous ape to Shakespeare. Twenty-three of the 37 adjectival compounds end in a present participle; 10 are found in A, 13 in B. If we assume that Shakespeare wrote A, we have a satisfactory explanation of the presence in it of ten compounds of this type; but if we assume another author for B, then we must look for a dramatist who has left us some proof that he was likely to have used thirteen such formations in 1662 lines of drama. My figures have proved that all known contemporary playwrights except Shakespeare used this type of compound very sparingly. Accordingly, if we must father B upon some author known to us we are forced to suggest Shakespeare. The other possibility is to accept the facts, confess our ignorance, and permit the play to remain authorless.

It will not have escaped the notice even of critics in whom the mass of arithmetical calculation may have induced somnolence that the facts and arguments adduced in favour of the Shakespearean authorship of *Edward III* apply with much greater force to a thesis which I firmly support—that Shakespeare wrote the plays on *Henry VI* and that the lines contributed by Marlowe are as many as the snakes in Ireland. When we consider the length of the plays, most unusual for that period, the large size of their vocabularies, the close inter-relations of these not only with those of *Venus* and *Lucrece* but with those of such undoubted plays as *Richard II* and *King John,* the almost exact agreement of *1 Henry VI* and *2 Henry VI* with *Richard II* and *King John* not only in the total but in the distribution of about 450 words commencing with certain prefixes, the high number of compound words and in especial the exceedingly high percentage of compound epithets in these plays, the peculiarly Shakespearean use of compounds ending in present participles, and many other important differences in respect of vocabulary from the plays of his predecessors, we are forced to conclude that not Marlowe, not Greene, not Kyd, not Peele wrote these plays but the man whom Heminge and Condell declare to have been the author.

I have taken care to present figures which I trust are accurate and may be checked by any one who has time and patience; my conclusions are, I think, reasonable inferences from the facts at my disposal. If I have not wandered far into the illimitable forest of conjecture, my excuse must be that I have

heard great argument
About it and about! but evermore
Came out by the same door where in I went.

What Shakespearean study needs at present is more facts and fewer guesses.

SHAKESPEARE AND THE VOCABULARY OF
THE TWO NOBLE KINSMEN

RECENTLY I re-read *The Two Noble Kinsmen* and came to the conclusion that editors of Shakespeare's plays might fairly be asked to justify the exclusion of this play from a canon that includes *Pericles*. Whatever effect may be produced on the mind, ear and feelings by a careful reading aloud of the third, fourth and fifth acts of *Pericles,* much the same or even greater effect must follow an equally attentive perusal of certain scenes of *The Two Noble Kinsmen*; I could not but think that I was listening to the voice and music of the master, to the language and verse of the man who wrote *Coriolanus, Antony and Cleopatra, The Winter's Tale* and *The Tempest.* In the hope of helping to make it clear that Shakespeare had a hand in writing this play, I decided to make a more thorough examination of the vocabulary than had previously been made, and I now submit the main results of this work. My conclusion is that Shakespeare wrote those scenes of the play which the subjective impressions of competent critics assign to him, viz., Act I; Act III, Scene 1; and Act V except the second scene, or 1091 lines in all. Fletcher or his ghost wrote the rest of the play, amounting to 1681 lines. Let us call Shakespeare's Part A, Fletcher's Part B. The vocabulary was examined in the following way. I selected from the play about 1000 of the rarer words or about a third of the total vocabulary, keeping in separate lists the words belonging to Part A and Part B. My experience with the vocabularies of nearly 80 plays makes it practically certain that all the ' rarer ' words of the play appear in one or other list. Though Part A amounts to less than two-fifths of the play I found it necessary to select more words from it than from Part B. Having gathered my raw material, I used Schmidt's

Vocabulary of Two Noble Kinsmen

Shakespeare Lexicon to reduce the number of the chosen words by classifying them in certain groups on the principle adopted in Table I. One hundred and eighty-eight words were not in the lexicon; of these 111 were in the 1091 lines of A, 77 in the 1681 lines of B—a surprising result and the reverse of what might have been anticipated. Next I used the *New English Dictionary* to find how many of the 188 words were new to our literature— ' new ' words I shall hereafter term them—and I further subdivided these into main words and compound words. The following tables give details of the results obtained; for comparative purposes I add corresponding figures for five plays assigned to the period 1608-11.

TABLE I

CLASSIFICATION OF THE ' RARER ' WORDS IN PLAYS NAMED

Play.	I. No. of Lines in Play.	II. No. of Words Peculiar to Play.	III. No. of Words found in 1 Other Play of Shakespeare.	IV. No. of Words Found in 2 Other Plays.	V. No. of Words Found in 3 Other Plays.	VI. Total No. of Words.
Antony and Cleopatra	3,016	231	152	103	71	557
Coriolanus	3,279	242	138	118	97	595
Cymbeline	3,264	219	132	105	94	550
The Winter's Tale . .	2,925	214	116	113	97	540
The Tempest	2,015	190	120	81	76	467
The Two Noble Kinsmen	2,772	188	107	92	74	461
A. (Shakespeare's)	1,091	111	54	52	36	253
B. (Fletcher's) . .	1,681	77	53	40	38	208

The totals in column VI of the table represent between a fifth and a sixth of the complete vocabularies of the plays named, and include almost all the compounds as well as any unusual words present. The figures given

243

for Part A, due allowance being made for its length, agree very closely with those for *The Tempest*; in this respect Part A fits well into this group of Shakespeare's plays. If we compare, however, the tabular figures for Part B with those for Part A and *The Tempest* and if we make changes in the respective totals proportional to the respective differences in length, we find that, within the range included in the table, the number of words in Part B is little more than a half of the number in Part A or *The Tempest*. The deficiency is greatest in words peculiar to Part B, that is, precisely where the conditions of the test should favour the author, for we are calculating these 'peculiar' words by using the concordance to Shakespeare, and consequently the greatest difference of vocabulary should appear in this column. The want of agreement between Parts A and B is too well maintained throughout the table to be accidental. Differences in characterization, moral tone, treatment of subject-matter, style and metre have combined to force critics into a division of the play in two parts and to postulate a different author for each part. The figures given above and other pieces of evidence drawn from the vocabulary also require the presence in the play of two authors, one of whom has a less copious and more commonplace vocabulary than the other.

The next table illustrates the rate at which Shakespeare revivified his vocabulary even during the last years of his dramatic career by a continuous inpouring of previously unused words into each new play; it also subdivides these fresh words into two groups and gives the percentage of compounds.

The number of words used by Shakespeare for the first time in a play represents an addition of this number to his stock; the ratio of the number of such words to the number of lines in the play in which they are found may be taken as a rough measure of the poet's activity in the world of words at the time of its composition.

244

TABLE II

	I.	II.	III.	IV.	V.	VI.
	No. of Lines in Play.	Total First-used Words.	Ratio of Totals in II to Totals in I.	No. of First-used Main Words.	No. of First-used Compounds.	Percentage of Compounds on Totals in II.
Antony and Cleo- *patra*	3,016	273	1 word to 11 lines	218	53	19·4
Coriolanus	3,279	267	1 „ „ 12¼ „	228	39	14·6
Cymbeline	3,264	231	1 „ „ 14 „	164	67	29·0
The Winter's *Tale*	2,925	225	1 „ „ 13 „	161	64	28·4
The Tempest ..	2,015	192	1 „ „ 10½ „	118	74	38·5
The Two Noble *Kinsmen*	2,772	188	1 „ „ 14¾ „	113	75	40·0
Part A . ..	1,091	111	1 „ „ 10 „	76	35	31·5
Part B . ..	1,681	77	1 „ „ 22 „	37	40	52·0

Perhaps it may be a measure of his imaginative and creative activity also, unless we must regard as a mere coincidence the facts that *Hamlet* and *King Lear* have not only the greatest numbers of previously unused words (equal to nearly ten per cent. of their entire vocabularies), but also have the highest ratios (calculated as in the table above) of all the plays written after 1596. *Macbeth* and *The Tempest* are not far below them in their ratios. This high proportion of previously unused words is distinctive of Shakespeare, and consequently in this respect Part A may be placed with *The Tempest* and other plays of this period. The ratio test exhibits very clearly the great difference between the two parts of the play; Part B does not belong to this period of Shakespeare's career. In the fourth and fifth columns of the table appear the totals of first-used main-words and compounds respectively. The main-words are incomparably the more important, compounds being as few or as many as the needs or whims of the author may require. It will be noticed that compounds increase as main-words decrease. The proportion of such words in Part A is rather high but is considerably lower than for *Hamlet* or *King Lear*; it agrees satisfactorily with the result for *The Tempest*. The ratio for Part B—one fresh main-word to each 45 lines of text—is I think lower than for any play of Shakespeare, and indicates the poverty of the author's vocabulary. The percentages of compounds in the sixth column illustrates the gradual reversion of the poet during the last three or four years of his working life to the more lyrical style characteristic of *Midsummer-Night's Dream, Romeo and Juliet, Richard II* and *King John*. Once more Part A may be grouped with *Cymbeline* and *Winter's Tale*. The percentage of compounds in Part B is exceeded only in *Richard II*; perhaps it would be more accurate to say that the high percentage of compounds in Part B conceals the poverty in the matter of fresh main-words. Tested by the totals of first-used words Part A and Part B are by different authors.

We must now sort out from the words peculiar to each play those which are recorded in the *New English Dictionary* as new to our literature—we may conveniently subdivide these 'new' words into two groups, main-words and compound words.

An important and unvarying characteristic of Shakespeare's vocabulary at any period of his career is the presence in his plays or poems of a large number of words previously unused not merely by himself but by any other known author—'new' words as I term them here for the sake of brevity. The numbers given for the plays in the above table are large, but are far smaller than the totals for the great

TABLE III

WORDS NEW TO OUR LITERATURE

	I.	II.	III.	IV.	V.	VI.	VII.
Plays.	No. of Words Peculiar to play.	No. of New Words.	No. of New Compounds.	Total New Words	No. of New Words Repeated from Earlier Plays.	Total New Words.	Ratio of No. of New Words to No. of Lines in Play.
A n t o n y and							
Cleopatra ..	231	51	47	98	21	119	1 new wd. to 25·4 lns.
Coriolanus . ..	242	58	31	89	22	111	1 ,, ,, 29·5 ,,
Cymbeline . ..	219	40	48	88	40	128	1 ,, ,, 25·5 ,,
The Winter's							
Tale	214	34	49	83	22	105	1 ,, ,, 27·9 ,,
The Tempest .	190	25	59	84	27	111	1 ,, ,, 18 ,,
Two N o b l e							
Kinsmen ..	188	34	47	81	25	106	1 ,, ,, 26 ,,
Part A ..	111	27	27	54	12	66	1 ,, ,, 16½ ,,
Part B ..	77	7	20	27	13	40	1 ,, ,, 42 ,,

tragedies, *Troilus and Cressida, Love's Labour's Lost, 1 Henry IV, 2 Henry IV, Henry V* and others. The various attempts to assign many of Shakespeare's plays to Marlowe, Greene, Peele, Chapman and others do not take this word-making habit of Shakespeare into account. J. M. Robertson said of Chapman, ' He is the supreme neologist among the poets '[1] of his time. Of his poetry I do not offer an opinion, but I have made a careful and methodical examination of all his signed plays. The total number of words ' new ' to literature which I have found in his twelve plays is considerably less than the combined total of ' new ' words present in *Hamlet* and *King Lear*; it is slightly less than the combined totals given in my table for *Coriolanus, Antony and Cleopatra* and *Cymbeline*. The highest

1. *Shakespeare and Chapman*, p. 54.

number of 'new' or invented words to be found in any play of Chapman's is 55, the total for *The Widow's Tears*; this includes both main-words and compounds. Nineteen of Shakespeare's plays have each over 100 'new' words or almost the double of Chapman's maximum. We may expect, therefore, that any play or any substantial portion of a play, written by Shakespeare during the years 1609 to 1613 will be found to contain a considerable number of 'new' main-words. Part A satisfies expectation in this respect, for the number of 'new' words present in it is, considering the relative lengths, almost exactly comparable to the number found in *The Tempest,* and proportionately exceeds the total in any other Shakespearean play of this period. Part B, on the other hand, contains, relatively to the respective lengths, little more than a third of the number of 'new' words found in Part A; the insignificant number (7) of 'new' main-words present is almost identical with the number (6) of 'new' main-words in the non-Shakespearean portion of *Henry VIII,* which is of about the same length, and was probably the work of Fletcher.

I now proceed to examine in detail groups of words and especially 'new' words.

About a fourth of the compound words present in *The Two Noble Kinsmen* are parasynthetic formations such as *black-haired, hard-hearted.* Shakespeare from the beginning used compounds of this type very freely; he has 350 altogether, the majority of his own coinage. He averages about ten a play, but *1 Henry IV* has 27 and *King Lear* 21. The numbers in plays written c. 1608-1612 are 4 in *Coriolanus,* 13 in *Antony and Cleopatra,* 11 in *Cymbeline,* 6 in *The Winter's Tale* and 10 in *The Tempest.* Part A has ten, all but two not in the Shakespeare concordance, viz., *bright-habited, clear-spirited, high-speeded, maiden-hearted, scythe-tuskt, best-tempered, foul-mouthed, leaden-footed, strong-hearted*; in Part B they number thirteen of which three are in the concordance. Four end in -eyed, viz., *fair-eyed, great-eyed, grey-eyed, red-eyed,* three in -haired, viz., *black-haired, hard-haired, white-haired,* three in -hearted, viz., *honest-hearted, soft-hearted, stout-hearted,* the others being *freckle-faced, round-faced* and *bare-armed.* Those in Part B connote simple attributes of person or of disposition, they are obvious epithets used in every-day speech, not unsuitable to drama but merely descriptive and without any poetic quality. How much more varied in form, compact and expressive are the similar compounds in Part A! Emilia, describing herself as ' bride-habited But mayden-harted,' epitomizes in five words her part in the play. The epithet *quick-eyed* in the couplet,

> Come all sad and Solempne Showes
> That are quick-eyed pleasures foes (I, v, 7-8).

gives a touch of fancy wanting in each of five such adjectives used in a literal sense by the messenger in his twenty-line description of a knight (IV. iii. ll. 117-136). The group of parasynthetic compounds in Part A reminds us of *Soft-conscienced, tender-bodied, tiger-footed* in *Coriolanus,* of *loose-wived, broad-fronted, onion-eyed, three-nooked* in *Antony and Cleopatra,* of *euil-eyed, full-acorned, truest-mannered* in *Cymbeline,* of *honey-mouthed, red-looked, stretch-mouthed,* in *The Winter's Tale,* and of *sour-eyed, wide-chopped, short-grassed, puppy-headed* in *The Tempest.* Those in Part A bear the hall-mark of the mature Shakespeare; every one of those in B could find a place in the most commonplace prose.

The parasynthetic type lends itself to word-coining; eight in Part A, five in Part B are ' new ' words. In addition three of the words in Part B are borrowed by the author from early plays of Shakespeare's. Chapman has 36 ' new ' formations of this kind in his twelve plays, or two more than are in *King Lear* and *Antony and Cleopatra* combined.

249

R

Shakespeare and the Homilies

A notable feature of the diction in Part A is the number of substantives which are used as verbs; they add vigour, vividness and imagination to the verse. Several critics have remarked on such passages as

> He will not suffer vs to burne their bones
> to *vrne* their ashes.   (I. i. ll. 46-7.)

and

>   give vs the Bones
> Of our dead Kings that we may *Chappell* them (I. i. ll. 52-3.)

and

> her Armes . . . shall . . . *corslet* thee   (I. i. ll. 196-8.)

and

>   Yet what man
> *Thirds* his owne worth   (I. ii. ll. 106-7.)

Quite as worthy of mention are,

>   Fortune at you
> *Dimpled* her cheeke with smiles   (I. i. ll. 69-70.)
>   (used participially only in Shakespeare.)
> You have *skift* Torrents   (I. iii. ll. 44-5.)
>   Our richest balmes
> Rather than *niggard* wast   ('I. iv. ll. 37-8.)
>   So hoyst we
> The sayles, that must these vessels *port* euen where
> The heauenly Lymiter pleases   (V. i. ll. 51-3.)
>   *Arme* your prize
> I know you will not loose her.   (V. iii. ll. 153-4.)

Eleven such verbs are to be found in Part A, six of which are 'new' words; only one in Part B.

>   The wolues would *iaw* me   (III. ii. 1. 7.)
> (This is in a scene that many critics give to Shakespeare.)

Most Elizabethan and Jacobean authors use nouns freely as verbs, but they are not very venturesome and usually follow custom in their choice. I find but seven unusual verbs of this kind in the sixteen plays of Marlowe, Greene, Peele and Kyd, and can trace but one such instance in the twelve plays of Chapman. The last plays of Shakespeare teem with daringly brilliant metaphors due solely to this use of nouns and adjectives as verbs. A few quotations may be taken as typical.

knee the way into his mercy   (*Cor.*, V. i. ll. 5-6.)
     and my true Lippe
Hath *virgin'd* it ere since.   (*Ibid.*, V. iii. ll. 47-8.)
Ile *mountebanke* their loues   (*Ibid.*, III. ii. ll. 132.)

From the same play may be added *bonnetted, fisted, feebling, furnace,* etc.

Holes where eyes should bee which pitifully
disaster the cheekes   (Ant., II. vi. ll. 15-6.)
The white hand of a Lady *Feauer* thee. (*Ibid.*, III. xiii. l. 138.)
     not th' Imperious shew
Of the full-Fortun'd Caesar, euer shall
Be *brooch'd* with me   (*Ibid.*, IV. xv. ll. 23-5.)

Other nouns used as verbs are *spaniel, barber, ghost.*

'Tis still a Dreame; or else such stuffe as Madmen
Tongue, and *braine* not.   (*Cym.*, V. iv. ll. 145-6.)
That Drug-damn'd Italy, hath *out-craftied* him.
     (*Ibid.*, III. iv. l. 15.)
     The blessed Gods
Purge all Infection from our Ayre, whilest you
Doe *Clymate* here   (*Winter's Tale*, V. i. ll. 168-170.)
     The good mind of Camillo *tardied*
My swift command.   (*Ibid.*, III. ii. ll. 159-160.)
The thunder . . . did *base* my Trespasse.
     (*Temp.*, IV. iii. l. 99.)
huskes Wherein the Acorne *cradled.*   (*Ibid.*, I. ii. ll. 463-4.)
     and *oared*
Himselfe with his good armes in lusty stroke
To th' shore.   (*Ibid.*, II. i. ll. 112-4.)

Such instances could be more than trebled from these plays alone; almost every play affords examples of such happy valiancy of phrase. The presence in Part A of so many instances not in the concordance of this peculiarly characteristic mode of compelling our attention compels us also to think that Shakespeare was the author, a conclusion to which the number of ' new ' verbs so formed points.

The six words in the next group are also not in the concordance and are all ' new ' to literature; they seem to combine the characteristics both of the parasynthetic type and of nouns used as verbs. Even Shakespeare's daring ingenuity could not compel certain nouns to do

Shakespeare and the Homilies

duty as active verbs; he therefore transmuted them into participles used adjectively by adding -ed to them. Usually the ' new ' word so formed is an adjective, sometimes it appears to be the past participle of a ' new ' verb which is used in the passive voice These formations are so numerous in the poet's plays that a large number of illustrative quotations is not necessary; those below come from his last group.

> faces pale With flight and *agued* feare   (*Cor.*, I. iv. ll. 37-8.)
> To helpe our *fielded* Friends   (*Ibid.* I. iv. 12.)
> My affaires Are *Seruanted* to others   (*Ibid.*, V. ii. ll. 88-9.)
> *Carbunkled* Like holy Phoebus Carre.
> (*Ant.*, IV. viii. ll. 28-9.)
> prorogue his Honour, Euen till a *Lethied* dulnesse
> (*Ibid.*, II. i. ll. 26-7.)
> the Token'd Pestilence   (*Ibid.*, III. x. l. 9.)
> *chalic'd* Flowres   (*Cym.*, II. iii. l. 21.)
> the prettiest *Dazied-Plot*   (*Ibid.*, IV. ii. l. 401.)
> *ditch'd*, and *wall'd* with turph   (*Ibid.*, V. iii. l. 14.)
> my third comfort.
> (*Star'd* most unluckily) (*The Winter's Tale*, III. ii. ll. 96-7.)
> The *fringed* Curtaines of thine eye   (*Temp.*, I. ii. l. 408.)
> *Leg'd* like a man   (*Ibid.*, II. ii. l. 35.)
> Thy bankes with *pioned*, and *twilled* brims. (*Ibid.*, IV. l. 64.)

Once more I quote scarcely a third of the examples present in these plays. The six examples found in *Two Noble Kinsmen* all occur in Part A. They are

> The *Helmeted* Belona   (*T. N. K.*, I. i. l. 80.)
> yet what man
> Thirds his owne worth (the case is each of ours)
> When that his actions *dregd*, with mind assurd
> 'Tis bad he goes about.   (*Ibid.*, I. ii. ll. 104-7.)
> My poore Chinne—'tis not *Cizard* just
> To such a Favourites glasse.   (*Ibid.*, I. ii. ll. 59-60.)
> A Cestron, *Brimd* with the blood of men. (*Ibid.*, V. i. ll. 52-3.)
> The *masond* Turrets   (*Ibid.*, V. i. l. 61.)
> Arcite is gently *visaged*   (*Ibid.*, V. iii. l. 52.)

The habitual use of these formations seems peculiar to Shakespeare; they are almost unknown to his predecessors and I have found three only in the twelve plays of Chapman. The presence of six such ' new ' words in

Vocabulary of Two Noble Kinsmen

Part A gives additional support to the opinion that Shakespeare wrote it. The important group of words beginning with the prefix un- amounts to nearly 4 per cent. of Shakespeare's vocabulary; about a quarter are 'new' to literature. It follows logically, therefore, that we may expect to find in a play of Shakespeare's, and especially in a tragedy, a large number of words beginning with un-, a considerable number used by him for the first time, and some 'new' words. Such are characteristics of almost all his plays, early or late; a short table will illustrate my contention.

TABLE IV
DISTRIBUTION OF WORDS BEGINNING WITH UN-

Play.	Total No. of Words.	No. Used for First Time.	'New' Words.
2 Henry VI	34	28	7
Romeo and Juliet	44	16	4
Richard II	52	22	8
1 Henry IV	39	9	4
Twelfth Night	33	17	7
Hamlet	71	35	17
Lear	55	21	12
Coriolanus	48	23	8
Tempest	20	6	3
Two Noble Kinsmen			
Part A	19	10	7
Part B	8	0	0

Part A satisfies the conditions prescribed above; a total of nineteen in less than 1100 lines agrees very well with the totals for *Hamlet, King Lear,* and *Coriolanus;* the number (10) not in the concordance is as many as we might expect, and the seven 'new' words, three being repeated from earlier plays, exhibit the author's power of invention. Part B seems to have been written by a man whose vocabulary is almost entirely derivative. None of his contemporaries or predecessors approaches Shakespeare in the number of coined words of this type; Marlowe has twelve in his plays and poems, whilst

Chapman has less in his twelve plays than are in *Hamlet*. It is a remarkable fact that in *The Taming of the Shrew, Pericles, Timon, Henry VIII, Edward III* and *The Two Noble Kinsmen* all the ' new ' words beginning with un- are in the portions usually assigned to Shakespeare.

Another characteristic of Shakespearean drama is a very free use of compound words consisting of a noun or its equivalent followed by a participle. This type is common in poetry, but Marlowe and the other predecessors of Shakespeare avoid it in plays intended for the public stage. Such compounds are infrequent in Chapman and Fletcher; Chapman has eleven in twelve plays and I have noticed only two in Fletcher's dramatic poem, *The Faithful Shepherdess.* Part A has five such formations, *blood-sized, heart-pierced, wind-fanned, all-feared,* and perhaps *bride-habited*; in Part B there is one, *beast-eating.* We find numerous compounds of this type in the last group of Shakespeare's plays. *Coriolanus* has eight, e.g., *brow-bound, wind-shaken, grief-shot,* etc.; *Antony and Cleopatra* six, among them *lust-wearied, war-exercised; Cymbeline* six, including *sky-planted, thief-stolen,* etc.; *Winter's Tale* nine, such as *Ear-deafening, fire-robed, soul-vexed, honour-flawed*; and *The Tempest* as many as twelve, including *cloud-capped, pinch-spotted, pole-clipt, sight-outrunning,* etc. Part A shares this characteristic of Shakespearean drama, Part B does not.

A century ago Spalding in his famous *Letter* remarked that

> verbal names expressing the agent . . . are in an especial manner frequent with Shakespeare, who invents them to preserve his brevity, and always applies them with great force and quaintness.

Shakespeare coined about 100 such ' verbal names,' but more than half are compounds such as *foot-licker, ape-bearer, master-leaver,* etc., a type which predominates in his last group of plays. He has more than 500 words of this type, but the proportion of coined words is lower than in other groups of words ending with English suffixes. Part A has ten, Part B four such words not in the concordance; not one is 'new' to literature. The number of these words in Part A suggests Shakespeare. Some other words in Part A are worth discussing. Three words *dove-like, Phoenix-like,* and *pig-like,* the two latter 'new' words, serve to remind us that Shakespeare has 74 such adjectives the majority of his own invention. *Coriolanus* contains no less than six, viz., *dragon-like, infant-like, Juno-like, picture-like, thunder-like* and *tinder-like;* in *Antony and Cleopatra* we find *dolphin-like;* in *Cymbeline, nurse-like* and *villain-like;* in *Winter's Tale, clerk-like;* and in *The Tempest, calf-like* and *fish-like.* All of these are 'new' words. Part B has no 'new' words of this type.

A group of three nonce-words, viz., *meditance, operance,* and *precipitance* suggests that in Part A Shakespeare was doing what is unusual with him, trying his hand at coining words from Latin stems. He did not invent many words ending in -ance; we have *transportance* in *Troilus and Cressida* and *reprobance* in *Othello* for the more common words ending in -ation.

Two 'new' words, *smel-lesse* and *tasteful,* both in Part A, recall Shakespeare's excessive use in his early plays of adjectives ending in these suffixes—there are 57 in *3 Henry VI.* He coined about 60 such adjectives; included in them are *aidless, napless, shunless, (Coriolanus), cloyless, graveless, useful (Antony and Cleopatra), chaffless (Cymbeline),* and *baseless, printless, useless (Tempest).* There are no 'new' adjectives of this type in Part B.

Importment is a 'new' word of a type that is a favourite with Shakespeare; words ending in -ment are especially frequent in *Hamlet, Troilus and Cressida,* and *Cymbeline.* In *Hamlet* he uses the amazing number of 44. *Bewitchment (Coriolanus), allayment, fitment, insultment (Cymbeline)* are 'new' words. None of his predecessors invented any words of this type and I find only one in Chapman's plays. Prose writers such

as Nashe delighted themselves by inventing jaw-cracking
words such as *concloutment*; Shakespeare is the only
dramatist who makes free with them.

In the last scene of the play two strikingly expressive
' new ' words, viz., *disroot* and *disseat* occur in the space
of four lines. Shakespeare coins 32 such words in all;
in his last group of plays he gives us *disproperty,
disbench* (*Coriolanus*), *discandy, dislimn* and *dis-
punge* (*Antony and Cleopatra*), *disedge* (*Cymbeline*),
dislike (*Winter's Tale*), and *disproportion* (*Tempest*). These formations were rarely invented by
his predecessors; Chapman has two ' new ' words, viz.,
disminion and *dissavage* in his twelve plays. In the same
passage we have another noticeable nonce-word in
jadery, apparently formed on the model of *stitchery*
(*Coriolanus*), *varletry* (*Antony and Cleopatra*), and
mappery (*Troilus and Cressida*).

In the last section of this article I may appear to be
following the practice of critics who, by marshalling a
medley of miscellaneous words and an array of parallel
passages common to play X and to play Y, deduce from
such points of resemblance that the two plays are by the
one pen. My method of investigation rests not on
sameness but on differences in vocabulary, and requires
rather the absence than the presence of identical phrases
and parallel passages. My arguments are based upon
words not common to Part A and Shakespeare's latest
plays, on ' new ' words of Part A not in the concordance,
on words that Shakespeare had not used before. The
diction of Part A I take to be his because nearly every
line bears the stamp of the essential qualities of his
vocabulary, simplicity, directness, originality and
copiousness, the whole shot through with imagination
and alive with metaphor. I submit that the evidence
drawn from a study of the vocabulary strongly supports
the claim made by many critics that *The Two Noble
Kinsmen* should be included in the Shakespeare canon.

INDEX

This index is selective not exhaustive. Numbers refer to the pages of the book.